ECONOMICS AND SOCIETY: No. 5

Price Determination
and Prices Policy

Economics and Society Series

General Editor: Professor C. D. Harbury

ECONOMICS AND SOCIETY SERIES

Price Determination and Prices Policy

by
JOAN MITCHELL
Reader in Economics
University of Nottingham

London
GEORGE ALLEN & UNWIN LTD
Boston   Sydney

ISBN 0 04 338084 0 hardback
      0 04 338085 9 paper

Photoset in 10 on 11 point Times
by Red Lion Setters, Holborn, London
Printed in Great Britain by
Biddles Ltd, Guildford, Surrey

Preface

A good shorthand description of economics is the study of every-thing that has, or could have, a price tag. The terms on which firms do business are prices; prices determine the welfare of households. Discussing prices fully would involve all important aspects of economic behaviour, a task to which this whole series is devoted. The purpose of this book is to discuss prices with prices policy in mind. Prices are increasingly a major preoccupation of govern-ments; price controls and prices policies are no longer exceptional. Designing a benign policy depends on knowing how prices are formed, or more precisely, what determines the changes that take place.

The state of the art of economics does not allow many useful generalisations or principles about pricing that apply throughout the economy; nor are the rules for distinguishing competitive from non-competitive sectors more than ground-clearing guidelines. Governments needing prices policies for counter-inflationary pur-poses and officials designing or applying them must consider price formation and practice in all sectors, in multifarious circum-stances. Though the general lines of policies owe much to econo-mics, the efforts of price controllers and watchdogs have arguably added as much to economic knowledge as they have derived from it. There is now a considerable literature of official reports and policy reviews, especially from the National Board for Prices and Incomes, the Price Commission and the Monopolies Commission. The Select Committee on Nationalised Industries and the National Economic Development Office have contributed to discussion of nationalised industry prices. These are the main sources for what follows. Evidence is often given, or more freely given, to official bodies than is made available through other channels. If readers are encouraged to explore this for themselves, with the interest it deserves, this brief survey will have served a useful purpose.

The market economy or private enterprise are terms to which economists (among others) react with emotion. It is important, therefore, to clarify how these terms are used here. A market economy can be supported as a matter of principle, the implication being that private ownership, individual freedom or minimal government interference are politically and socially desirable, and attainable as a corollary of a market system. This is neither the sense in which it is used here, nor part of any conclusion readers are intended to draw. A market economy is also a matter of fact; it is the basis of the system in which we live. Even if we deplore it, or wish to change or reform it, it is still necessary to understand how it actually works. Moreover, market responses are more general than private enterprise. The essence of a market system is offering goods and services at a price, to which buyers and sellers respond by independent decisions. Since those decisions are the result of all of us trying to make the best of our lot in an uncertain world, market forces are very strong, whatever the political or ownership system. Even in a highly controlled, administratively organised sector, like housing, suppliers and customers exercise choice in a 'market' way. Consequently, it is merely prudent to inquire what market forces are, or what they would be, partly to weigh up the forces pent up by administrative action, partly to check how effective intervention really is. So considering market reactions or solutions is not to be taken for approval, either of a political system or of the desirability on principle of unbridled market responses.

The text is arranged in four parts. Part One concerns general issues about prices, including the ambiguities of the term itself. There is also some historical background to pricing policies, very necessary to an understanding of official policies. Part Two concerns the private sector, Part Three the public sector. Part Four discusses prices policies (meaning official action to influence the price level), and also the growing concern of governments with consumer affairs apart from pricing directly.

Finally, the author is pleased to acknowledge the support given by the Social Science Research Council to her continuing interest in price and income determination.

JOAN MITCHELL
University of Nottingham

Contents

Part One

INTRODUCTORY

Chapter 1

Prices in General

Consumers (and economists) are sometimes baffled, astonished or outraged to find that businesses do not seem to take prices as seriously as they should. A wide range of prices for identical goods is not uncommon. The same goods are repriced on the shelves by having new labels stuck on. Complaints can lead to apparently casual reductions, suggesting that the original ones might have been decided equally casually. Investigating what firms do rather confirms the impression of casualness. Small firms may refer to price lists compiled by their suppliers; large ones may leave them to be decided somewhere down the management hierarchy, according to vague rules or no rules at all. Senior management may not know the prices; even if they do, they may well not know what final consumers actually pay. No very purposive activity is suggested.

Equally, businessmen (and economists) can despair over consumers' behaviour. Shoppers can have mistaken ideas, or no ideas at all, about goods they have just bought, let alone the ones they did not choose. Others positively seek out high-priced goods, or high-price shops, entertaining the belief that high price means high quality (or scarcity, or exclusiveness). No very active discrimination appears to be exercised.

There is plenty of evidence that such behaviour is far from rare or untypical. But there is also evidence for the more careful calculation of prices by businesses, and keen awareness of prices and products by consumers, that an active market system implies. Hardly any simple generalisation about price behaviour or principles really applies in practice, without much qualification. The variations depend on market structures, and on the peculiarities of different sectors of the economy. But how the behaviour varies has profound effects on the performance of the system, and on the welfare of its households. Price provides producers' income, which helps to determine investment for the future. It sets limits to the goods and services most consumers can command. If consumers respond little or slowly to changes in price, production is likely to adapt slowly to changing demand. If firms price by convention more than by regard for current conditions, consumers get less out of available resources than they might. The workings of the market, and the prices it throws up, have increasingly been thrust on the attention of governments. Their activities have at least made us more aware of how prices actually are determined, through the growing pile of reports on firms or industries. Those reports form the basis of what follows as a background to government prices policies.

THE MEANING OF PRICE

Price itself is an ambiguous concept, fundamentally different in the way it appears to producers and consumers. Producers and traders are interested in average revenue rather than price; that is, the unit selling value of their output. Even small, single-product firms sell different units at different prices. Perishable foods may be sold at top prices early in the day, lower prices later on; either because the lettuces and strawberries are past their best (a change in supply), or because the customers are not keen to buy (a change in demand). The practice of date marking packaged food has induced some traders to reduce prices as the date approaches. Hairdressers may charge children and pensioners less than other customers for an identical service, or less on particular days. Short-lived special offers are becoming more and more common, from pork chops to permanent waves. The same goods in the same quantities may be sold at a discount to other traders but at the full price to ordinary customers. The price to which the customer's (and therefore aggregate) demand adjusts is what he actually paid. The return to the seller per unit sold is the average of what he achieved, given his pricing policy.

But most firms are multi-product enterprises. Even small businesses (shops, farms, builders and so on) sell a range of products. Large or small, they may sell at firm prices from a price list; or by a process of bargaining with each customer; or at constantly changing, though listed, non-discriminating prices.

When it comes to large enterprises, it is difficult to think of one which produces something so standardised that it has one unambiguous price. Coal, for instance, is distinguished by size and characteristics, some suitable for domestic use, some for industrial use. Domestic coal is sold in five grades. Industrial coal is classified by size and ash content among other specifications. Some varieties are virtually distinct products, selling in particular markets. Each has a different price, and working out or changing the whole schedule is a technical business, completely known only to the National Coal Board's marketing division. The NCB itself is interested in the total and average revenue of the enterprise, and that only on the occasion of restructuring in prices. Bricks come in different grades and specifications; the kilns can be made to produce more or fewer common bricks (not fit for finishing) or facing bricks. The various specifications are set out in price lists. Average sales revenue defines the producers' returns. Chocolate confectionery is not dissimilar. Standard ingredients go in one end of the production line, and after processing come out as a range of products, each of which eventually has its own price and is, to the consumer, a distinct product. The ·assortment and price list is mainly of concern to marketing or sales managers; at the top level, average sales realisations per ton is the concept that matters.

These differences are important as prices change. Prices (paid by consumers) may rise, while average revenue falls, or rises more than prices, depending on the mix of products an enterprise sells and the way it loads increases on various items of its range. A price control which restricts prices by restricting increases in enterprises revenue may still allow unexpectedly high price increases if it does not control the loading as well.

Average revenue is also different from price for public utilities charging by multi-part tariffs (like gas, electricity and phones). The charge has a fixed rent element as well as a unit commodity price. To the producing enterprise, the price is the average revenue per unit of the product. To the consumer it could be the running rate, or the lowest running rate, or the total average charge per unit to him. The perceived price differs to consumer and producer; and the perceived or realised price differs to different consumers, according to level and time of their consumption. This is a situation fraught not only with confusion but with resentment and suspicion between customer and supplier, especially when the structure of charges is changed. Again price and average revenue can change in opposite directions, or one can change without the other.

Where there are many varieties of branded goods, other difficulties arise. The price of a jar of jam is clear enough; but how are price changes to be noted? At any one time there is a band of prices for jam. The individual prices within the band tend to change roughly in line, but not in step. One prominent supplier raises his price; others follow quickly or slowly, to an extent depending on their costs and whether they are actively seeking a larger market share. Shops may start or withdraw 'special offers'. The result is a round of price increases, liable to vary each time. If or when 'jam' has increased in price, in a policy context, depends on an average movement, which can only be measured by an index.

Custom-made goods present even more problems of identifying price changes than mass-produced ones. Builders and civil engineers, shipbuilders and process plant contractors, produce a different product for each customer. The 'price' is the sum paid in settlement of a contract. But a price change, or the size of the change, is difficult to substantiate. An index showing changes in the 'cost to the client' of building and civil engineering work has been compiled by the Central Statistical Office, taking into account changes in the cost of inputs, modified for estimated changes in input per unit of output, the whole adjusted for changes in the proportion of overheads and profit in cost. But this is far from a normal price.

Price only has meaning for a definite product. Individually producers, sellers and consumers usually have clear notions of products, but their definitions do not tally. When it comes to prices Policy this problem is of major importance, since the policy applies to producers or traders in the interests of consumers. Products, as consumers understand them, may start off as only a small part of the business of a large enterprise, handled and passed on by many other businesses. Controlling the prices of 'shopping basket' products is an administrative nightmare, because the control has to apply to parts of integrated businesses. Controlling the activities of firms is administratively tidier; but it may prove ineffective on retail prices, because the controlled firms supply only part of retail sales.

THE PRICE LEVEL

Price is an imprecise concept; the concept of price level is equally so. Strictly speaking it is only measurements of change that give it meaning. But prices never do anything uniformly; even during strong inflationary surges, some prices fall; and prices at various stages of production rarely change in parallel.

The price level is necessarily an index of only a few items among a vast population. Which items are selected, and how they are combined, influences the result significantly. There is no incontrovertibly right index, still less a complete one. The nearest to a general index taking account of all stages is the Gross Domestic Product (GDP) deflator; that is, the price index implied by deflating current value GDP to a constant price base. It is not much used, however, partly because its remoteness from recorded data must leave an unusually large margin of error, and partly because changes in the pattern of production are reflected in it as well as price changes.

The Retail Price Index
The appropriateness of an index of changes in the price level

depends on its purpose. The most frequently used in a general policy context is the Retail Price Index (RPI), since this most nearly represents price experience determining changes in the real income of households: it is a suitable index of the performance of governments or economies in terms of their final product, domestic consumption. In principle, the relevant items to index are clear. The major difficulties relate to choosing representative retail outlets, since prices vary so much among them, and to weighting products and product groups to represent a general structure of consumer expenditure. The basis of both is the annual Family Expenditure Survey (FES). Budgets for two separate weeks in summer and winter are kept by a sample of 7,000 households, classified by income group, household size and composition, age of the head of household, occupational group and region. The items are summarised in nine product groups (food, drink and tobacco; housing; fuel and light; durable household goods; clothing and footwear; transport and vehicles; miscellaneous goods; services; meals consumed outside the home), as well as outlets. The FES is used to define the 350 items, priced by purchasing each month in specified outlets in 200 areas, the data collection being organised by the regional offices of the Employment Services Agency on behalf of the Department of Employment. Special offers, sales and similar transitory price changes are thus included; Value Added Tax (VAT) and other taxes are also included. The accuracy of the RPI depends critically on the accuracy of the FES. 'Accuracy' is itself a misleading term in relation to such an averaging process; the greater the differences in expenditure between groups or the greater the changes over time, the less the average represents the experience of any one group, still less of individual households. Expenditure by pensioner households is distinguished from the rest because the differences are thought to be significant, and the highest income groups are excluded altogether. Other possibly significant differences, for instance relating to large families, or large, poor families, or regional differences, can be traced only very imperfectly with so few budgets, as a considerable number of 'cells' in the detailed figures contain too few instances to be representative. Among products, drink and tobacco are known to be underrecorded (and corrections are made); housing is conceptually difficult to record generally; and infrequent purchases, like fuel and furniture, are likely to be inaccurately recorded with figures for only two separate weeks. No doubt general changes of direction or rates of change in retail prices are reflected well enough; but small changes and differences are as likely to be statistical quirks as reality.

A valuable supplement to the RPI data is the Price Commission's quarterly reports on the retail prices of selected fresh foods, collected fortnightly from representative cities and large towns, less frequently from medium and small towns. The prices, collected and published in considerable detail, show the persistent, but not consistent, variations between shops for a single product (non-branded fresh foods) narrowly defined, variations which lie behind all the index figures, revealing the considerable ranges compressed into the group or overall averages. The Price Commission's data, collected by its own regional officers, are combined into product group indices (relating to, for instance, beef, home-killed lamb, imported lamb and pork, as well as 'meat'), using the FES weights, and into indices relating to the types of shop (by product group). Thus at any rate for fresh food, retail price changes are monitored and indexed in the detail necessary to link market changes experienced by the customers to the changes in the price level to which governments direct their attention.

Wholesale price indices
Changes in the price level so far as enterprises are concerned are substantially different. The experience of industry as purchaser is summarised in the index of wholesale prices of materials and fuel; and as supplier by wholesale prices of goods for sale (on the home market). Both are constructed for over thirty industrial sectors (as defined in the Standard Industrial Classification, which groups firms by the goods or services 'principally sold'). Monthly price quotations are collected, for representative items, based on the Production Censuses, relating to orders currently placed for goods of constant specification; that is, adjustments are made for changes in product quality, all including revenue duties but not VAT. The total indices, constructed with and without food, drink and tobacco industries, are not merely the average of the sector indices, but are appropriately weighted to represent industry directly. Each price is averaged for the month, expressed as a percentage of the price in a base period, the 'price relative'. The price relatives are combined, on the same lines as the RPI, by weighted arithmetic averages, the weights relating to expenditure in the base (Census) year. Finally, all are multiplied by a constant 'scale factor' to make the index equal to 100 in a convenient 'reference base' year. Since adjustments are frequently made for product changes, but the weights are revised less often, the wholesale indices represent the actual experience of individual firms even less than the RPI represents that of individual households.

Prices of imported materials and other goods are indexed

separately. An additional problem in valuing occurs: imports can be valued as an industrial input, that is, at prices in sterling, as paid by industrial or other purchasers. Changes then reflect both changes in supply prices and changes in the value of sterling. Indices of world prices, denominated in foreign currencies, of foreign currency prices of UK imports, and of current sterling prices of those imports, all have their uses according to their context. As a great deal of substitution goes on between sources of supply and between products, influenced by relative prices and availability, the task of weighting the indices appropriately is far from straightforward. There are in consequence a number of series, serving rather different purposes. The two official series include one for unit import values, derived from the overseas trade statistics, valued in sterling, and implicit-weighted by current expenditure patterns; the other is the wholsesale price index for commodities wholly or mainly imported, covering twenty selected commodities, in sterling prices. The Price Commission compiles its own index of the world prices, in sterling, of basic materials imported into the UK. Indices of world prices in foreign currency are compiled by the National Institute for Economic and Social Research and the *Economist*.

The limitations of indices representing changes in price levels in whole sectors are revealed whenever they are needed for operational purposes, rather than for merely describing a situation. Adjusting accounts to show real profits or changes in assets, net of inflation, is an important instance. Generally, the purpose is to remove the effect of a rising price level; specifically, a choice of index must be made. The RPI is the most widely used and probably most reliable general index of the price level. Nevertheless it is entirely inappropriate to businesses, since it is weighted by household expenditure rather than by the very different expenditures of enterprises, as well as covering so wide a range of products (after they have passed through distributive trades) that it represents no industrial sector, let alone firm, at all closely. The Sandilands Committee on inflation accounting firmly proposed indices relating as closely as possible to the specific expenditures of firms, having explicitly rejected the idea of a general index of the price level as unquantifiable and hence operationally useless. Price indices need to relate to three distinct sets of values: fixed assets, namely plant and machinery; stocks of materials; and stocks of goods for sale, the relevant items in all three sets varying with the firm's activities. Consequently, the CSO produced not only new indices but a whole bookful of them, giving figures for the three sets; for plant and machinery in twenty-five industrial sectors, and for stocks in twenty-one retail sectors, eighteen wholesale sectors and thirty-three industrial sectors, plus construction, gas and electricity. The thousands of price quotations necessary, even for an undoubtedly imperfect exercise, can be envisaged from the following example of the items for one industrial sector, motor vehicle (and wheeled tractor) manufacture. Plant and machinery includes: metal-cutting machine-tools; elevators, conveyors, lifts and escalators; cranes, lifting and winding devices; powered industrial trucks and tractors; scientific and industrial instruments; welding machinery and electrodes; metal-forming mechanical tools; mechanical engineering products not included elsewhere; electric motors; and computers. Stocks of materials include: steel sheets and steel manufactures; vehicle parts and accessories; commercial vehicles, chassis and engines; miscellaneous metal goods; electric motors, wires and cable, electrical equipment and batteries; fuel, chemicals and allied products; wrought aluminium, copper and zinc; ball and roller bearings and transmission chains; packaging and wrapping materials; textiles, glass and glass fibre. Stocks of goods for sale is naturally for an assembling industry a shorter list: passenger cars; vehicle parts and accessories, wheeled tractors; commercial and public service vehicles; three-wheeled vehicles; and trailers and caravans. The lists and the indices would be unimportant details if the prices of various items or at successive stages of production moved together. The more refinement in the indices, the more evidence there is that this is not so: the prices and unit costs of inputs do not move together; different outputs use inputs in different proportions; firms have different policies about pricing and about the timing of changes. Consequently there are considerable, significant divergences between contributions to the average change in the price level, even at one stage or in one sector.

However, since the various sectors of the economy are interdependent a systematic relationship between changes in price indices is to be expected. Increases in import prices increase manufacturers' or wholesalers' (for fresh foods) costs; eventually their output prices increase, raising wholesalers' and retailers' buying prices, and eventually their selling prices. Such a process is indeed shown by the series of indices; but the time lags are not constant, nor are the changes at earlier stages matched by later ones. Prices of some commodities are reflected in manufacturers' or retailers' prices sooner than others, depending on the complexity of the processes through which they go. For instance, crude petroleum has to be refined to petrol or diesel oil for transport, or put through chemical processes to make plastics, textile fibres or fertilisers; the former process is considerably shorter (taking into account the usual transaction lags between one sector and another) than the latter. If all import prices move together, perhaps because sterling has depreciated, the different sectoral time lags would average out to a recognisable general linked movement in other price levels. But if an increase in average import prices is disproportionately due to a few specific materials becoming dearer, the time lags may change, reflecting particularly long or short production processes, or non-average pricing practices down the production stream.

Price Commission indices

The Price Commission has contributed to the better understanding of the relationships. It added a new set of indices of a novel kind, relating to *proposals* to increase prices put before it during the life-time of the Counter-inflation Act. Though the proposals related only to the largest firms, many were price leaders. Hence they gave a significant indication of price increases soon to appear in wholesale prices, and in due course in retail prices. For instance, the turning point from accelerating to decelerating monthly increases in 1975 came in March in the Price Commission index, in May in the wholesale (output) index and in June in the RPI. But the three series, thoroughly averaged as they all are, nevertheless show varying time lags at various periods. No doubt the wholesale-retail gap appeared rather short in 1975 as no outstandingly large retail increase for heavily weighted items (such as housing, fuel or fresh food) occurred, largely for seasonal or administrative reasons.

The Price Commission also studied the effect of changing material prices (falls as well as rises; sterling prices of primary commodities fell by one-third in the first half of 1975) on a number of specific products, some with high material inputs, some with lower. Naturally the short-process, high-material-content product reflected changes in material prices most fully and most quickly, the specific instance being copper going into copper tubes for domestic central heating, the copper accounting for nearly two-thirds of manufacturers' costs. The time lag in passing on rises (and falls) was negligible, and institutionalised since buying and selling prices are both linked to current quotations on the London Metal Exchange. At the other extreme, changes in the price of wool incorporated in women's jumpers affected retail prices up to eighteen months later, though there were (in 1975-6) signs that manufacturers were reducing the time lag by three or four months. The extent to which the material price change is reflected in material costs, and hence manufacturers' prices, also depends on manufacturers' policy. Substantial stocks bought wisely (or with luck) may avoid price peaks altogether. The method of valuing stock taken into production varies; last-in-first-out (LIFO) shortens the lag between material and output price increases, first-in-first-out (FIFO) lengthens it. A change of method from FIFO to LIFO (or nearer to it by averaging) might considerably shorten the lag and push the index of output prices up more than previously. Also the indices at times of shortage sometimes reflect prices at which few transactions actually take place. Moreover, the extent or speed at which manufacturers can pass on cost increases depends on competition. Intensified competition would lengthen time lags when prices were rising, and might well account for the levelling of prices in relation to fluctuating input prices, output prices rising and falling (other costs being equal) less than proportionately to input prices.

Consequently, though general relationships between the price indices can be traced clearly enough in pushing the final price level up more or less, the time path or the ratios of one increase to others are not easily predictable from averaged data only. The price level, though the phenomenon to which economic stabilisation policies generally and prices policies in particular are directed, is a kaleidoscopic one, fully deserving the array of statistics which surrounds it.

COSTS

Marked cost increases are naturally passed on into final prices; but the extent to which they are passed on varies continually. Firms may take less profit when the market presses; they may postpone minor price increases until an accumulation of minor cost increases necessitates a larger one (perhaps for a new season's supplies). They may use less material, waste less or use lower qualities; materials or goods for sale may be in stock for a longer or shorter time. Though it is generally true that costs are passed on, there is no mechanical process at work. In the end, all prices are determined by costs and profits (profits being partly the cost of capital); the trend of prices follows the trend of costs. But prices changes at a particular time or for particular products need not be on trend, nor need the casual connection be from costs to prices. Constraints on prices, such as competition or price controls, may determine costs and profits.

Most output most of the time comes from on-going enterprises; therefore many costs are virtually unavoidable. The premises give rise to various charges, mostly fixed and unavoidable: rent and rates; lighting; heating; cleaning and other maintenance; expenses of complying with fire regulations or insurance. Vehicles must be licensed, taxed and insured. Machinery, vehicles and tools must have a minimum level of servicing; office staff, equipment and supplies are needed, if only to arrange payment of costs and to collect revenues. Employees' costs must then be met: employers' National Insurance contributions, pension fund contributions, training levies, redundancy payments, expenditure to comply with health and safety regulations. There may be royalties or licences to pay, or interest on borrowed money. In practice these are fixed and unavoidable for day-to-day management purposes. Most of them are also overheads rather than operating costs.

Cost of materials, bought-in services, operating labour and capacity are also practically fixed, once orders are going through, or a particular batch or design is put in production, or once the season starts on farms or in fashion trades.

With a rather longer time scale, or at a higher level of management, more costs are avoidable. Material costs per unit of product are controllable, and to a certain extent avoidable. Different suppliers can be sought once contracts run out. Alternative lower cost mixes can be used, such as oils for margarine or soap; alternative materials can be used, such as plastics for metals in building fitments, or the product can be redesigned to use less or less expensive materials, as in car components of many kinds.

Energy and water requirements are often determined technically by equipment or process. But both can usually be adapted; for instance, by better insulation or temperature control for heating installations, and by recycling water.

Production labour costs are in principle avoidable, but changes can often more easily be made upwards than downwards. Overtime is usually welcome (to employees), short-time is not. Recruitment can be stopped and started; but stopping the inflow of apprentices, trainees and beginners soon upsets the age and experience structure of a large labour force. In manufacturing, the more mechanised a production flow, the less production labour varies with output. In distribution and services, labour required varies more with capacity and organisation than with sales. In any sector, a skilled and experienced labour force is a valuable asset, not lightly damaged, with legal rights to notice and redundancy pay. Rates and conditions of work are based either on statutory minima or on collective agreements between unions and employers' association, above the heads of most firms, supplemented perhaps by company agreements. Increases in pay may be limited by law, as in the Pay Code 1972-4; or by a mixture of law and agreement, as in the social contract of 1975-7.

However, as output or sales increase, greater changes in production methods and hence in costs are possible; pay costs per unit of output depend on productivity, and this must ultimately be controllable everywhere. Some production lines may require a fixed labour force, but the capacity of the line can be changed or worked more hours. Ancillary equipment or processes can speed it up, or replace ancillary labour. Where the technology is not so inflexible, better methods, more versatility of function, and so on, help to limit labour costs in face of rising wages and conditions.

Capacity costs are only avoidable in the time span for planning new production. This can be anything from the weeks or months it takes to order off-the-shelf vehicles, tools or standard machinery, to the ten or fifteen years for complex industrial plant, or for acquiring land with development planning permission. Matching capacity to demand for the product can involve difficult forecasting exercises, as well as a fine balance between having enough to meet the peaks of fluctuating demand at the expense of under-use at other times, or more continuous full production at the expense of some frustrated customers at peak times. The right aim (the average intended degree of utilisation) is not easy to set. Given the aim, the longer the forecasting period, the easier it is to achieve it.

Depreciation
Meanwhile, today's capacity costs are the result of past planning decisions, wise or foolish as they may now appear. Even if they were wise at the time, new ideas and new processes overtake them. Depreciation is a proper element in cost, whether regarded as a notional charge for the deterioration in the value of the assets employed, or as a contribution to financing their replacement. But exactly what the depreciation should be quantitatively is highly controversial. Up-to-date valuation of capital employed is a complex matter. Inflation increases the value of existing (still useful) capital; depreciation and obsolescence reduce it. Neither involves a transaction, so there is no market value; accounting conventions must provide a substitute. Valuing assets at replacement cost may involve estimation, in spite of the proliferating indices for capital goods and stocks. The Sandilands' Committee recommended that assets should be valued at the future loss an enterprise would suffer if deprived of them, the value-to-them of existing assets rather than notional replacements, a change which partially overcomes the difficulty of deciding what is replaceable before it is replaced.

For computing costs and cost changes, enterprises naturally have a convention for handling depreciation. So long as the convention is unchanged, the difficulties of the concept affect profits and profitability rather than costs changes. The Price Code sidestepped the problems by requiring firms to compute depreciation according to their own usual accounting practices. But there is no absolutely 'right' practice, nor a simple one.

With the main elements of cost representing commitments of different kinds, avoidable or flexible over different time scales, it is not surprising that costs seem to determine prices. Moreover, prices have to be decided for each order or model, as major increases of input prices are announced or as management routines turn out revised accounts. Price decisions for all but new products relate to costs at their least flexible.

PROFITS

But market forces, namely demand and competition, have to be reckoned with. In order to translate costs to prices, profit must be added. Some firms aiming at administered prices add a required margin as though it were a cost. In the end, all or part of it is the cost of capital; but this depends on profitability. Profit is the residual, left after total costs have been subtracted from total revenue. However, total profits having been established, they have to be related either to products, to get profit *margins*, or to capital employed, to get *profitability*. To get profit margins on products, revenue and costs for the products must be computed. Revenue raises no problems; costs do. As we noted in relation to prices, many enterprises produce a range of products, with the same management, many common services, and very often some common plant. Overhead and possibly some operational costs must be allocated to one or other of the range of products. In the absence of any other obvious principle, pro rata allocation of costs according to output is often practised. But whether this is the right procedure depends on the circumstances, and the problem in hand. If some products are essentially by-products of other main products, there is no reason for allocating them their share of indirect or overhead costs. What is a by-product and what is a main product changes according to the markets for each. Any cost which can be escaped by a particular product not being produced should obviously be allocated to that product—so long as escapable costs can be estimated in the required form. For instance, the escapable costs of a particular kind of freight on the railways are not self-evident, and are in fact estimated by rules derived from lengthy researches into the various elements of railway costs. Allocating the remaining joint costs between joint products is in practice usually done by spreading them proportionately to an appropriate indicator. But there is an element of arbitrariness about it. Consequently profit margins are equally questionable. Changes may be less so, unless average overhead and operating costs are changing in different directions, or to a different extent.

Profit on capital depends, like depreciation, on the valuation of the capital. Revaluation of precisely the same assets, used in precisely the same way, can alter returns on capital radically, as frequently happens when properties are revalued. The profitability of capital employed in one product or product range is often relevant to the behaviour of potential monopolies, or to price increases permissible under a price control. Allocation problems arise, of what are essentially corporate assets, used jointly for other purposes, as well as of referred or controlled products. They are usually solved in the same rough and ready way, often with firms and the Monopolies Commission disagreeing about their significance.

Profitability is in the end the single most important aspect of a firm's performance. The management of a profitable enterprise will probably be rewarded in higher income, certainly in repute. The profitable firm will have relatively little difficulty in borrowing more to finance investment, whether by new equity sold to the public or by loans from institutions. Profit is taken to be the mark of success; and though it may not always indicate efficiency, its absence may well indicate inefficiency. Yet measures of profitability are controversial and often far from exact. Moreover, the concept of profit as used in analysis is radically different from profit (and equally obscure) in a policy or practical context.

The economists' profit is the sum of 'normal' profit and monopoly profit. The normal profit is that return on capital employed which will keep it so, given the economic parameters. The return will vary according to degrees of risk (mainly of instability of earnings). The rewards for risk taking having been allowed for, the remainder represents the value of the contribution of capital to the total value of sales, and the income required by lenders or owners to continue holding their assets in the same form. Managements strive to improve profits, by increasing the value of the productivity of capital to induce lenders or owners to maintain (or increase) their investments. Competition prevents their efforts securing more than the normal (average) profit, since any excess will attract more capital, or enable a rival, who by assumption has access to the same technology and factor supplies, to trim his prices and take a larger share of the market.

Actual profits are variable, as can only be expected of a residual.

One year's result may reflect the cycle of economic activity generally or that specific to the industry; or an occasion when the risks manifested themselves (in, for instance, breakdowns, blow-outs and other disasters, or in unpredicted shifts of fashion); or a period of adaption and reorganisation to new circumstances; or a change in the normal (average) amount of organisational slack. Averaging over a run of years is a rough-and-ready correction for particular, non-continuous influences, so long as an appropriate number of years can be chosen rationally, and so long as choosing different starting points does not give a markedly different result. But this is only a beginning. The exceptional current year needs to be compared not only with the past but with what can reasonably be expected to come, if it is to guide lenders and owners into holding, disposing of or increasing their investments.

Profits are also the source of finance for new investments. Farms and small businesses may find it difficult or expensive to borrow. Large firms may find self-financing the cheapest source, especially where taxation on transferred earnings can be avoided. Many firms work to a *required* rate of profit. Required revenue exceeds estimated costs by required profit. Average revenue follows, when divided by estimated sales. Prices are then set to produce the required average revenue; so supply prices include the required profit. If prices are market-determined, the required profit may or may not be earned; if it is not, costs must be reduced, sales increased or price structures altered to raise average revenue. But a viable alternative, when competition is not pressing, is to raise prices. The object of prices control is often to stop or reduce this practice where competition is weak or market reactions slow. Administered prices, including required minimum profit, are widespread though by no means universal in manufacturing and public sector enterprises.

Prices, then, may be determined by costs, in the sense that changes in costs plus any deficiency in required profit margin makes up firms' supply prices—if the market will bear it.

MARKET STRUCTURE AND BEHAVIOUR

Whether cost-based prices will stick in the market is partly determined by competition, partly by consumers' resistance. Firms in competitive markets take a going price, and adapt their behaviour to it, trimming costs to make that price profitable at the turnover their market will allow, improving product, service or marketing to make a margin above the going price. Monopolies make their prices in a captive market. They 'administer' prices, that is, construct prices on the basis of whatever costs they incur, and whatever turn-over a corporate plan implies. The customers can take them or leave them; they do so according to their incomes. The customers of the competitive firms take or leave the offers primarily accord-ing to price, as there is always a substitute product. Incomes will determine aggregate sales, which will eventually influence how many firms stay in or enter the market.

A supplier's relation to his customers can account for as much influence on prices as the existence of rival producers. A monopoly supplier faced with a monopoly buyer can be as much a price taker as the small business faced with many rivals. Equally, the price maker may be the enterprising proprietor in a competitive trade, taking the extra trouble or exercising his ingenuity about his product. The discerning customer, domestic or commercial, can refuse to buy at cost-plus prices, because they are not felt to be fair or reasonable, or because he is prepared to go without. The availa-bility of alternative suppliers or products obviously makes obstinacy easier, but it is not always necessary. But generally, the most important subverter of cost-based prices is relatively falling or stagnant income.

Competition and price leadership

Competition requires that there are enough suppliers for no one of them to set the price, and enough alert, bargain-hunting customers to make an active market. How many is enough for competition depends on the size and level of the market more than on the number or size of firms. Industries of many small firms can behave in a far from competitive way if markets are local (small shops, local brickworks, printers, haulage firms) or stratified (fashion shops and fashion wear manufacturers). Large firms operate in regional or national markets, the largest in international markets. International competition may be the fiercest of all, since there is a greater range of input prices, especially for labour, and output costs, due to different standards of work. In industries of large firms prospective gains and losses are bigger, but managements are more sophisticated. Professional managers are not necessarily more averse to risks than owner-managers; their lack of financial interest in particular projects may make them more free to take cal-culated risks, making for more competitive behaviour. Chemicals and oil operate in international markets, largely with salaried executives, but are keenly competitive despite the size of the firms. These were two industries where the market held prices consider-ably *below* the level allowed by the Price Code in 1976.

Competition is also a matter of organisation. Commodity and

fresh food markets are organised to establish market prices by bringing together many buyers and sellers: monopolistic pricing as practised in manufacturing is impossible. Entry can be restricted, for instance by admission restrictions, or space in produce markets, and market operators do their best to differentiate their product in terms of service and range of goods. But their function is essentially competitive, as both the National Board for Prices and Incomes (NBPI) and the Price Commission found them during their inquiries in 1967 and 1974.

Transactions among manufacturers and their customers depend on firm-to-firm contracts and continuing supply arrangements, as for instance between motor manufacturers and suppliers of components. Constantly shopping around for new suppliers is not possible on the same scale. Searching for new supplies is itself costly and changes disrupt production flows. The Monopolies Commission found the motor firms generally satisfied to bargain with customary suppliers, though the possibility of alternative supplies, or manufacturers making more of their own components, helped to keep costs and prices at competitive levels.

The range of sizes of firm in one industry can be as important as the size of the largest. Price leadership is a common form of modified competition, and is widely found in the many industries of a few large firms among many smaller ones.

The price set by the leader limits the price for the rest, though it does not necessarily prevent others going above it. Such industries commonly show a cluster of prices, the leader's price being neither highest nor lowest, the distribution of the cluster depending on variations in product, location or service that go with it. The general level of the cluster depends on the costs of the leader. A typical range is described in the NBPI's reports on bricks, with strong leadership from the London Brick Co. (LBC). The Board recommended that the current price restraints be applied to LBC, leaving the other few hundred firms to adjust their prices as best they could. A leader with as large a share as LBC is practically impossible to dislodge, as he can maintain a price covering his average costs plus required profit; if the followers threaten his market share, he may lower costs as well as prices, having the resources for investment. The leader's price determines the followers' costs and how long they survive. In the brick industry, it was not long. In 1967 there were five 'fletton' brick producers; by 1973 only LBC remained, with 100 per cent of fletton capacity, and over 40 per cent of all building bricks. In this, price leadership was a stage in the rapid concentration towards one dominant producer.

Price leadership often seems to be transitory, though not

necessarily on the way to monopoly. National newspaper prices clustered round the *Daily Mirror* in 1967, all waiting until its proprietors put in a notification of increase, though its need for revenue was plainly the least. But the *Daily Mirror* lost its leadership by the early 1970s. Similarly, Turner and Newall had its leadership in some asbestos products eroded, though more slowly, by more successful competitors.

Competition between leader and followers may depend on large-scale distribution arrangements and national promotion campaigns. The leader can advertise to reach his customers over the heads of followers and distributors alike, as Walls and Lyon's Maid have done for icecream, and Bird's Eye and Findus for other frozen foods. National firms, like Ever Ready (batteries), can offer frequent deliveries and a range of models beyond the resources of smaller firms. But national operation is not always an advantage, especially when markets are changing rapidly; offering a complete range of a product virtually anywhere may involve marketing some unprofitable lines, alongside the profitable 'cream'. But some of the cream may be skimmed by smaller firms concentrating on one product or size, as happened with replacement car batteries. Similarly, the small firms processing aluminium remained profitable, when the four majors were barely profitable or making losses.

Oligopoly
Secondly, we come to oligopoly, competition among few firms well aware of the interdependence of their own and their rivals' policies. Open collusion is barely possible in view of the Restrictive Trade Practices Act (except for approved cases such as books and drugs); so deliberate joint profit maximisation is virtually impossible. Market shares are defended instead since aggressive selling might provoke profitless retaliation. Prices are sticky, increases occurring after new wage agreements, or major increases in material prices. The four aluminium semi-manufacturers, still then sharing 80 per cent of the market between them in 1967, were in this position. The result was a scramble for orders, even for non-standard sizes and small lots, involving considerable extra cost. In such industries price plateaux are separated by rounds of price increases, extended where there is product differentiation, quickly completed for standard products sold to other businesses. Beer is an example of the first, newsprint and aluminium examples of the second.

In all these cases, prices for the main products will ultimately follow costs upwards; but costs must also respond to sales and prices, if demand is price-sensitive. Price changes are likely to be uniform for unavoidable cost increases; but market constraints or company strategy may delay the adjustment. Prices can only remain much in excess of costs where entry is difficult, *and* where firms are content to defend market shares. Even this situation is only stable until demand sags; then the weaker firms are absorbed by the stronger ones, with financial and management resources to get costs down and sales up.

When the Monopolies Commission investigated price leadership and oligopolistic behaviour in its report on 'parallel pricing', it emphasised the possibilities of both structures being eroded by new competition, either by causing prices to be restrained by the threat of newcomers, or by a firm (other than the leader) breaking into entrenched market shares. New products, expanding markets or technological change are usual occasions for such erosion to occur. Each new product variation led to renewed competition between the two leading detergent producers, Unilever and Proctor & Gamble. In the early 1960s, technological change upset the previous stability of compound fertiliser producers. On the other hand, the five industries the Monopolies Commission particularly reviewed, namely bread, electric lamps, gramophone records, petrol and tyres, had all reached technological stability as well as a high degree of concentration. But at any one time, oligopolistic pricing is widespread in manufacturing, as seen in the Monopolies Commission evidence; various public authority buyers listed dozens of cases.

Monopoly

Thirdly, there are the monopolies, the price makers and profit takers. However, there are few enduring monopolies on a world scale. Some operate nationally, protected by import controls or tariffs, as Courtaulds had for viscose yarn; some acquire such a monopoly in a product or process without protection, as Mallory did for mercury batteries. Courtaulds' monopoly gradually lost its value as other yarns were developed, in more competitive conditions. Mallory's lost its force quickly, when other firms (like Varta) in effect reintroduced the process. Even control of raw materials does not always protect a monopoly indefinitely. Turner and Newall (T & N) strengthened its monopoly in asbestos products by acquiring mining interests; the monopoly has since been weakened by two rivals, Cape Asbestos and BBA, the first a mining group moving into product markets, the second an industrial textiles group, extending into asbestos materials and buying its fibres from a subsidiary of T & N. Both of these have taken a larger share of the growing market for friction materials (for vehicle brakes).

There is no conclusive evidence that monopolies are exceptionally profitable. The NBPI considered only Courtaulds and Mallory's to be too profitable in any sense. The Monopolies Commission found some of the biggest UK firms, LBC, British Plasterboard, Pilkington's (for glass) and Metal Box to be on the whole only reasonably profitable, and generally efficient. The Roche drug company and Kellogg's (breakfast cereals) were thought to be pricing too high, to keep profits undesirably high. Large firms, including monopolies, are often run by highly qualified managers to whom it is a matter of pride or reputation to keep costs down. T & N, a monopolist already slipping, gave the Monopolies Commission most cause for doubt, though about its efficiency and restrictive agreements rather than its profits. Prices are not generally above average or marginal cost, and the costs not unreasonably high. Managers may also be wary of potential competition or unwelcome attention from governments. Reasonable prices are a protection against both. Nevertheless, a 'reasonable' price is not easy to define. Clearly it is a price related to average cost. But costs include selling and research and development expenditure. For a monopoly, or for competing giants, like Beecham and Glaxo, it must be a matter of commercial judgment to decide how much should be spent on either; there is no market-determined cost here in the same sense as average production cost. Skilful marketing is as necessary a function in large firms as efficient production. Even monopolies need to inform, to ward off potential competition, and to compete in the stores for the customers' attention.

Research and development is necessary to improve production methods, to improve the product and design new ones. But how much is justified or reasonable is difficult to say even after the event. There may be no standard of comparison apart from what is thought to be socially necessary on the one hand, or practice by similar firms overseas on the other.

Competition and welfare

One of the reasons for economists' concern with pricing in different market structures is welfare. Competition promotes welfare if it aligns prices with the costs of efficient firms. If efficiency is encouraged, more consumption can be provided from given resources. Long term, taking into account new technology or products, or the need for extending investment, prices should be based on the marginal cost of the best method to meet prospective demand. Allowing for all the uncertainties attaching to each of these magnitudes, the most we can expect in practice is either market pressures pushing prices in the right direction, or firms adopting these pricing principles as a matter of policy. The occurrence of either of these is at best patchy. In a potentially competitive industry, prices may cover the costs of the least efficient sufficiently to keep it in production, if rivalry is sufficiently lethargic. Inefficient firms may be on the way out (by merger, selling out, new management or diversifying), but so slowly that the underlying conditions change faster. Competition concerns products as much as price, and consumers can only value what is on offer. Monopolies or ologopolies may or may not be technically efficient and enterprising; if they are not, they may still be very long-lived. On the other hand, the competitively organised markets may not encourage least cost procedures. Bulk contracts for specified products between producer and customer may be much more efficient while being much less competitive.

Administered, or cost-based, prices are often assumed to be against the interests of consumers. But this is not always so: it depends on the form of the competition. Prices can be driven down or deliberately reduced to cover marginal or escapable costs only. But selling all the output at marginal cost may be neither viable nor desirable. Escapable costs leave out the inescapable overheads, and the minimum return on capital necessary to keep the business going; someone has to pay them. Where a multi-product firm sells in competition with a single product firm, the multi-product firm might sell at marginal cost, recovering its overheads on other lines, whereas the single product firm can only recover them from the one product. A high-cost, multi-product firm could supplant or take over a low-cost firm by this means. Consequently, 'cross-subsidisation', or using profits on one line to support the production of other lines, is a practice often officially disapproved in the interests of greater competition.

Though costs seem to dominate price formation, starting with costs and building up to prices is a one-sided view of the economy. Sales depend on price; price depends on costs; costs depend on output levels; output levels depend on sales. The circle is complete. Differences between markets are differences between the strength of the links. A good management can stretch or weaken the links with a novel, well-promoted, well-designed product that can be less dependent on price. Being first in the field with a new process weakens the link between costs and market price. Improving the productivity can lessen the dependence of costs on production. However, market trends, arising from social changes, give expanding total markets for some goods, declining or static markets for others, limiting the possibilities of firms' shaping demand. Technology limits or expands the possibilities of altering supply conditions.

Prices áre formed in different ways, at different times.

Price *determination* suggests a purposive activity, whereby someone or some Board deliberately decides each price, through to final prices; or the market continually adjusts demand to supply until the right market-clearing price emerges. Prices for new products may be determined in such a way. For the bulk of goods and services, prices are more formed than determined, by a process of accretion, as materials and components go from one industry or trade to another. Such deliberations that go on are as likely to be about average revenue as price, and more likely to be about the timing and size of changes than about price as such. On the way, there are many influences on costs or prices, or particular pricing practices important in one sector, irrelevant in another. Products and services eventually bought by domestic customers end with prices and charges vaguely perceived, soon forgotten, often ignored; and traders are often able to vary individual prices by percentages much larger than profit margins. Market behaviour bears little resemblance to a coherent system, let alone an optimising system.

The market system is essentially an arrangement for adjusting changes in supply, demand and price to one another. It works, that is, it succeeds in making stabilising adjustments so long as the changes are small and acceptable. If not, various non-market behaviour emerges: grabbing storable commodities, from the hoards of sugar, toilet rolls and salt built up by consumers in response to a comparatively minor, even merely rumoured shortage (1974), to the 'corners' in commodities or insider dealing in shares that the law or regulatory bodies have to prevent. Market adjustments are bargains between buyer and seller, each having weaknesses in the urgency of the buyers' needs and the number of rival sellers; each having strengths in the weight of buyers' budgets, and the common costs and behaviour of rival sellers, or the superiority of the product of particular sellers. Domestic customers only bargain themselves for minor service jobs: house decoration and repair; possibly car maintenance and repair; caterers or entertainers for parties or voluntary societies. Most retail prices are set by bargains between firms. Small shops buying through wholesalers may have as little influence on market prices as their customers. But the larger wholesalers or various buying agencies then do the bargaining. It is the main bargainers through whom the market works.

The function of the market system is to allow producers, sellers and buyers to make their own decisions about acceptable combinations of price and product. The perfect market logically results in a 'best' combination of price and product. There is not much evidence of such bliss in actual markets. But while decisions are diffused through active markets, at least there is more participation by final consumers in relatively better combinations. Markets do not automatically work smoothly or benevolently; not all bargains are good or socially desirable, nor do they necessarily aggregate to a best or better national interest. So intervention by law and policy is widespread. However, the market suitably constrained is a most powerful and useful regulator of price.

Note on Further Reading

The literature on price determination is vast. The aim of the notes on reading is to suggest references which discuss the topics here included in more detail, and contain references for pursuing the discussion further still. The emphasis is on official sources, and books based on experience of pricing and prices policies. Students who wish or need to consider the elementary concepts of market economics should consult *Economics in Society: A Basic Course* by King and Hamilton, or *Economics of the Market* by G. Hewitt. As to costs and enterprise behaviour towards them, *Social and Business Enterprises* by Jonathan Boswell covers this and other general industrial issues admirably. *An Introduction to Industrial Economics* by Devine, Jones, Lee and Tyson, should be consulted, especially on forms of market structure.

References for Chapter 1 are:

Price Index Numbers for Current Cost Accounting, Central Statistical Office (1976).

Method of Construction and Calculation of the Index of Retail Prices, Studies in Official Statistics, no. 6, HMSO (1967).

Price Commission quarterly reports (beginning April-May 1973).

Chapter 2

Governments and Prices

Governments in the UK began to become involved with pricing practices and controls early in the century. Prices policy, in the sense of an attempt to stabilise the price level, emerged only during the Second World War.

Before the First World War, pricing was no concern of officials or politicians except with respect to the government's own contracts. Monopolistic pricing or collusion to maintain prices or share markets was subject only to the law on restraint of trade, interpreted in so narrow a way as to make almost anything legal. Restrictive agreements in restraint of trade were regarded as unenforceable, and so no concern of the courts, except incidentally in disputes between the parties.

After the First World War, the growth of trusts and trade associations was officially considered by a Committee on Commercial and Industrial Policy (1918) and a Committee on Trusts (1919). Both saw merit in combination among firms, though both also admitted the danger of detriment to the consumer. The Committee on Trusts suggested that an annual report should be made to the Board of Trade, with a special tribunal to investigate cases (an idea which could have produced a Monopolies Commission or a Prices Board thirty or forty years before they actually appeared). An addendum (signed by Ernest Bevin, of the Transport and General Workers' Union, and two Labour politicians) actually recommended price control for any monopolies which could not be undermined by competition. Soon afterwards (1921) the Parliamentary Committee of the TUC suggested a permanent Costing Department, publishing costs, profits and prices, and a consumers' council to advise on cases; this would be reinforced with government powers to limit dividends and prices (another Prices Board or Prices Commission-like idea). But such ideas were not taken up in political circles, and official attitudes did not change.

RESALE PRICE MAINTENANCE

'Orderly marketing', as practised by monopolies and restrictive trade associations, inclined more and more to resale price maintenance (RPM). It was often introduced at the behest of retailers' organisations, themselves aiming to restrain competition. Manufacturers specified the *minimum* price, in practice usually the fixed price, at which their products were to be resold, wholesale and retail. Some associations enforced *collective* RPM, whereby all members withheld supplies from the traders guilty of cutting prices on the products of any one.

Manufacturers are dependent on distributors to reach their customers; hence maintained prices are set high enough to cover the costs of most if not all the distributors, including the less efficient, thus providing the more efficient or well-located shops with ample profits. Collective RPM prevented new firms or new methods coming into distribution on the basis of cutting some of the generous margins; costs were higher than they need be, as were profit margins, with lower turnover. Yet price cutting was regarded as something less than respectable.

As early as 1920, a Sub-Committee on Fixed Retail Prices was set up to report whether minimum price fixing was desirable. It concluded that it was. It prevented 'undue profit' being made out of market fluctuations, since when demand was buoyant, 'fair' prices (lower than unrestrained market prices) were maintained, and when it was slack, prices were high enough to provide a 'fair remuneration' for labour, an early and somewhat odd view of prices-and-incomes. By 1930 RPM was so widespread that it was again considered, by the Committee on Restraint of Trade. It was again upheld. This time the emphasis was legal: the right of freedom of contract must be upheld, in spite of admitted disadvantage in the form of higher prices than necessary to the public. Not until the Second World War was this legalistic, anti-competition view really undermined in official circles; but the war brought into the administration very different officials (many with trade or academic experience), and more radical politicians into government.

After the Second World War another committee, the Resale Prices Committee (the Lloyd-Jacobs Committee), reconsidered. Manufacturers were thought to have a legitimate interest in the resale prices of branded goods, it being as it were part of the property (or monopoly) in the brand. Price cutting might actually be against the public interest, it was said, as it might be more difficult to keep quality up, or to provide continuous production and supply, or to provide adequate after-sales service without it. On the other hand, there was a great need to induce new and better methods of distribution, and to encourage price reductions. Freedom of entry for newcomers was vital for this. The main recommendation was far-reaching, though somewhat unexpected. *Collective* RPM should be prohibited; individual RPM should continue.

Policy to promote competition began somewhat obliquely, in the shape of the Monopolies Commission, set up by the Monopolies and Restrictive Practices (Inquiry and Control) Act 1948. This was to examine restrictive practices case by case, and report according to the circumstances. Meanwhile RPM continued. A White Paper, *A Statement on Resale Price Maintenance* (1951), actually proposed to make individual RPM illegal too, unless it was made clear that the price was a *maximum*. Nothing came of this (partly due to the change of government in 1952); but the subject refused to die. The Monopolies Commission reporting on *Collective Discrimination* (1955) was also against individual RPM, on the grounds that it restricted competition in distribution, and restricted consumers' choice. The Restrictive Trade Practices Act (1956) finally made collective price agreements illegal (with a few exceptions); but individual RPM actually became easier to enforce legally, as a specific power was created by the Act.

The Council on Prices Productivity and Incomes (1958) urged that the law be reconsidered. The (Moloney) Committee on Consumer Protection (1962) reported that the repeal of the relevant part of the Restrictive Trade Practices Act would benefit consumers. Meanwhile the supermarket, self-service revolution in food retailing was already under way. Retailing was concentrating, with much more ruthless managements, prepared to drive a harder bargain with manufacturers for their increasingly valuable custom; and intent on expanding by the most effective means, price competition. The Resale Prices Act (1964) finally put an end to legal rights of enforcement, even for individual RPM; but it was already breaking down by then, led by the larger retailers in the food trades.

Public policy then began to pursue the remaining shadow RPM, 'manufacturers' recommended price' (MRP). The Monopolies Commission (1969) found that on the whole MRPs did not damage the public interest. There was, it thought, enough competition in most distributive sectors to make them of limited effect; and they were a necessary convenience to small traders. They were also a protection for manufacturers and the public against overcharging, especially for new lines. However, the Price Commission (1976) took a different view. Reporting on the prices of small electrical goods, it recommended that MRP should be stopped since it can mislead consumers by suggesting a better bargain than is the case, where prices generally are below MRP. RPM-like habits have persisted patchily, but too widely, in spite of the complete (though slow) revolution in official attitudes to competition.

PRICE CONTROL

Price control, meaning statutory constraint keeping prices below market levels, was suggested as a technique for controlling monopolies, but was not used as such, except incidentally to policies used for other reasons. Price control was mostly a wartime device, at least until the 1970s. The exception was housing. After small house rents were frozen at 1914 levels, by the Increase of Rent and Mortgage Interest (War Restriction) Act (1915), house rents have remained controlled, with varying coverage and variously restrictive standards.

During the First World War the severe shipping losses imposed severe shortages of some foods. Demand-determined prices would have been unthinkably high; so rather than allow this a few goods were rationed. This in itself would have restrained the rise in prices, since rationing removes the incentive for the rich or eager customers to offer higher prices then market-clearing prices for the ration. However, prices were kept below this level by maximum price controls, to ensure that the poor could buy the rations, and more particularly to stop 'profiteering'. Apart from the rationed goods prices were allowed to find their own level, and a high level it was: the price index almost doubled in five years. After the war rationing rapidly ceased, the price controls were removed, and they did not reappear until the Second World War.

By the outbreak of the Second World War, a good many economic management policies had been prepared, heavily influenced by the experience of the First World War, the files and some of the officials still being available. At the outbreak of the war import prices rose dramatically, partly due to devaluation of sterling, more to very great increases in shipping costs. Food and industrial materials were bought by government departments from 1939 onwards, the purchasing departments being instructed to charge replacement cost to customers entitled to receive supplies administratively allocated according to 'essential' needs. Though it was recognised that price controls would be needed generally, these were not forthcoming at first (apart from more widespread rent control, introduced in 1939). But controlling the demand for credit necessitated some control on prices at a later stage. The Prices of Goods Act (1940) gave powers to control the prices of specified goods by restricting profit margins to pre-war cash values.

Meanwhile leading economists, notably J. M. Keynes (then a Treasury official, as he had been in the First World War), campaigned for a more comprehensive anti-inflation policy, designed to prevent excessive expenditure (namely an income-price spiral) developing, rather than merely to direct price policy to limiting credit creation. From 1941 onwards these policies were adopted. Direct limitation of wages was considered to be impossible, as collective bargaining was a right not to be sacrificed even in wartime; but limitation of prices was to be the means of in fact limiting pay. In the budget of 1941, food subsidies were introduced to stabilise the cost of living. Later that year the Goods and Services (Price Control) Act gave powers to fix prices of any non-food product, food already being controlled as a result of government purchase.

Wartime conditions were abnormal in making widespread government controls more acceptable, and the pursuit of private interest less acceptable. However, the costs and benefits of price controls were mostly typical of the problems arising in disequilibrium market economies. The first problem is that of conveying information about prices or price changes to the controllers. Seventeen local Price Regulation Committees, reporting to a Central Committee, were set up under the 1939 Act. Their main function was to receive and investigate consumers' complaints, a function similar to that of the Price Commission's regional offices (set up in 1973). But the Central Committee found itself a more positive price-restraining technique by getting some manufacturers of branded goods to nominate 'permitted' retail prices, thus turning monopoly and RPM to some beneficial, if temporary, use. The Committees soon acquired more powers and functions under the 1941 Act, by which their parent department, the Board of Trade, became responsible for setting maximum prices and profit margins for almost anything (other than food, rents, gas and electricity, controlled by other departments).

However, even with draconian powers and thousands of officials, not all the price controls were effective nor were they all conducive to efficiency. The powers (under the Prices of Goods Act) to limit cash margins were sometimes impossible to apply, simply because firms cannot distinguish costs and profit margins on individual products, among an integrated flow of many joint products. Controls applying maximum prices instead (under the Goods and Services Act) had to specify the goods more and more elaborately, in terms of design, quality or freedom from fault, to prevent evasion by product variation; 'new' products proliferated. Clothing could not be effectively controlled at all—in spite of great restrictions of supply—until the Utility Scheme made it possible to prescribe at least the cloth exactly, if not making-up standards. The right level for maximum prices was no easier to set. A complete freeze was impossible, since higher prices for materials, some increases in wage rates and sometimes lower productivity were pushing costs up; subsidies to offset all cost increases were not contemplated. Consequently prices had to relate to costs. But linking prices too firmly to costs (the 'cost-plus' system) effectively preserves producers with their existing practices, however inefficient. In wartime the control could not move far from cost-plus, since firms were either on essential work or had already survived severe planned concentration, their capacity having been assigned to permitted non-essential work. The worst cost-plus system is that applying a percentage margin to costs; there is then positive incentive to incur high costs. Extensive accounting and the supervision of accounts and the activities reflected in them are then needed as safeguards against unnecessary expenditure. But there were many sectors, especially producing for government purchase, where no other system was practicable, though it might have been better to have made more use of the US system where the 'plus' was a cash sum rather than a percentage.

The price controls were supported either by rationing, for the more important consumer goods, or by allocation of materials and labour (all workers in age groups liable to national service being subject to direction). Rationing prevented demand from pressing too hard on controlled prices, and secured near-equal distribution; allocation of scarce supplies prevented suppliers from devoting themselves to producing non-controlled goods.

The end of the war relieved some shortages, especially of shipping; but the immediate removal of controls would undoubtedly have led to considerable price increases. It was taken for granted (in the UK) that an orderly transfer of resources from war to peacetime purposes required price controls, allocation and rationing to continue. The controls in fact became less effective as increasing production allowed much more variety of consumer goods. As supply approached demand (at current cost-based, controlled prices), rationing or allocation became less effective—and less worth opposing. It was not unusual for traders or associations to recommend an extension of controls when officials were considering removing them, no doubt to avoid the increased uncertainty and risk involved in unfamiliar competition. A slow, piecemeal dismantling of rationing, allocation and government purchase of materials, with price controls removed soon afterwards, began in 1949. The winding down lasted steadily through 1950, when over half of consumer goods were still subject to some price regulation. The Korean War of 1951-2 brought soaring world commodity prices, and renewed shortages; allocation schemes were tightened again, but no price controls were reimposed. Rising import prices were allowed through into internal costs and retail prices. Remaining price controls on non-food consumer goods were removed in 1953; private trading was restored, and rationing and price control removed for most foods in 1953 and 1954, sausages, canned sardines, and canned apricots, peaches and pears being the last to keep their controls. One wonders why these particularly deserved such extended administrative care.

Removing the food subsidies was a more difficult operation. Supply prices did not increase very fast during the war, but immediately afterwards they leapt up. By 1948 total subsidies (mainly food, but including coal) had reached over 5 per cent of GNP, and nearly one-third of central government non-defence expenditure. The *subsidies* had to be stabilised in 1948, leaving the way open for steep increases in retail prices. A considerable reduction in the remaining subsidies in 1952 (by a newly elected government) allowed another noticeable increase in prices; most of the rest of the subsidies were removed gradually, with some left, and with price control also remaining on milk and bread until the late 1950s.

PRICES AND INCOMES POLICIES

The idea that prices and incomes are interdependent, and that both must be controlled in order to moderate inflation, has a considerable history, again stemming from the problems of managing a war economy, so far as official opinion is concerned. There was in fact a Treasury memorandum in 1929 on *The Course of Prices in a Great War*, concluding that the problems of financial policy, controlling profits and labour costs must be dealt with jointly. Since wages could not be effectively limited by taxation (unlike profits), a wartime programme must include 'fixation of wages and prices', or prices and incomes policy as it is now called. But the purpose was to limit the potentially inflationary demand for credit. When war was imminent a decade later, this was still the basis of government policy.

The government nevertheless acted weakly and cautiously in 1939-40. It was not until 1941 that there were either powers for an effective general control of prices, or subsidies to stabilise cost of living supplements in wages. Thereafter, what was in effect the first UK prices and incomes policy was pursued more vigorously.

The policy of stabilising wages through stabilising the cost of living was extremely successful. The success was to a significant extent due to its being imperfect, selective and incorporating a safety valve. At that time an index of the cost of living of the working classes (weighted by expenditure as shown in budgets collected in 1914—candles and all) was compiled, to which some wage rates were linked; and those that were not tended to ride on the index, as an increase in the cost of living was accepted as a good reason for a wage increase.

At the end of the war the policy was rapidly eroded. World food prices started to rise steeply, as erstwhile enemy countries came back into world markets, constricted as their output was by damage, shortage of shipping and labour, enhanced by unusually poor harvests. Pay restraint collapsed as employers, anxious to get into civilian production, competed for scarce labour. By 1948, after a balance of payments crisis had been suppressed with exchange controls, rising labour costs threatened the government's export drive, and expenditure from excessive personal incomes was diverting potential exports to domestic consumption. Earnings had increased by no less than 17 per cent between 1947 and 1948 and the cost of living was 10 per cent up. As there had been no statutory control of wages during the war, none was thought feasible after it. A White Paper, a *Statement on Personal Incomes Costs and Prices*, embodied the government's hopes and entreaties for voluntary restraint. Price controls under the Goods and Services Act still existed, though the government (unwisely) allowed some relaxation from maximum price orders, only a month after the White Paper, since costs were rising fast. However, the policy held for a critical time. Wage rates rose only 5 per cent between March 1948 and March 1950; retail prices rose 7 per cent. The TUC actually recommended a wage standstill for 1949, provided the price index rose by less than six points; but prices rose persistently, and the unions were becoming impatient. The devaluation of sterling in September 1949 effectively ended the first post-war prices and incomes policy, as the subsequent price increases were far beyond what had been expected.

Though there were no more attempts at prices or incomes policies, official concern about increases in the price level scarcely disappeared during the 1950s. The Council on Prices, Incomes and Productivity appointed in 1957 were intended to influence 'public opinion' (clearly the trade unions) by recommending ways of moderating the rise in prices. Their appointment and their recommendations were both controversial; their influence was minimal.

The next government attempt to halt the upward trend of the price level was the 'pay pause' of 1961 (after another balance of payments crisis). If wages, salaries and dividends were all frozen for six months, the underlying improvement in average productivity would enable costs and prices to be stabilised if not reduced. Thereafter income rises in line with average productivity (the 'guiding light') would keep the price level stable. The policy met with determined opposition from the trade unions, and so came to nothing. But it was notable for calling forth the complaint, among the reasons justifying the opposition, that it involved no explicit policy for prices. Thereafter, an acceptable incomes policy was taken to be a *prices* and incomes policy.

The first comprehensive prices and incomes policy was introduced by the next government (a Labour government coming to office after twelve years) in 1965. It involved establishing a National Board for Prices and Incomes (NBPI) to supervise unprecedentedly detailed rules for prices as well as incomes (discussed fully in Chapter 9 below). This lasted until the next change of government in 1970. The incoming Conservative government was elected with a programme explicitly rejecting the interferences with market forces implied by prices and incomes policies; but it found that it could not remain agnostic about the rate of increase of either prices or incomes. By 1971 both were rising considerably faster than before, and much faster than in the early 1960s; but this time inflation was accompanied by unemployment, approaching the politically critical one million. As relations between TUC and government were bad, industrialists as represented by the CBI actually proposed their own prices policy, the so-called 'price initiative'. Two hundred of the largest firms (many represented on the CBI Grand Council) agreed to limit price increases to 5 per cent for one year, with few escape clauses for exceptions. Their hope was that the unions would offer some wage restraint in return, a hope entirely disappointed. Nevertheless a prices policy had reappeared, without benefit of government.

The government could not remain totally indifferent, nor totally silent, on so important a policy. Nor could it plausibly disapprove a development industrialists evidently thought in their own best interests. Tangential approval was signalled by ministers urging the nationalised industries to join the 'initiative', a policy which led to larger and larger sums being granted to finance deficits as costs rose. As the initiative neared its end, the CBI insisted with growing anxiety that the government declare its own policy to moderate inflation. Once more even a government originally pledged to sweep it away had arrived at a conjuncture when it had no alternative to a prices and incomes policy.

Talks between government and unions began, aiming at another 'tripartite' agreement between themselves and industrialists. When the talks failed the government introduced the Counter-inflation Act (1973), which brought in the most rigorous of imposed policies up till then. Closely following a prices and incomes policy introduced in the US the previous year, the new policy began (November 1972) with a ninety-day freeze on most prices and all incomes. From the spring of 1973 to 1974 (when the government lost an election), income increases were subject to the rules of the Pay Code and price increases were subject to the Price Code (discussed in Chapter 9 below). The Pay Code mainly imposed a limit on permitted increases. The Price Code mainly limited price increases to cost increases, up to a profit ceiling. The Pay Code was monitored by the Pay Board, the Price Code by the Price Commission.

The next incoming government (the Labour administration of 1974) abolished the Pay Board and the Pay Code. The Price Code, much revised, and the Price Commission were kept in being by two extensions of the Counter-inflation Act, up to the summer of 1977.

The content and results of the prices policies are discussed later. First we consider the pricing practices in private and public enterprises, on which prices policies have to work.

Note on Further Reading
Further report on Commercial and Industrial Policy. Cd 9035 (1918).
Report of the Committee on Trade. Cd 9236 (1919).
Sub-Committee on Fixed Retail Prices. Cmd 662 (1920).
Report of the Committee on Restraint of Trade, HMSO (1930).
Report of the Committee on Resale Price Maintenance, (Lloyd-Jacob). Cmd 7696 (1949).
A Statement on Resale Price Maintenance. Cmd 8274 (1951).
Reports of the Central Price Regulation Committee (up to 1946).
Reports of the Council on Prices, Productivity and Incomes, HMSO (1958, 1959 and 1961).
Collective Discrimination, Monopolies Commission (1955).
Recommended Resale Prices, Monopolies Commission (1969).
Small Electrical Household Appliances and Recommended Retail Prices, Price Commission (1976).
How to Pay for the War, Keynes (1940).
Statement on Personal Incomes Costs and Prices. Cmd 7321 (1948).
The Great Inflation, 1939-51, A. J. Brown (1954).

Civil Industry and Trade, Hancock and Gowing, Official History of the Second World War, HMSO (1949).

The British Economy 1945-50, Chapters XIII and XIV, Worswick and Ady (1952).

Machinery of Prices and Incomes Policy. Cmnd 2577 (1965).

Prices and Incomes. Cmnd 2639 (1965).

Part Two

THE PRIVATE SECTOR

Chapter 3

Commodities, Agriculture and Food

Market structure, market performance and pricing practices vary between sectors of the economy, especially between the primary products, manufacturing and services. The more important private sector services in determining prices, as reflected in the RPI, are distribution and housing.

COMMODITIES

'Commodities' is understood to mean natural materials and foods traded internationally on a large scale. All of these have markets in the usual sense. However, commodity markets are often understood to be those where trade in 'futures' is organised. Commodity prices therefore are influenced by three sets of conditions: the conditions of supply in mining or agriculture; the market for commodities in the ordinary sense of buying and selling; and the operations of commodity markets in the special sense of future trading.

Agricultural crops
For agricultural crops, long-term supply depends on trends of land use and productivity, in turn dependent on government policies, and the amount spent for improvements in irrigation and drainage, machinery, plant, breeding, fertilisers and marketing arrangements. Though the main sources of supply of most crops are localised for climatic reasons, there are enough sources of supply for strong competition between sellers. If the producers are still the sellers, they have very little market power at all even for plantation crops, but monopolistic or co-operative marketing boards are much more usual. These may be in fierce inter-country competition, especially where the product is still standard (grains, sugar, cocoa, rubber, timber). Great efforts are made to differentiate the product (Ceylon tea in competition with Indian); and some differentiation occurs naturally (Latin American and African coffee,

American, Egyptian, Pacific cottons). Price leadership from one of the main producers or producing areas is therefore not uncommon. 'The' world price is often a particular price for a given description in a main producing area, with a flexible range of prices for other descriptions in other places. The changes in relative prices are due to changes in relative output, due in turn to seasonal factors in the short term, and changes in the economic structures of supplying areas in the long term. Changes in price level are more likely to be due to demand changes, or general changes in input prices, such as fertilisers.

Production lead times are long and inflexible: coffee bushes mature in five to ten years, rubber trees in seven. Once crops are planted, nature and previous investment in water supplies, fertilisers and machinery determine the maximum output. Greater capacity for storing supplies carried over from season to season has given sellers more power to stabilise supplies, but some crops deteriorate. All storage has become relatively more costly as interest rates have risen, and standards become more exacting. Short term, changes in demand and hence in price can have little effect on supply. Long term, the response is naturally greater (and often underestimated); but even then it may be slow if there are few opportunities for farmers to turn to other crops or other sectors for employment or investment. In spite of many sources of supply, the marginal ones generally being able to switch to alternative crops, agricultural prices are notoriously unstable. The trouble is partly the sheer size of the markets; the main suppliers may not be able to switch to other crops. Storage on a large enough scale to stabilise prices may not be feasible, in the light of competing demands for investment funds.

Demand conditions make the instability of prices worse. Demand for food crops is unresponsive to price, sluggishly so to incomes. With low price elasticities of demand and supply (short term), changes in supply or demand cause changes in price. Cycles of excess and deficient supplies are characteristic of uncontrolled agricultural markets (and very often of controlled ones as well). A shortage and high prices tempts too many farmers into increasing output for the next harvest, and subsequently investing in extra capacity. Supply then becomes excessive in relation to demand, prices fall sharply below expectations and incomes below plans; too many disappointed farmers withdraw, preparing the way for the next shortage and high prices.

However, in the longer term demand changes with income, product innovation and technology. Instant coffee, machine-washable wool, synthetic fibres, mixtures of cotton and synthetics, soft vegetable-oil margarines have all increased the price elasticities of demand for the natural crops.

Minerals

Supply conditions for minerals have some features in common with those for crops, notably long production lead times. The underlying trend of supply often depends on the investment decisions of large enterprises, taking a view of prospects more than ten years ahead, and as a result is unusually risk- and uncertainty-prone. Political risks also face some of the expatriate multi-national companies. Investment in new capacity is usually very costly, and the returns dependent on natural conditions. The large amounts needed for investment and the special conditions have made mineral production a highly specialised sector, of large firms. The returns usually reward the risk takers generously.

Short term, supplies are more controllable. Mines can be worked more or less fully, and stocks can be run down or built up. Where the sellers and buyers are large enterprises, the market can be stabilised by contracting for regular supplies. However, demand, even from the largest users, is also subject to major uncertainties.

The underlying trend of demand depends on the incomes of the ultimate users. For instance, the demand for copper depends not merely on the demand of the electricity suppliers for cable, but on the trend of demand for the electricity. Technical development changes the demand for the material relative to the demand for the product (telephone cables carry much more traffic per unit weight of metal than formerly). Substitution of one metal for another depends also on relative costs and prices.

World demand for most materials is rising as the rich countries get richer and the poor countries enter the industrial field. But the demand for industrial materials is subject to cyclical booms and slumps, these cycles tending to coincide more closely in the major industrialised countries. Demand for minerals is therefore more volatile. Market demand is made still more unstable by changes in the purchasers' stocks. Stocks of materials, work in progress and ex-factory products are run down and built up in anticipation of booms and slumps, price changes, or changes in governments' commercial policies. Consequently prices are also highly unstable, except where lack of competition allows a dominant producer to administer prices regardless of cycles, meeting declining sales with postponement of price rises, and booms with more rapid increases. But where there is competition and market determination of prices, boom prices can be 50 to 100 per cent higher than slump prices (as 1974 prices were above 1975 prices).

The market response to be expected from a cyclically unstable industry is collusion to control the supply, firmer contractual arrangements or forward integration. All occur among mineral producers. Aluminium producers have long been suspected of collusion (and investigated by anti-trust bodies in the US and Canada). The most successful of politically organised cartels is the Organisation of Petroleum Exporting Countries (OPEC); but in the absence of strong political common interests, other mineral producers find it more difficult to reconcile their conflicting interests for long. Large companies find it easier, by keeping prices in line, where outright agreement is illegal. Contracts are used increasingly. Forward integration into fabrication, and even down to processed products, occurs in aluminium and asbestos (and pulp and paper companies).

Supply and demand in conditions of low price elasticities often determine commodity prices. However, we must quickly add that there is no general rule applying to all commodities all the time. Substitution gets more responsive to cost increases as industrial sophistication grows. Some commodities enjoy high income elasticities (as most metals and oils do); some have none. Drought, flood and more human disasters, such as strikes, lockouts and accidents, rarely hit all producing zones in the same year.

Long term, prices must cover costs of supply. If demand rises higher than current supply capacity, prices must rise enough to make marginal supplies worth exploiting. If demand falls below supply capacity, prices will be very weak as existing suppliers try to avoid contracting production. Short term, the stability of prices depends on the organisation of the suppliers.

Oil and Gas

The fossil fuels, especially oil, are an outstanding example of the effect of monopolies in naturally scarce materials, and the natural variations between the productivity of one producing unit and another. The idea of economic rent, or the extra income the owner of a prolific resource derives from its superiority over others, was developed to explain the consequences of differences in soil fertility. But few farmers have enjoyed economic rents, considerable though some of them are, on the scale of oil companies.

Accessible oil reserves are among the most valuable monopolies in modern economies. Surface and air transport both depend almost completely on oil; and where there are substitute fuels, for electricity generation or heating, oil has had much lower costs than the alternatives. Until the 1970s, demand for energy continuously increased with increasing production and trade; oil-propelled transport has increased even faster. At the same time cheaper, more prolific oil-fields were still being discovered and exploited in the Middle East and Africa.

Most oil is produced by a few multi-national companies. However, with competing producers and varying costs of production, supply and demand could still balance at a market price just covering the costs (including required return on capital) of the marginal suppliers. But demand has increased fast enough to keep ahead of supplies. Oil prices fell relatively to other things for nearly thirty years after the Second World War impelled by new low-cost sources, as well as competition; but profits kept up. The producers were enjoying economic rents, the surplus they could earn through possession of oil wells, over and above cost. Even if competition is fierce enough to bring prices down to marginal cost, some producers still make handsome surpluses.

Governments of oil-bearing countries began to take a share in the monopoly surpluses by taxation. A royalty per barrel was levied, to be paid sometimes in a specified overseas currency, sometimes in oil (subsequently either sold on international markets or sold back to the producing companies). The percentage take was gradually increased. The oil companies remained profitably in production, partly attracted by the remaining slice of the surpluses, partly by exploiting the captive parts of their markets. The taxation screw was finally turned much tighter by a unique pricing device. The royalties are a percentage of 'posted prices', that is, offer prices for oil of a given quality at a given port. But posted prices were in fact like list prices in many other sectors, an initial figure from which commercial negotiations start rather than a price actually paid. As the governments of the Arab oil producers came together politically they took advantage of their joint monopoly, to take over the regulation of posted prices. The higher the posted price the higher the tax revenue, even with a given royalty percentage, or both could be screwed up. As all the major oil companies were affected by this policy, they could all pass on the extra import to their customers. The producers go on earning surpluses at the expense of consumers; but a high proportion of a much higher total goes to governments.

When natural gas and oil were discovered in the North Sea, the UK government had to decide how to deal with the monopolies conferred on successful licensees. Natural gas was the more straightforward. An effective curb on any monopoly supplier is a monopoly buyer. The British Gas Corporation (BGC) was established in 1973, a much stronger national body than the twelve virtually autonomous boards it succeeded, with a statutory monopoly for buying all natural gas. The exploration and development companies then had to agree beachhead prices and offtake conditions with the BGC. The tougher the bargain BGC drove, the better its own income would be, through larger sales or lower costs or both. On the other hand, the tougher the bargain, the greater the danger of restricting further exploration and development. Producers would adjust their plans so that costs including required returns, and taking into account imported risks, were covered by the price offered, at the margin. Nevertheless, intra-marginal producers and intra-marginal wells would still be earning surpluses.

Oil was a different matter: there was more of it; the repercussions would be greater (more of it is likely to be used as feedstock for other products, as well as its needing more complex refining); and no monopoly purchaser existed. The alternatives were to create a monopoly purchaser, to take some of the surplus by taxation, to control prices, or for the state to go into the business. Once the existence of oil had been proved, the government possessed part of the monopoly in the form of licences to drill. If the size of reserves and the unit costs of bringing them to shore were not so uncertain, an appreciable slice of the surplus might be transferred by auctioning the licences. The government decided to use administrative means, mainly to influence the rate of activity: those whose proposals involved faster progress got preference. Meantime the world price had been successfully jacked up by OPEC. As the oil flowed, so would the surpluses.

At first a royalty (12½ per cent) on production, plus the Petroleum Revenue Tax (PRT) on profits (in addition to the normal Corporation Tax), was instituted, with generous grants on investment effectively offsetting the tax in the early years on production, and for marginal ventures. But only the royalty was effective. The North Sea companies, mostly subsidiaries of the multi-nationals, managed to slide out by using the ubiquitous posted prices. By charging themselves posted prices instead of market prices on transfers from producing companies overseas to the associated refineries or distribution companies, they produced losses rather than profits in the companies on which the PRT was to be levied. The next government's answer was twofold: to establish a notional ring-fence round the North Sea for taxation purposes, allowing no imports of 'losses' from elsewhere; and to set up the British National Oil Corporation (BNOC). The BNOC has a 51 per cent share in production, enforced as a condition of licences to explore; and it handles oil taken as royalties.

The effect of this on prices is to leave them to be determined in world markets, though the UK price will be to some extent influenced by the increasing availability of high quality oil so near major refineries and markets. For all its size, the BNOC operates in a competitive world market, and probably has less influence on prices than some other nationalised industries.

Government policy

Few other commodities lend themselves to inter-government control of prices to the same degree as oil. But as commodities sold on international markets are often a large part of the income of developing countries, their governments naturally take an increasing interest in the stability of that income. Long-term agreements are constantly advocated. However, successful commodity agreements are hard to come by. Consumers want agreements at times of shortage, to cut off the top of boom prices, and to share out scarce supplies fairly. Producers want agreements at times of glut to put a minimum to prices and guarantee purchases. But at boom times, as prices rise, producers have every incentive to break agreements and sell as much as possible to the highest bidder. In slump times, consumers have strong incentives to buy outside the agreement at knock-down prices, from weak sellers, such as new producers trying to get into markets, or unorganised operators profitably exploiting the fringes of markets, with destabilising effect.

As serious a problem for governments in consuming countries is the effect of commodity prices on manufacturing costs. Price rises affect all users equally, at any rate before they have time to try substitutes. All therefore know that their rivals have roughly equivalent cost increases to take into their prices. Prices rise in line, however competitive the structure seems to be. In some cases, like metal processing or milling, prices are based on movements in raw material prices anyway. Where other inputs are a higher proportion of costs, material cost increases can still be passed straight through to consumers further down the production chain. This has been one of the strongest cost-inflation generators in advanced countries.

Commodity futures markets

The most important characteristic of commodity *markets* is that they deal in titles to goods rather than the goods themselves. They are consequently highly speculative. The principal commodities traded in London are the metals: gold, silver, copper, lead, zinc and tin; and the 'softs': cocoa, coffee, sugar, cotton, wool, rubber, grain and soya beans.

Sellers and buyers of commodities must both decide not only at what price to trade, but whether to trade at all now (spot) or whether to stock it for a time and sell or buy it later on (forward). The problem is endemic to crops because of their seasonal production. Production must necessarily be concentrated at harvest-time; with consumption spread virtually evenly through the year stocks must be held and financed by someone. The stock-holders bear the costs of physical storage, and the risks of the price in future not rising enough to cover the costs of stocking plus interest on the capital involved. The incentive is the handsome reward if prices do rise. Producers and consumers of commodities both bear their own risks involved in production, and may not welcome another set where the expertise required for success is very different from their own. Specialised commodity markets dealing forward have therefore long been a feature of international trade between dispersed producers and manufacturers or processors.

However, forward as well as spot contracts greatly increase the scope of a market; each part of the supply has a range of possible prices and delivery dates. Not only have purchases to match sales in terms of quantities and specifications, but delivery dates have to be matched to suit buyer and seller too. Markets can be 'thin': that is, sellers or buyers can have difficulty in finding a taker for a sale at the right time. Futures contracts cover the thin patches by multi-plying the number of contracts, and make 'hedging' possible to accommodate more of the risks.

A futures contract is an agreement to sell or buy a quantity of a commodity at a future date; but the contract itself (the future) is bought and sold. The same physical supply can thus be bought and sold many times over before settling day finally transfers its owner-ship. Successful dealing in futures depends on guessing future changes in price. Given the selling price of a future contract for a given period hence, a potential buyer will buy (the obligation) if he believes prices will rise more than that. If he is right, spot prices will rise more than expected, and futures with them. Long before he gets to settling day, our buyer can sell the future at a profit. (If he is wrong and the prices fail to rise, he may also hasten to sell his future in order to minimise his losses.) As futures, or 'terminal', markets (in the UK) only require buyers to pay a small percentage of the nominal amount of their contract at the time of the contract, very large profits indeed (and very large losses) are possible.

The main function of futures markets is to provide facilities for hedging, that is, covering a current physical transaction with an opposite futures one. A producer can not only sell forward; he can remove more of his risk by buying a future as well. Similarly, pur-chasers can sell a future at the same time as they buy forward. (Futures markets make it a commonplace to sell something not yet in your possession.) Then, nearer the date of delivery, the futures contract can be sold (or bought). If prices fall, the physical transaction represents a loss to forward buyers; and if they rise, a loss to sellers. But as futures prices will also be affected, the sellers of futures will gain as prices fall, and the buyers as they rise. So hedging removes some of the potential loss to one party or other, and may even bring modest gain. Prices are thereby stabilised; this in turn has the effect of stabilising producers' incomes and manufacturers' costs.

However, this is only part of what actually happens. Futures markets are essentially speculative: that is, they operate through buyers and sellers backing their judgment about future prices. If speculators interpret price rises as a sign that further rises are coming, rising prices lead to an increase in demand instead of a fall, and each rise makes another more likely (and vice versa for falls). A limit to speculation is set on commodity markets (unlike foreign or stock exchanges) by the physical needs met by the commodity. Demand for the commodity cannot be totally inelastic to price rises, and neither is supply. New harvests, new mines opening eventually moderate the wilder flights of buying.

Commodity markets show a process of price determination as near as any to the classic idea of higgling until demand and supply balance—which does not by any means result in the best of all possible results in the best of all possible worlds. The volume of speculation is a subject of constant criticism. As speculators come into the market as 'investors' only, prices are influenced more by speculation and less by real supply and demand. Moreover, if the speculation is destabilising, producers will suffer lower incomes than they might when prices fall, and industrial costs will rise higher than they might when prices rise. *Short term*, commodity markets which offer hedging facilities through futures may help to stabilise prices, incomes and costs. But if longer term, the speculative activity they encourage increases the uncertainty of incomes, suppliers or cost, it is often questioned whether the short-term advantages outweigh the longer-term problems (anxieties which led to a Select Committee of the House of Lords investigating commodity prices in 1976-7).

Speculation can be modified by regulations requiring higher margins, by licensing or otherwise supervising dealers authorised to enter markets, or by establishing commodity commissions. These would have monopoly powers statutorily created to buy all produce offered to them, and sell on the best terms they could get. Monopoly powers of this kind were exercised by government departments in the UK during and after the Second World War. But these were times of acute shortage, with supplies allocated to consumers always eager to receive them. Informal, non-statutory supervision of markets is exercised by the Bank of England, a role it attracted as part of its responsibilities for exchange control or supervision since most commodities with London markets are imported.

Some commodity markets (especially the London Metal Exchange, LME) have far more influence on prices than the proportionate amount of trade they do. Sales of metals such as copper, which have not gone through the market at all, may nevertheless be automatically priced at LME prices. It is quite possible therefore for a price inflated by speculation, or unduly sensitive to marginal buyers merely topping up their normal contract supplies through the market, to be reflected much more widely in costs and prices in metal-using industries. Such a rise is not caused by a cost increase at all. A market price that is in fact formed only by marginal uncontracted supplies sold to marginal buyers is bound to be much more volatile than a market price influenced by total supply and demand, since the proportionate changes are so much larger. The international price of sugar is similarly only a marginal price, as the bulk of sales are controlled by international agreements.

To sum up, price formation for commodities is a result of market activity with a strong speculative element. However, the prices set by the market also influence the growth of supplies, though often with long time lags. Commodity prices rising faster than their costs will make some crops more profitable than others, and make it worthwhile to use poorer land or open more difficult mineral areas. Commodity prices rising sluggishly in relation to costs will eventually depress production and discourage investment, especially in capital-intensive mining. The great weakness of supplies being regulated by market trends is shown most starkly on commodity markets. The response to either rising or falling prices is exaggerated because producers cannot or do not fully take into account the effect of their collective actions on future prices. Consequently cycles of boom and slump are very common. If these were predictable, buffer stock schemes would counteract them and stabilise producers' incomes and consumers' costs. But there are long-term trends also, depending on secular changes in demand which make the amplitude, period and average level of each cycle unpredictable. Buffer stocking has its own risks, the costs of which may be far above the costs involved in speculative markets. There is no obvious choice between the two. As is so often the case, the 'right' policy is as much a matter of politics as of economic analysis.

AGRICULTURE

Agriculture (and horticulture) is an industry of homogeneous products and many small firms often owner-managed. It should be the archetypal competitive market. Yet agricultural prices are everywhere supported and markets controlled by governments. Free market prices are extremely unstable. Consequently farmers' incomes are unstable, in spite of price and quantity produced varying inversely; and in most countries they are lower than incomes in industry (without government support).

Demand and supply

The conditions of demand for food in the UK compound farmers' problems and inhibit easy stabilisation measures. Demand for food as a whole has a low price elasticity. Demand for the cheap bulk foods, grain and potatoes and sugar, shows a persistent downward trend as real incomes rise. Potatoes have managed a spectacular revival in a processed form as potato crisps. Biscuits, cakes and breakfast cereals have not quite managed the same revival for flour, nor have ice-cream and sweets for sugar. Milk and eggs show signs of increasing market saturation. Consumers go on buying the daily loaf or weekly joint, lettuces at the weekend, especially when warm weather strikes, tomatoes on Saturdays (to go with the lettuce), the average three eggs a week. Proportionately large price increases or decreases do not much repel or attract them into buying less in shortage, or more in abundance. General food price changes merely impoverish or enrich them.

However, demand for particular products may respond readily to relative price changes. One meat is a fairly close substitute for another; changes in the relative prices of beef, lamb, pork and chicken cause substitution, especially given time for adjustment. Some green vegetables or root vegetables (but not potatoes) are easily substituted. Dried, canned and frozen fruit and vegetables are close substitutes when prices rise, as well as more strongly preferred as incomes rise. But if regulations permit, imports are much the more important source of substitutes in consumption.

Catering is an important part of the market. Commercial or institutional caterers can be even less price-sensitive than their customers. The cost of even the major item of food, ham for the sandwiches, hindquarter beef for the lunch or dinner trade, chicken or forequarter beef for pies and savouries, is a relatively small part of total catering costs, most of which is labour and the cost of premises. But the caterers may well be very discriminating between sources of supply.

On the supply side, technological developments have increased productivity at an impressive rate. Research into plant breeding, methods of cultivation, control of pests and weeds, animal health and selection, livestock management techniques, has produced steady improvement. Increasing use of fertilisers and much greater capital has added to the returns. Output has increased at a persistently faster rate than consumption. Consequently, the proportion of UK food supplies produced at home has increased steadily. Almost all UK farmers are multi-product enterprises, with considerable flexibility between products. As relative demand, prices and costs change, the pattern of output has changed. Most farmers have prospered most of the time. But this has only been possible by much greater government regulation of the market than has ever been exercised in any other private sector.

Co-operative selling (collusion) among farmers to regulate supplies has not developed much, no doubt due to the large number of independent producers, and conflicts of interest between large and small, lowland and upland, one product sector and another. Moreover, the rewards are great for individual members selling on the open market when prices are high. Governments have stepped in to eliminate the competitive weakness.

Four different methods are used: creating a monopoly, by requiring all supplies to be sold to a marketing board; guaranteeing minimum prices to farmers; restricting supply by controlling imports by quota; and raising market prices by import duties, or buying for stock, or both.

Marketing boards

Two of the longest lived statutory marketing boards in the UK are the Potato Marketing Board and the Milk Marketing Board (MMB). The Potato Marketing Board does not itself buy or sell. It controls acreage, lays down minimum standards for normal sales (mostly by size), and advises when imports or exports should be regulated. For the rest, it bases acreage quotas on estimates of yields and the size of the market, aiming to keep the first-hand price reasonably above estimated average cost, in order to give an adequate return on capital employed. The monopoly is not complete: potatoes destined for processing into crisps or 'instant' dried mash do not come within the control, and are mainly sold forward on contract. Prices are kept within a narrower band than a free market range.

The MMB is an effective discriminating monopolist. All milk must be sold to it (except small quantities withheld by licensed farmer-retailers). It then sells milk for sale as liquid milk at one price, and milk for manufacture (into cream, butter, cheese, yoghourt and so on) at another. The price elasticity of demand for liquid milk is very low, for manufacturing milk rather higher, because dairy products have close substitutes in imports. Consequently the MMB can increase its revenue (and farmers' income) by charging more for liquid milk than it does for manufacturing. It bends its best efforts to selling more liquid milk; and if supplies dwindle the market is kept supplied, while the creameries get the remainder at a much more variable price. Being a statutory authority it does not *maximise* its returns, as it is intended to control the division of welfare between consumers and producers. It probably could charge far higher prices for liquid milk and increase its income.

Milk producers receive a pool price from MMB for all deliveries, the weighted average price of liquid and manufacturing sales. Consequently the price of marginal supplies from the producer is higher than its market price for manufacturing, the marginal use. Marginal costs can thus be above price, the loss or revenue being borne willy-nilly by the MMB. Farmers are encouraged to produce more milk than consumers of dairy products are prepared to pay for at resource cost; too many resources might thus be kept in dairy farming.

Retail prices and distributors' margins are both fixed periodically by the Ministry of Agriculture, Fisheries and Food (MAFF) in relation to cost increases revealed by a sample survey. The price structure is extremely simple—even crude. A uniform price for three grades (Channel Island, homogenised and 'ordinary' pasteurised) applies in all areas, with the exception of the more remote parts of Scotland. Consequently the retail dairies have to average the very different costs of delivering to compact urban and scattered rural areas. Milk in towns and milk sold in shops probably has a higher than free market price, delivered milk in scattered areas a lower than free market price. In return the quality is uniform, and uniformly high, and the transport operation from farm to dairy probably organised as well or better than otherwise.

A marketing board controlling the supply by acreage quota increases supply prices. The extra value is the rent or monopoly profit created in the quotas. The usual detriment of monopoly to consumers is that inefficient producers in possession of a quota may continue their malpractices indefinitely. A market-type solution adopted by the Hops Board (a statutory body originating from the Agricultural Marketing Act 1930) is to make the quotas saleable. Their value is greater to the efficient grower, with uniform prices covering a range of average costs. The extra costs of the quotas squeeze the profits of the inefficient, putting pressure on the weakest to reform or retire. The creation of the monopoly puts up prices to consumers, as is intended; but this arrangement means the consumer does not have to suffer doubly, by having to pay the higher costs of inefficiency as well as the monopoly profit.

Not surprisingly, farmers have often been in favour of more marketing boards, and more have existed, though uniformity can be a disadvantage for some products. In addition, the marketing has not always been done as well as the best producers can do for themselves. The Meat and Livestock Commission seeks to improve the quality of the product offered for a given price rather than raise producer prices as such. The farmers themselves responded to this 'weakness' by setting up the Fatstock Marketing Corporation, their own competitor for the wholesale meat trade. This is probably the most important example of collusion among farmers, apart from the few co-operatives.

Government support before 1972

Guaranteed minimum prices were the main support to agriculture in the 1950s and 1960s. Before UK accession to the European Economic Community (EEC) these prices were fixed at the Annual Price Reviews, based on joint surveys by MAFF and the National Farmers' Union of changes in costs, investment required to meet estimated demand and returns on capital. The guarantee was an average for all suppliers, implemented by a periodic payment to farmers of the difference between this average and the average realised market price. The subsidy actually received by individual farmers could therefore be far removed from the difference between their own costs and receipts. Farmers still had an incentive to reduce unit costs and increase receipts; but the subsidy and hence the farmers' total returns were highly unpredictable, and the total government commitment still more so (unless all the estimates were fulfilled). The principle is straightforward enough; the practice became more and more tortuous. Market prices vary for seasonal and cyclical reasons, especially for livestock. Cereals are easier to store than livestock products, and have an entirely predictable production period. The problem is the period over which the average applies. If the period is too short, the average merely follows market fluctuations up and down—or worse, follows them with a lag, so that the guarantee goes *up* when supplies are ample and market prices falling, and vice versa. If the period is too long, seasonal and cyclical fluctuations get averaged and flattened so much that too little indication of demand comes through at all. All this on top of administrative delays resulted in so complicated a system at its worst that it is questionable how many farmers really got any market signals to respond to.

The most serious political disadvantage was the unpredictable and growing cost to the Exchequer. The lower world or demand prices, the larger the gap between them and the guarantees. The more produce sold from farms at home, the larger the total subsidies to be paid. However, the great advantage of this type of deficiency payment price support is that it is consistent with consumer prices at the world market level. Indeed it was the UK's large imports from world markets that led to this system being adopted in the Agriculture Act of 1947.

Horticulture has mostly been protected by restriction of supply through import quotas, especially by seasonally varied licences. Market price is raised, and otherwise submarginal producers can stay in business; the intra-marginal ones make higher profits. But there are special problems attaching to perishable crops. Once they are grown and packed, a price covering hardly more than the cost of distribution will be better than destroying them. Short-term gluts (aggravated by sluggish demand, perhaps, as well as abundant supply) can result in abysmally low prices in the few countries allowing imports. If home producers then go out of business, the consumers may suffer from higher prices or lower supplies in future less favourable seasons. At least so the argument goes. But growers themselves have stabilised their markets by developing more standardised crops and selling more by contract to distributors or processors. For salad crops, fresh vegetables and fruit, longer cropping or selling seasons also help. For processing, uniform ripeners at one time may be more important to cut harvesting costs. The plant breeders and crop management experts both assist in improving and 're-designing' the product.

The Common Agricultural Policy

Protection by maintaining high market prices, supported by official stock-piling, was the system adopted for the Common Agricultural Policy (CAP) of the EEC. As in so many agricultural policies the principle is simple, the practice positively labyrinthine. So what follows is an outline of the most mind-boggling price policy yet.

The common policy requires uniform competitive prices throughout the EEC. The protection requires barriers to imports from outside. The prices are decided by the Council of Ministers once a year; the protection consists of either common external tariffs or variable levies on imports. The system requires no less than three common prices: the *target* price, the *intervention* price and the *threshold* price. The target price is the basic price that producers are intended or expected to get from the market. The intervention price is up to 10 per cent lower than this, obtainable by selling to intervention, the minimum guarantee. The threshold price is the one to which import prices are compared to calculate the levy and should be that price at the port of entry which would actually secure target prices in the market (allowing for distribution costs and profits).

If market prices fall below the target level, farmers may sell to intervention (in the UK the Home Grown Cereals Authority and the Meat and Livestock Commission). If import prices are below the threshold, levies are imposed. But free market prices are far from uniform. There are differences in quality and characteristics even for cereals, let alone livestock; and variations in transport and handling costs between surplus and deficient areas. Consequently 'the' common prices become schedules of prices, in the case of cereals, for instance, aligned with the most deficient areas for wheat, with lower prices for the (named) surplus places. For imports, supplies coming from different suppliers at different times are bought at different prices. The levies therefore are related to the lowest c.i.f. price, and as these vary day by day, so do the levies.

For pigmeat, eggs and poultry the import levies are more complex. About two-thirds of the cost is the cost of feeding stuff. Therefore there is a levy (on imports of pigmeat, etc.) based on the difference between world prices and EEC prices of feeding stuff; plus another levy levelling up the prices of the product.

With separate national currencies, common (administered) prices can only exist if rates of exchange are fixed. If they are not, the differences must be compensated. Hence the monetary compensatory amounts (the mca). If one currency floats down (or is devalued), its produce becomes cheaper in terms of the currency of the rest. Its farmers get an extra competitive advantage against those with stable or appreciating currencies. To prevent this, amounts enough to close all or part of the gap (to restore wholly or partly the old parities for farm produce only) are paid on imports into the devaluing country. A 'green pound' is established, above the value of the pound used for other purposes. The effect is a considerable benefit to consumers in relatively devaluing countries, like the UK, because the mca's reduce the price of food imports, keeping domestic prices down. But the further the 'green pound' is away from the current real pound, the bigger the contribution by way of the mca's that comes from EEC funds. The EEC and the UK farmers both gain at the expense of consumers and importers by moving the 'green pound' nearer the real pound.

For the transition period, between the Treaty of Accession and various dates up to 1978, accession compensation amounts (aca's) also applied. These had a similar, additional effect to the mca's. They were decreasing amounts paid on imports from other members, with the full 'common' prices to reduce them nearer to the lower UK market price. Like the mca's, the aca's reduced food prices to the consumers, at the expense of farmers, though in this the sacrifice was only relative consisting in a smaller step upwards towards the common prices.

When we add to this different food distribution methods and different costs and margins in the various member countries, it is not surprising that the last thing the CAP establishes is common food prices. It holds a complex range of prices linked to European farmers' costs and incomes, rather than world prices. Whether they are above or below world prices depends ultimately on relative efficiency, but more immediately on supply in relation to demand on world markets.

However, food retail prices are considerably more than farm-gate prices, the gap being highly variable according to the channels of trade by which produce gets to consumers. Some goes through the fresh food markets, some to food manufacturers; thence both kinds go to the retail distributors.

FRESH FOOD MARKETS

Fruit and vegetables
Fruit and vegetables can go through two or three distribution levels. Most is sold first by primary wholesalers operating from the few large 'primary' markets. Consignments from growers or importers are generally sold on commission, with percentage commissions varying from product to product. The Price Commission found, for example, commissions of 6 to 10 per cent on the main vegetables. There is also a standard cash handling charge per 'package'. The primary wholesalers sell to secondary wholesalers, large retailers or institutions. The secondary wholesalers buy on their own account, and sell to retail greengrocers. Some imported fruit is handled by a monopoly selling one country's produce. In 1967 the NBPI found these boards had considerable market power, as they each had a virtual monopoly in the markets at certain seasons. But by 1974, when the Price Commission surveyed the trade, the dominance of the produce boards had been weakened by changes in the structure of distribution. Supermarkets or stores increasingly stock fruit, and the national chains want high quality, standard all-the-year-round produce, preferably prepacked, at the

lowest handling cost their size makes possible. Direct contracts with overseas growers, rather than selling intermediaries, have increased. At the same time, the larger growers have gained bargaining power as demand increases; more growers demand outright purchase before shipment rather than commission sales.

The same trend has allowed and induced the growth of a few large wholesalers, importing a wide range of produce on their own account, graded to meet the specifications (in terms of size, appearance and percentage damaged) of the different firms. These operate through many markets as well as their contract business. Industrial and commercial caterers also buy on contract from importers and large wholesalers, and from primary markets.

Prices are determined in the markets by the pressure of demand, as the sellers or auctioneers feel their way towards the market-clearing level. However, large customers buying from large importers or importer-wholesalers reduce transaction costs considerably compared with the traditional channels. This reduction could either increase profits for wholesaler or retailer, or result in lower prices. But fruit and vegetables are not cheaper in national supermarkets than in small greengrocers'. It is possible that quality is better, though few shoppers would agree. The competition of contract sales with market trading has not made much inroad into the markets' prosperity, and some supplies going outside markets are priced at current market prices nevertheless. Within markets, competition from the larger firms (though not necessarily the very large national firms) has caused some concentration and induced greater efficiency, which in this context means greater discrimination in buying and more sales per salesman. Both mean less waste of resources, and less real cost. Prices are generally as competitively determined as anywhere.

The banana trade is a special offshoot, in that the green fruit must be shipped at a set temperature and ripened after landing. The special capital required has prevented competition beyond oligopolistic forms. Three large firms undertake almost all the trade in the UK, Geest buying from the Banana Board in the Windward Islands, Fyffes and Jamaica Producers from a government Banana Board in Jamaica. Yet the Price Commission found there was 'adequate measure of competition' between them, with selling prices covering only reasonable costs and profits.

The most important determinant of final prices for fruit and vegetables is the constantly changing balance of supply and demand. Neither market wholesalers nor greengrocers can fix selling prices by adding a mark-up to costs, though some supermarkets may do so. But the customers are very sensitive to rising prices. The short term is all important, since profit depends as much on selling quickly as on selling at a high price. The specialist greengrocer stays in business by careful buying, and choosing the right mix of quality and price. The supermarkets stay in the business by carrying smaller ranges, at less variable, on average higher prices, keeping their sales by the convenience of adding green-grocery to the trolleyloads.

Meat

The meat trade has been plagued by suspicions of profiteering, from both producers and consumers. It has consequently been combed officially a number of times (without the profiteers being unmasked). The channels of meat distribution are broadly the same as those of fruit and vegetables: from producer or importer to wholesalers; from wholesalers to retailers, caterers and institutions, the primary wholesale stage being the auction market. However, about half the home-killed beef, nearly as much lamb and most of the pork is sold by private contract to wholesalers, retailers or bacon and meat product factories. Again like greengrocery, most of the retail trade is still with the specialist butchers, about two-thirds of it being with independent butchers; multiple butchers, co-operatives and the supermarkets share the remainder. More of the retail trade goes to large integrated firms, while the independents gradually diversify away from fresh meat, to cooked meat products, provisions or tinned goods.

Meat is sold with successively more complex price structures as it passes through. At first sale, the price is merely an average for either the whole live weight or the deadweight carcase. After that, beef is sold at considerably different and very variable average prices for forequarters and hindquarters.

The retail butcher has pricing structure problems at least as complex as those of greengrocers. Wastage is far higher; the exact proportion lost depends on the quality as produced (which determines the minimum bone and fat to saleable meat ratio). After that a good cutter can leave more higher value meat for sale than a poor one; the quantity of each cut left after different methods of cutting varies appreciably. Prices of the cuts also vary, with different relationships between one cut and another, and different ranges between highest and lowest prices among shops. Different cuts of beef fetch up to fifteen different prices (the highest being perhaps three times the lowest), cuts of lamb at least five, pork perhaps six or seven (in addition to beefburgers, porkburgers, sausages and offal). The level of prices is to some degree made by the market: there must be *some* price at which sirloin or fillet steak would fail to sell in the grandest of shops, and there certainly is a level in reasonably shopped centres above which mince, stewing meat or 'roasting joints' will not sell fast enough to keep sales up and costs down (for storage and deterioration) to be normally profitable. Prices for the same cut in the same shopping area vary greatly (up to 40 per cent or more) in different shops, partly reflecting quality or service. But in the end, the butchers' judgment of their trade in the light of the fluctuating general demand for different cuts, determines pricing. There is no uniquely 'right' price, since all (or most) survive satisfactorily.

All official investigators so far have found market-determined, competitive pricing, from retail butcher back to livestock producer. Short term, from day to day or week to week, butchers and wholesalers buy what they can reasonably expect to sell at expected prices; but they deliberately flatten their selling prices compared with buying prices, taking lower margins when firsthand prices rise, for seasonal or cyclical reasons, and higher ones when they fall. This is the practice which leads to suspicions of profiteering, at times of low prices because margins are 'too high', at times of high prices because prices are too high. But as consumers respond more to price rises than to falls (no doubt for income reasons), this is a reasonable way to maximise sales and revenue, and it is compatible with competitive behaviour. Average wholesale and retail prices move reasonably in line with producers' prices, as might be expected. If meat is more costly to produce, its price must go up enough to cover the costs of the quantities demanded. But demand also responds to changes in relative prices, with both wholesalers and retailers competing by a mixture of price level, quality and price structure. But the strongly centralised multiple butchers and supermarket companies both operate by adding a margin to buying-in prices. In the end they must charge what their customers will pay, which is heavily influenced by competition from the specialist butchers. Were the trade to be more concentrated in the large organisations, administered prices might become more common, probably tempered by 'special offers' more like grocery and provisions. But the concentration proceeds slowly.

Eggs and poultry

Eggs and poultry production have become specialised and concentrated, largely by passing the produce markets. Poultry costs have been greatly reduced by capital-intensive methods of rearing, resulting in more continuous supplies from fewer sources. Wholesaling is largely carried out by packers, a few of whom are part of integrated producer-packer firms. The packers usually sell to supermarkets, grocers or dairies on contract. The Price Commission found the key price to be the packers' weekly selling price. As packers hold very little stock, the price is aimed to keep supplies moving through, given the supply expected from producers. Demand is not very responsive to price reductions, so retailers are not particularly discriminating. Competition between packers is therefore not very active, and they can dictate prices. The producer gets a price based on the packers' selling price, less the packers' margin, which remains relatively level whether or not enough is left to cover production costs. With consumers indifferent to price reductions and producers over-reacting to price increases, the industry is unstable. The largest integrated produce with the lowest costs can well withstand low prices when supply outruns demand, the smaller producers having to endure the worst fluctuations sales or profits. The packers are content to maintain their income in a far from competitive trade, while the passivity of retailers and their customers allows.

Frozen or chilled poultry meat has become more a grocery than butchery product, produced overwhelmingly by very large specialist firms, and priced as other supermarket lines, by adding a stable margin to buying in prices. Demand depends on prices for butchers' meat; if meat prices fall or stabilise, extra poultry meat can only be sold at lower prices. With managed mark-up policies, the price fluctuations are passed back to the producers. Periodic pressure on producers' returns as retail prices and demand fluctuate has induced a high degree of concentration. The retail price is competitively determined like manufactured foods, through the retailers' exerting their buying power limited by consumers' price-sensitivity.

Consumers' expenditure on food is about half fresh and half manufactured; so on fresh foods consumers spend one-tenth to one-eighth of total expenditure. The market system, and market influences on price formation flourishes for most fresh foods. Integrated firms covering production or importing down to retail distribution operate through branches in all the main markets. Increasing quantities of fresh food are sold through even larger national supermarket chains. But still there are few exceptions to what is usually understood by competitive pricing. Consumers complain about quality and high prices, and perpetually suspect profiteering by 'middlemen'. The middlemen of the more traditional style have their weaknesses, as the decline in their number shows; but their weaknesses are of *low* profits; high *costs* and wasted resources are the penalties of excessive handling. With free entry and relatively little capital required, high profits are soon followed by an increase in the number of outlets (or slackening in concentration). At the retail end, the resilience and adaptability of the successful independent firms stands out. At all stages the response of enterprises to changing demands and resource costs is marked.

Note on Further Reading

Agriculture and the State, Davey, Josling and McFarquhar (1976).
Trading in Commodities, Granger (1974).
Costs and Prices of Aluminium Semi-manufactures, NBPI No. 39.
Fuel Policy, Posner, Chapter II (Price of North Sea Gas) (1973).
United Kingdom Offshore Oil and Gas Policy. Cmnd 5696 (1974).
Political Economy of North Sea Oil, Mackay and Mackay (1975).
Distribution Costs of Fresh Fruit and Vegetables, NBPI no. 31.
The Marketing of Eggs, Price Commission no. 1.
Fruit and Vegetables Interim Report, Price Commission no. 2.
Prices and Distribution of Bananas, Price Commission no. 4.
Fruit and Vegetables Final Report, Price Commission no. 5.
Prices and Margins in Meat Distribution, Price Commission no. 7.
Prices and Margins in Poultry Distribution, Price Commission no. 11.
Prices and Margins in the Distribution of Fish, Price Commission no. 14.

Chapter 4

Manufactures

CONSUMER GOODS

All manufacturers buy from and sell to other enterprises. Professional buyers and sellers can be expected to know their market and exercise their bargaining power, whereas consumers cannot usually do this. However, cost structures and pricing practices vary with types of product or production. Products vary from consumer goods for mass markets to materials and components for the assemblers of capital goods, or special one-off products designed for the customer. Production costs may be sensitive to material prices and costs, to pay costs or to capital charges. Markets also vary from price competition in local markets to international competition among giants, or effective monopoly. We examine below some of the more important categories with distinctive pricing environments or practices.

Food manufacturing
Food producers serve a market where demand depends on households, the least organised of customers. Yet the manufacturers include some of the largest firms, and their immediate customers, the wholesalers or retailers, are also among the largest and most expertly managed. The result is product differentiation, lavish marketing and promotion and more concentration.

Production techniques are basically simple: mixing, crushing, heating or cooling, packing, bottling or canning, all lend themselves to automatic or electronic control, and the whole process can be organised as a continuous flow. Unit costs are very sensitive to continuity of production and high capacity utilisation; regular sales and good stock control, right down the distribution channels to the final customers, are necessary to minimise costs. Large-scale marketing and product development is therefore crucial to profitability.

Distributors can be induced to buy regularly only if the consumers can be induced to do so. Their awareness of the product must be constantly stimulated; advertising and supplementary promotions are as important as production, particularly as many purchases become habitual. Marketing, distribution and advertising together actually cost twice as much as production for tea, distinctly more than production for ice-cream, nearly as much for margarine and chocolate.

Manufacturers aim to capture more of the floating, weak-preference consumers. As the floating occurs most readily between close substitutes, this leads to the marketing of different products as near as possible to competitors' trade, punctuated by an occasional significantly new product. Hence the extraordinary proliferation of lines, and the characteristic follow-my-leader appearance of near-imitations of every successful new product. One firm producing 137 different ice-cream products and another 125, the two of them sharing 65 major lines, as the NBPI found, is choice indeed. The cost is considerable, as production lines are slowed, stocks increased and distribution more costly with more separate lines. The starting-up and launching costs for a new product are considerable, and must be recovered from the revenue from a successful product before the 'copiers' catch up (rather like R and D). But food cannot be patented; a temporary monopoly must be created by promotion aimed at building up sales to planned production capacity as quickly as possible.

Advertising and selling are often subject to economies of scale to a higher level than is production. National advertising with national distribution allows the best fit between the audience reached by the advertising and the potential customers. Major advertisers can bargain for better terms; a good salesman can service a national distributor to more advantage than smaller ones. Physical distribution has its own economies. Equipment and vehicles can be kept more continuously occupied in large operations. Large lorries are more economic than small ones, even if they are made to pay their full road costs.

There are many examples in food manufacturing of massive concentration, based on distribution and marketing skills. Brewery companies have reorganised to minimise physical distribution costs, and expanded to make better use of marketing capacity. Brooke Bond established its large share of the tea market by advertising, and consolidated its dominant market power with its own van deliveries and skilful marketing, skills applied later to Fray Bentos (meats) and Oxo (meat extract) and other foods. Cadbury-Schweppes, which also includes Typhoo, another major tea company, is based on massive resources in distribution and marketing, the further exploitation of which led to the proposal to merge with Allied Breweries. The two dominant ice-cream makers maintain their dominance because their delivery costs are lower than smaller firms or potential newcomers can achieve; the large frozen food processors have largely driven smaller ones from supermarkets by superior distribution. Once national firms with national distribution networks are established it is difficult for smaller firms to match either their costs or their selling power. However, there is still room for specialised firms in new outlets to thrive; smaller frozen food firms supplying home freezer centres and caterers, a trade where advertising and promotion is on a much smaller scale, work successfully.

'Standard' bread (made by the plant bakers) is a manufactured food whose sales depend on ready availability in the supermarkets. Service in distribution and discounts to the retailers are more important than consumer advertising. The 'shelf life' of bread is minimal, as the customers prefer it fresh; deliveries daily or more often are necessary to keep the supply going in the larger outlets. Profit depends on turnover, and turnover depends on the retailers' willingness to give a bulky, low-value product sufficient shelf space. The main technique of competition is therefore the discounts (from uniform retail prices). As each supplier tries to increase his market share by increasing the discount for large orders (22½ per cent being standard in the 1970s), the discounts tend to increase and profits to fall. It is hardly surprising that all the national firms sell fancy breads, rolls, buns and cakes, to maintain profits in these less price-sensitive trades. During the price policy of 1973-7 the Department of Prices actually controlled the maximum margins for a time, to prevent a price increase intended to meet extra production costs being passed on into retailers' margins.

Many of the large firms make a wide range of products with joint costs of production and distribution. Pricing them to get the required average revenue can be a complex business. Chocolate confectionery is a good example. Sales are very responsive to advertising, but ready availability in as many outlets as possible helps to maximise sales. The high-selling lines need to be sold in convenient cash units as much as weight units. (Hence the practice of reducing the weight of bars or packets when costs rise, rather than raising the price, maddening for consumer organisations if not for the customers.) Confusion about price changes results. When costs rise, consumers expect prices to rise pro rata; but as the markets for the products are subject to differing and varying competition, this would not maintain or improve average revenue. Average sales revenue is as sensitive to the product mix as to average prices. The NBPI thought that scale economies in production were offset too easily by all the indirect costs. Constant promotions and the extra cost of supplying many small outlets add appreciably to prices. The Price Commission found that the recommended margins on diabetic chocolate, a tiny part of the total turnover, and a captive market, were actually lower than those on non-diabetic chocolate, mainly because the distribution cost was almost entirely the cost of delivery to warehouses, with no advertising cost to be added.

With so much activity in selling, it is not surprising that manufactured food prices are not entirely competitive. A successful brand manager is one who knows his market and how best to exploit it, not one who constantly fusses about unit costs; such preoccupations would yield far lower percentage improvements in revenue than a successful sales campaign. An industry of firms, all devoting themselves to selling, may well have higher average *costs* than necessary, whether or not profits are also above competitive levels. The four large chocolate firms had allowed indirect costs to inflate, in the NBPI's view; and Brooke Bond, though undoubted price leader for tea, had neither the lowest costs nor the highest profit, and was at the time of the NBPI investigation (1970) striving to reduce distribution costs by administrative action.

Some constraint on prices is set by competition intermittently, by firms diversifying into related fields when profitable opportunities appear. An established brand name can be used to sell another range of products (another way of making fuller use of capacity); a successful brand is a valuable monopoly, created by past investment. But above all, serious competition comes from retailers' own brands. Own brands make inroads into national markets; more costly selling campaigns may be incurred as the market leaders fight back. But prices may still be lower with own brand competition than without, at the expense of manufacturers' profits, or manufacturers' costs, or the number of firms remaining in business.

The direction and pace of price changes are correlated closely with cost changes. Material costs are naturally a large part of these; though they are not strictly unavoidable (recipes and ingredients can be changed), there is usually a narrow limit to substitution in the short term. But use of capacity, including distribution, also influences unit cost. Specific product price changes do not correlate as closely with costs as in some other industries.

Does all the advertising and promotion make manufactured food prices higher than they could or should be? It is often contended that high marketing makes mass production possible; and reductions in production cost outweigh increased selling costs. This is possible, and no doubt it sometimes happens. But in the nature of things it cannot be proved, since concentrated national production is not possible without national, and therefore costly, distribution and marketing. Competition concerns the product as much as the price, but price can still be an indispensable element. Competition for the retailers' custom is essential to the manufacturers. If the retailers' customers are price-sensitive, which better information and mobility allows them to be, or if retailers behave on the assumption that the customers are price-sensitive, some pressure on cost, prices and profits is exerted on manufacturers. It is impossible to demonstrate whether on balance we are better off, taking into account the penalties by way of resources occupied too lavishly in non-production, with the innumerable choices of very similar lines, than we would be with lower-key distribution of more standard products. Changing to such a system would be extremely costly. Perhaps so long as there are own brands and competition in retailing, the final consumers have keen prices consistent with the range of goods for which they are willing to pay.

Other consumer manufactures
Some 'shopping basket' consumer goods other than food, like soap and detergents or the more necessary toiletries (dental preparations and shampoos), have very similar markets and marketing practices to those of manufactured food. *Detergents* particularly show typical pricing behaviour for an oligopoly (selling branded consumer products). Consumers are not very price conscious in choosing between brands, though short-term price reductions considerably increase sales of one brand, partly because retailers buy more 'special offer' packs, partly as a result of consumers' stocking up at advantageous prices. The NBPI observed that price competition (apart from short-lived promotions) only occurred when one of the two major companies felt threatened by rivals or innovation; prices otherwise moved closely in step, mostly on the occasion of increases in material costs. Relative prices of the main products, such as soap-based and synthetic powders, also moved in step, even when relative costs changed. Consequently, lower costs through increased efficiency resulted in higher profits rather than lower prices; the fierce competition concerned advertising and marketing. Constant advertising at peak times and rates are characteristic and obvious; less obvious is the high discount from recommended prices offered to traders (20 per cent in 1965). However, the manufacturers' promotional efforts reduce distributors' selling costs, thereby making it more difficult for smaller firms to expand, as they can only compete by offering higher discounts from the prices set by the leaders.

The firms themselves recognised the uncontrolled momentum of their advertising in a curious agreement reached in 1961, an agreement consisting of three intentions: to cease reduced-price packs (special offers) on certain lines; to reduce advertising expenditure by 10 per cent; and to establish a code of practice for promotions generally. Actual consultation on prices would have fallen foul of the Restrictive Trade Practices Act; nevertheless, the agreement led to a uniform reduction in prices on the same day. But the agreement held for only a year, each firm being suspicious of the intentions of the other, and each worried by the prospect of a newcomer taking advantage of a less well-protected market. Advertising is the main form of competition; so long as the firms still aim to compete, voluntary restraint of advertising is intolerable. The Monopolies Commission also reviewed the industry and they too found advertising inexcusably high. Their remedy was a minimally advertised line from each company selling at correspondingly lower prices, so that consumers' could at least have more choice. This was done, but the low-advertising lines did not make very serious inroads into the major markets. Shortly afterwards a number of larger distributors introduced own brands at still lower prices (for slightly different products), again with something less than spectacular results, and affecting the dominance of the national brands very little. Prices have remained determined as much by selling expenses as by production costs, with changes following major changes in material costs. Average revenue more than covers the costs of the less efficient producer, with exceptional profits to whichever is the current leader.

Toilet preparations also carry heavy advertising and marketing costs. Materials (three-quarters of which are packing materials for cosmetics) accounted for a third of costs, manufacturing costs and general overheads about one-eighth, leaving no less than two-fifths of total costs spent on advertising promotion, selling and distribution. The toiletries section (including more of mundane necessities, dental and hair preparations, sold in supermarkets as well as chemists) spend more on advertising and promotion than the cosmetics section. Cosmetics particularly shows stratification of the market into three price brackets, the cheapest having the smallest share, with relatively little competition between them. Even within the strata price response is low, the customers behaving as though high price and quality are presumed to be correlated. This is no doubt accentuated by another peculiarity of the market, namely that a very high proportion of purchases are gifts and the generosity of the giver is represented in the price. Manufacturers defend or expand market share by maintaining the price and creating the appropriate brand or company image, perhaps restricting outlets to create exclusiveness. But in spite of the apparent weakness of price competition, manufacturers' prices increased less than costs in the mid-1960s, as larger firms merged with smaller ones and the large ones strove for larger market share over which to spread heavy overhead and selling expenses. Nevertheless profits were high and unusually stable, especially in the medium-price stratum.

Textiles, clothing and footwear are similar to food in producing necessities as a group, though with so large a range of choice that the market for a specific product can be very sensitive to price or selling pressure. Yet the supply conditions are markedly different: branding and promotion is less important; manufacturing is far less concentrated; and the industries have been declining unprofitably (on average, that is, with a few untypical prosperous sectors or firms).

One major difference in demand is fashion: many purchases are socially determined; but conventional behaviour is to follow annually changing fashion. Brands are less successful since attractive colour and design does not require expensive research so much as individual flair; and economies of scale in styling are not important. Even household textiles respond to fashion trends, for the all-important, profitable increments of business. Chains of department stores buying standard items of clothing in bulk, and selling with the backing of their own name are far more important than national promotions. The store buyers are price-sensitive, even where their customers are not; and their greater control over the quality as well as styling often gives customers more reliable goods than market responses alone secure. As in food distribution and manufacture, the growing bargaining power of the stores tends both to erode manufacturers' profits and to reduce production costs by offering outlets to long runs. But the whole textile and footwear sector is much weaker than food in grappling with dominant distributors since there are few barriers to competition, without decisive scale economies, even in selling and distribution. Consequently overseas competitors, with markedly different input costs, have found it easy to under-cut British producers on large contracts with the distributors. Prices and sales have been increasingly constrained by imports, mainly from poorer countries.

The industries tend to blame 'dumping' (selling at prices below cost, or selling for export at lower than home market prices) for the rapid penetration of markets by one newcomer after another. Their critics tend to blame the industries for not reducing their own costs, or improving their marketing. Neither factor is sufficient to account for the size of the problem, which is common to all the more industrialised economies of Western Europe. Price competition from new entrants, based on lower input prices for one factor of production, should, within the laws of the market system, induce adjustments by the substitution of relatively cheaper factors, or by eliminating less efficient firms (their talents being better occupied in some other sector). But any such adjustment takes time. It evidently takes less time for new entrants to build up production than it does for old ones to re-equip, relocate, redesign or redeploy. Moreover, capital is as readily transferable between countries as are goods; so cost advantages in labour supply cannot easily be offset by cost advantages in capital supply. With textile materials, natural and synthetic, being easily and cheaply transported, and easily available on world markets, the only result is the elimination of whole industries. With major cost and price differences to compete against, the established producers become far less profitable, being deprived of both financial resources for re-equipment, and evidence of the wisdom of anyone else doing so. Government support does not halt the decline, with continually renewed competition from new producers offering successively lower prices and better products.

Protection by import controls has much the same effect as a collusive cartel in raising prices enough to keep the inefficient in business and the efficient earning unnecessarily high profits. Moreover, it deprives the consumers of low-cost, low-priced ranges of goods, a loss more widely spread, and possibly more regressive, than the increased welfare of the protected industry. Governments of the richer countries have rejected national protection in principle since a lower level or declining trend of world trade could harm any of them far more than temporary gains from introducing particular commercial barriers.

This is the background to an innovation of commercial policy, the *Arrangement regarding International Trade in Textiles*, known as the Multi-Fibre Agreement (MFA), jointly negotiated by textile importers through the organisation supervising the *dismantling* of commercial barriers, the General Agreement on Tariffs and Trade (GATT). The MFA, negotiated in 1973, secured three main principles: that all existing unilateral or bilateral restrictions on textile imports were frozen; that all such agreements should be notified, and arrangements made for their phasing out; and that multilateral restrictions under joint surveillance of producers and importers should replace them. The exporter-members of the MFA were to be allowed 6 per cent annual increase in quotas as notified. Importing countries could apply to have a quota fixed, where imports cause 'market disruption', as defined in the MFA. A procedure for consultation between exporters and importers was laid down.

Fifty countries signed what was in effect an agreement of international market supervision, designed to support production and prices. Price-competitive markets can mean intolerably rapid transfers of resources where developments are rapid or cost differences large. The MFA itself was liable to be undermined by new producers taking up some of the market left by the 6 per cent limit on expansion by members. Prices in the importing countries are determined either by the costs of the home producers remaining in business, aligned to average or marginal costs according to the buying policy of the larger customers (the big stores); or by the costs and required profits of the importers. With their market restricted below the uncontrolled level, the importers may either accept higher profits or still compete on price, the latter being a policy which might better preserve their market share in the longer term.

Consumer durables

Markets for consumer durables (cars, bicycles and motor cycles, furniture, electrical goods and consumer electronics) have also suffered increasing competition from imports. Lower costs overseas are the main reason; but past crudities of government economic management have handicapped some. These have been the growth industries as real incomes have increased. Apart from some of the high quality furniture and electronics, the durables are mass-produced with considerable economies of scale, with well-known, easily transferred technology. Capacity in the UK and overseas has increased faster than the market. Demand has been cyclical, partly because of the cyclical growth of incomes, partly because of government's credit restrictions and relaxations. Consequently competition is fierce, though it is not always price competition directly.

Furniture is an industry of a few fairly large firms, with dozens of relatively small ones, mostly specialised on a limited range (chairs, upholstery, tables, cabinets, pine furniture, wall fitments). Costs vary considerably, and often depend on the length of run for one model. The market is extremely varied too, from a price-competitive cheap end to a quality and style end, where virtually any price seems to stick provided the product is right. Retail prices include very large distribution margins, as distribution is unusually costly, mainly because of the space taken up in transport and showrooms, together with relatively slow turnover. High margins in the conventional trade has attracted increased competition from new methods, such as pack-flat designs, cash-and-carry trading operations, mail order and discount warehouses, operating on narrower margins with higher turnover, few or no showrooms, and standard ranges. The result is an even wider range of prices and products, with the larger stores bringing down margins and prices through much larger orders of standard products from the larger producers.

Much of this applies to *electrical and electronic goods* also. Margins are high, and display space costly. Competition with the conventional outlets, department stores, electricity boards and specialist shops, comes from discount warehouses and cut-price chains handling large quantities of cheaper imported goods, sometimes with a minimum of display or demonstration. As with furniture, conventional margins are large enough to allow a great deal of price cutting below manufacturers' recommended prices. Consumers' electronics are also similar to furniture in range of products and prices. At the experts' end, the quality of the equipment is far more important than its price, and prices are not necessarily very closely connected with production cost. A good write-up from the critics of the trade press is the most important selling point, and these rarely make much of the price. The industries have been concentrating to keep their unit costs low enough to retain some share of the market against imports. A number of manufacturers supply a larger number of varied outlets; but margins are high, as the market is on an expanding and apparently insatiable path, and a well-stocked electronic department is lucrative.

Hire purchase and other credit is the main means of payment for all these manufactures. The terms, particularly the deposit and the size of the instalments, are at least as important as price as such. Offering low or no-deposit terms and a long repayment period is therefore more important than trimming cash prices. But these are risky and costly terms, whether the credit is supplied by the store or by finance houses. The money itself is costly, as finance houses pay high rates to depositors or other lenders, and competition between them only increases the rates. Their own operating costs are not inconsiderable, and the level of bad debts is significant. To avoid too striking a difference between cash and terms, the cash customer probably pays more than he otherwise would in trades or stores where he is an unimportant source of revenue.

Some customers have only a hazy impression of the price they pay for the goods financed by HP or other credit. Even the discriminating customer must choose among a limited number of alternatives with high margins over cost. Price competition originates rather with the distributors, who can bargain with furniture makers or electrical equipment makers for special lines at low prices, or organise cheaper imports of fridges and freezers. It was the innovating distributors, like the cash-and-carry warehouses, which gave customers a choice of a cheaper cash transaction as an alternative to credit with conventional mark-ups, and terms on price-maintained goods.

Governments have frequently used controls on HP and hire terms or changes in indirect taxes as a quick way of controlling personal expenditure. Effective it may be for economic management: for the industries affected it has been a serious burden, and must have increased costs and prices. The changes in taxes or controls have been abrupt; demand and output change abruptly also. Idle capacity gives low returns and drives labour and capital out. The boom which follows is also likely to start abruptly when controls are removed or taxes reduced; whereupon shortages of skilled labour and up-to-date capacity leave unfilled orders which imports surge in to fill.

Cars are also bought by households largely on credit, many being also secondhand. Most car buyers are exchanging; so current credit terms and the difference between buying and selling price is the 'price' which decides the purchase. But cars are unlike the other durables in that the distributors, the franchise dealers for new cars, and the dealers in secondhand cars, are much weaker than the manufacturers. Price competition cannot come from the distributors' bargaining; it occurs either among UK producers or from imports. Rounds of price increases for the different size or price ranges occur, as for many other branded goods produced by oligopolies.

Two-tier pricing is widespread for car components and accessories. Many have two markets: the initial equipment market, for assembly into new cars; and the replacement market for spares and repairs. The customers in the initial equipment market are the vehicle manufacturers, generally larger than the component suppliers, with highly professional, discriminating buyers. With the larger part of their costs made up of bought-in components, and themselves selling in highly price- and product-competitive markets, they have to be. The customers in the spares and repairs market are private car owners or managers of company fleets. The private car owner may be discriminating, but he often buys a service or repair job from a garage rather than a replacement component as such. Furthermore, garage labour charges and overheads can account for far more of the bill than parts. There is a strong tendency for car owners to replace with the same make as the original equipment. But garages doing the repairs often make the choice of parts; and they may not be discriminating enough to choose the cheapest product. Consequently, the market for replacements is far less price-sensitive than the initial equipment market.

Component manufacturers commonly make most profit from replacements, even where initial equipment sales are larger, by charging far higher prices for replacements than initial equipment, price differences well beyond the extra costs. The component manufacturers can discriminate with the connivance of the vehicle manufacturers, or sometimes in competition with them. The largest of the clutch manufacturers (Automative Products) actually bought clutch linings at two prices for incorporation in initial equipment or replacement parts. The Monopolies Commission recommended in 1968 that the practice cease, and it did so for clutch linings. In 1972 the Commission found the practice still persisted for brake linings, a market where strong price leadership from Ferodo had not been eroded by competitors.

Naturally, so lucrative a protected market has attracted smaller firms, supplying only replacement components at lower prices. Vehicle and initial equipment component makers responded by dubbing initial equipment makers' products 'genuine' spares, the other 'spurious'. But though the gap between initial equipment prices and replacement parts has narrowed through competition, it can still exist while there are monopolies among the component makers, or while initial equipment brands are preferred.

Given the trade's captive profitable market, it is not surprising that RPM has been a major characteristic in it. RPM was usually defended, as component makers defended it, on the grounds of keeping up quality and giving distributors a wide enough margin for them to provide proper service, such as stocking large ranges or doing repairs or fitting. But those same wide margins allow inefficient distributors to remain in business. The Monopolies Commission had no doubt that the public interest lay in its abolition. 'The arguments as to the possibility of deterioration in service are based on the premise that the customer does not know what is good for him'; and the Commission indeed acknowledged that some do not, and are hence liable to exploitation or poor service. But despite the fact that it foresaw some temporary confusion, the Commission argued that RPM and its shadow, recommended prices, should be ended. Distributors' prices would then be tested by competition, the expected result being not necessarily to reduce profits but rather to put more pressure on costs. The Commission did not even expect much immediate change in selling prices, with the exception of those paid by large fleet owners with the biggest bargaining power. Less organised customers would get their benefit from more efficient and cheaper distribution, with a variety of prices, depending on the level of service chosen.

There are few consumer goods industries that are not competitive, though there are specialist firms in most of the consumer durables sectors with highly differentiated products, selling in a particular stratum of the market. But whether the competition concerns price rather than product or market shares depends on the product and the channels of distribution. Products of frequent purchase, where preferences are weak among the offerings of competing suppliers, are more likely to be price-competitive. Most manufactured food, the less cosmetic kinds of toiletries, some clothing and footwear all show this. But the pressure on price is exercised directly by the large retailers, using own labels as well as size for leverage. For the same reason, there is more price competition in standard lines of clothing and a good many durables. Price competition accounts for much of the import trade; but inadequate supply at boom times is also to blame. Prices are ultimately related to production costs. Whether these costs are those of the lowest-cost producers depends on whether branding is strong, what attitude retailers take, and how important imports are. Effective branding can detach price from lowest cost, though brand leaders (like other monopolists) may well have the lowest costs through having the resources for efficient production as well as high capacity utilisation. But sales costs add to unit costs, economies of scale keep them down; the rewards of successful promotions keep them up. Price changes follow cost changes for product *ranges*; but where the ranges include many separate lines, price structures can change also under the varying pressures of competition and preferences.

MANUFACTURING: INTERMEDIATE GOODS

The common characteristic of the remainder of manufacturing industries is that they sell to other industrial enterprises. Professional salesman sells to professional buyer, both of them backed by specialised skill and, in the larger firms, a sizeable staff for costing and pricing. The main aims of sellers and buyers are to keep their own costs down, by continuity of production and supply at a high level of capacity use; and to keep out of trouble with their own production managers, by accepting only profitable or worthwhile business in relation to the costs (especially of unusual sizes or specifications, short runs and unusual rushes).

The relationship between supplier and customer can be extremely close, and essentially technical, such as aero-space or electronic firms supplying Ministry of Defence equipment, boilermakers and generator builders supplying the Central Electricity Generating Board, civil engineers building roads and bridges, process plant builders constructing an oil refinery or chemical plant, roll makers supplying a steel-rolling mill, car or aircraft component makers working on parts for a new model. Metal Box, the largest can-makers, advises its customers on canning processes and canned products as well as on suitable cans. British Gypsum employ plasterboard salesmen specialising either in particular sectors among their customers (architects, surveyors, specialist builders) or in particular buildings (hospitals or schools). In addition, the company has a technical service to teach contractors to use their products, to train their employees (at the company's own training centre), and to keep in touch with the industry training board, government training centres and technical colleges. LBC maintain a programme of visits to its works and technical discussions for its principal customers. British United Shoe Machinery supplies comprehensive service facilities with its machinery, since most are leased; but its advisory services on designing and factory layout, justified by the wide range of machines produced, also serves as an effective barrier to smaller competitors. Firms supplying critical engineering components, such as the roll makers, employ sales engineers not only to sell but to assess the technical problems and requirements of their customers, backed by other technical staff. Morris Cranes have actually established a separate company, Crane Aid Services, to maintain and repair all cranes, a company which however has grown out of technical support services for their own products. Close relationships are also established in organising deliveries, such as building materials going to the construction firms, boxes, cans and bottles going to those who fill them, metal sheet sections and tubes going to processors. Continuity of production for both suppliers and users is hardly possible without reasonably stable relationships.

Price differences can be only one among a number of other considerations determining trade, even where competition is active. This alone means that pricing is only one aspect of selling policy: reliable quality, regular dependable supplies and access to good technical advice or service are others. A keen price may get serious consideration for new custom. Prices alone may not keep market share, but price may be the means of active competition to increase it.

There must be almost as many answers to the question how manufacturers' prices to other manufacturers are formed as there are sectors. Standard general purpose goods (like packing materials, processed metals, building materials) sell on price plus the security of a familiar supplier. Where performance is critical, as for machinery or machinery components, price can be a minor consideration; cost in use depends much more on reliability and low maintenance, given good design. Some of the outstanding differences arising from product characteristics relate to discounts and rebates for standard products; custom-made products; research and development in science or technology-based industries.

Discounts and rebates

Standard products sold in large quantities to many users lend themselves to mass, probably flow production, with considerable economies of scale for the whole operation, including distribution. Continuous and high capacity use and a minimum of office work reduces unit cost to a minimum. Large, regular orders are necessary for this; consequently quantity discounts and loyalty rebates are widespread. Such discounts are clearly cost-based, and a valuable way of keeping costs down throughout a production process. Nevertheless, discount structures can be an effective barrier to competition for dominant suppliers. Metal Box, for instance, defended itself as much from the competition of its customers making their own cans as of other canmakers by an elaborate structure of discounts and support services.

Discounts relate to size of order, out-of-season purchases, and long-term commitment to Metal Box, all of which the Monopolies Commission found cost-saving and broadly justified. However, the effect was a serious disincentive to buyers to split their orders. Metal Box's quantity discounts were cumulative: that is, a higher rate of discount applied to the *whole* of a larger order, rather than merely the next higher tranche of it, resulting in steeply decreasing marginal prices for large customers. As competitors could not enter the market with the same range of sizes as Metal Box, the really large customers could not move to another supplier exclusively. But if they ordered from Metal Box, the lower discount meant a higher price for all remaining purchases. The competitor's price would have to be low enough to meet Metal Box's relevant quantity discount, plus the lower discount on all the rest; and the structure was such that competitors' prices needed to be 15 to 20 per cent lower than Metal Box. An 'exclusivity' or loyalty rebate was added to Metal Box's price advantage. This was not cost-related, but an extra device for preventing customers going elsewhere. The Monopolies Commission has recommended against the practice as anti-competitive.

However, it is not always easy to distinguish one kind of rebate from another. Where suppliers deal with large customers by contract, especially public authorities, the discounts on sizes of order merge into separate negotiations with very large customers. Cable makers apply special discounts to government departments, electricity boards, the Atomic Energy Authority and the National Coal Board (NCB). British Ropes supply wire ropes to the NCB, the British Steel Corporation, British Wire Products and the Ministry of Defence, and sometimes shipowners and builders by contract at negotiated, secret terms.

Pilkington's used discounts to support merchants. They offered the most generous discounts for float or plate glass to glass wholesalers, based on their purchases from all sources, including Western European suppliers. (In return, the Western European suppliers matched Pilkington's discounts and prices in the UK, a plainly anticompetitive device.) The purpose of the discounts was, in the company's view, to enable and encourage the merchants to provide proper storage and processing services (cutting, silvering or decoration, and contract glazing). Stockholding by the merchants is an efficient way of reconciling the continuous production process with variations in demand, especially from builders.

Bulky materials, like bricks and cement, are often sold at delivered prices, with the usual discounts or rebates from list prices. *Delivery Charges* may also be a barrier to competition. If a standard charge is made regardless of, or too little variable with, the distance travelled the near customers pay more than the cost of supply, the distant customers less. Where less than cost is charged, competition from a local producer may be inhibited, though the resource cost would be less than the distant production plus transport. For this reason both the NBPI and the Monopolies Commission took the view that delivery charges should reflect delivery costs (relating to London Brick Company's supplies, cement and plasterboard). But if competition from a new entrant is still not possible, the charge merely redistributes the cost among customers, whereby their own relative costs and prices will be altered. This would tend to increase price differences between the well-populated central areas and the scattered peripheral areas. In all these cases the firms controlled a number of plants. Convenience, and capacity to supply overall cost-minimisation to the producer means some orders being fulfilled by plants other than those nearest the customer. Some pooling of delivery costs is inevitable to avoid customers' trying to dictate the exact source of supply, a development which can increase total costs. Economies of scale in distribution are important in such industries; they cannot be fully exploited unless the large suppliers in fact control the total operation. Charging the cost of particular consignments according to distances may be an aid to such control; but it cannot be a universal rule where production, deliveries and consumption have to be co-ordinated to minimise total average costs in the long run.

The labyrinth of discounts, rebates and negotiations makes it difficult to be sure what the prices of such manufactures are, or even to define a price. The price is certainly not the list price, which possibly no one pays; rather it is the discounted price, whatever it is, known perhaps only to buyer and seller. There is hardly a market price at all in the proper sense. But competition may still have some effect.

The definition of 'large' orders, to which the most generous discounts apply, can be changed; and the size of the largest buyers may justify the particular, negotiated discount, not so readily divulged. Salesmen may be given a minimum such as avoidable cost, or avoidable cost plus a contribution to overheads, or profit below which no customer may buy, or possibly not without reference back to higher management. The salesman can then meet the competition as he finds it, at a discount within a given range. It would be for higher management to judge whether the long-term value of the customer's business, or the urgency of keeping out the competition, might make it worth accepting an unusually low return. Equally, divulging to competitors discounts given to a particular customer could be a way of restricting competition, as the Monopolies Commission thought was done by British Ropes after the termination of an explicit price agreement among rope manufacturers, and hence a 'thing done' for preserving a monopoly position against the public interest. Instead of 'as long as a piece of string' a substitute colloquialism for vagueness might well be 'the price of a piece of rope'—or a tin can.

Any complex tariff, including discount structures, become embedded in their institutions and badly out of date. While reviewing discount arrangements, not necessarily with disapproval, the Monopolies Commission has heard many witnesses say that the discount structure was under review, or would be so. Costs are seldom a good enough guide, because of the problem of allocating the many joint costs. The market may be equally insufficient to indicate wrongly structured discounts where those of different suppliers only partially overlap. We note also that where the Monopolies Commission or NBPI disapproved discounting practices of market-dominating firms it was rather for pitching some prices too low than for charging too much.

Custom-made goods
In contrast to pricing by discount or list for the standard off-the-shelf products is the costing of custom-made one-off jobs designed

to meet particular needs. At one extreme are the nuts and bolts (literal and metaphorical), standard motors, tools, fans, pumps, trucks, cranes, metal sections and extrusions, chemicals, fibres, dyes, paints, cans, bottles and boxes, paper, plastics, oils and building materials (though all of these are on some occasions, or for some customers, designed to a specification); at the other extreme, oil refineries, steel-making or heavy chemical plant, buildings and bridges. Engineering especially covers the range, some of the firms regularly making both off-the-shelf and individually specified products (such as cranes and other lifting gear).

Buildings, heavy electrical equipment or a new generation of weaponry for the Ministry of Defence are all major examples of the one-off operation. Payment is made according to the terms of the contract between purchaser and main contractor. Contracts, especially for buildings, are often put out for tender, as UK local authorities are statutorily obliged to do. Firms wishing to compete send confidential estimates of costs and prices, according to their interpretation of the client's specification. The purpose, to ensure that such prices are competitively determined, has often been frustrated by the formations of 'rings' of suppliers who share out contracts by arranging lowest bids in turn. Suspicion or evidence of such behaviour has led to a number of Monopolies Commission cases, especially before the Restrictive Trade Practices Act made such agreements more difficult. For major contracts, much negotiation remains to be done after a tender is accepted. The final product consists of an assembly of many components, some of which may themselves be purpose-built, even of purpose-made materials (such as special alloys for technologically advanced generators or aircraft, or special finish or colouring for building materials). The more elaborate and technologically complex the product, the more technically qualified the purchaser needs to be. Chemical firms ordering new (usually larger) plant for heavy chemicals or plastics, the British Steel Corporation, CEGB or Post Office Telecommunications ordering new equipment, the Ministry of Defence developing and ordering a new missile or aircraft, a hospital board ordering a new hospital—all have technical costing staff, cost analysts and accountants as well as the engineers or architects and designers working on contracts. Much of the detailed work is costing the project. Costs have to be estimated; and for a large project taking years to complete, the probability of actual costs being different from estimate is considerable.

Fixed-price contracts put the risk on the supplier. He then has the maximum incentive to complete on time and organise his operations efficiently to keep his costs down to the estimates. If he can beat them, he makes extra profit; if he does not, he loses—and some spectacular losses have indeed occurred, not least to the shipbuilders in 1973-5, locked in to completing fixed-price orders placed before the accelerating inflation of those years.

Cost-based contracts put the risk on the purchaser. This is obviously an unsatisfactory arrangement in general, as the purchaser is not responsible for production management the quality of which in the end determines the costs. But where there is no previous experience of materials, design or production on which to base the cost estimates, or public authorities have to induce reluctant contractors to accept the business, there may be no acceptable alternative. The most outstanding example is the cost-plus contracts for military equipment and supplies, the 'plus' being a percentage profit (relating either to capital or costs) or a cash sum.

However, many other contracts have elements of cost-plus in cost escalation clauses, commonly relating either to wages or materials. If wages increase, or the price of materials, or certain named materials, increases, the contract price is automatically increased. There may also be penalties (reduction in price) for late completion, or a bonus (increase in price) for early completion. The 'price' paid is a series of payments at regular intervals, with a final settlement, taking in the penalties or bonuses, and any sharing of excess or saved cost that may have been provided for in the contract.

Costing and pricing fixed price contracts, such as the Ministry of Defence contracts, is lengthy in itself; so 'price-to-be-agreed' contracts occur. In principle the contract is fixed price; but 'agreement to proceed' can be reached long before the costing is complete enough for a price to be fixed. In these circumstances, the contractor has the advantage over the client in actually having some experience of production costs to use in his estimations in the later stages of negotiation. To prevent the greater risk of overcharging (as happened spectacularly in the Ferranti guided missile case in 1964) the only solution is 'equality of information', or access for the client to contractors' cost records.

Thus the price of a contracted, complex product is an amorphous concept, possibly with neither buyer nor seller having much idea how it will relate to costs or profits. But these are the extreme cases, though many of the large value cases. The more usual custom-made products have more continuity of experience to aid seller or buyer with accurate costing and management of production. Rolls for steel-rolling mills are all purpose-built; but materials, processes and specifications have enough standard elements to make stable and high-capacity working easier for the roll makers than aero-space or nuclear engineering firms. Office blocks, libraries or housing estates may be of different specification, but there are enough contracts in enough areas to give more experience of the likely variation of cost than can be gathered in building power stations or the Channel Tunnel. Where the variations are small or reasonably predictable, contract prices are firm and become little different in effect from the list prices for ranges of off-the-shelf products.

Sub-contractors or component manufacturers working for the large assemblers have some of the pricing problems of custom-built products, when designing and costing components for new products or designs. The car component manufacturers take part in designing parts to fit into new models, in close collaboration with the assemblers' designers,. The price has to be based on estimated costs. However, whether or not the price is profitable depends on the production run of the car. Once the design has been accepted and the car is in production, the component is very much off-the-shelf.

Science-based industries

Science-based industries live by product innovation, the products mostly being standard, requiring unusually high research and development expenditure. Research and development (R and D) is unlike most other forms of investment in that the return is uncertain and unpredictable for reasons other than the normal commercial uncertainties of business life. Moreover the lead times can be very long, from research to discovery, to pilot production,. to successful marketing on a continuing scale. Much expenditure is abortive because no commercially useful product results, or because the market proves to be less impressed with the value of the innovation than expected, or because a competitor unexpectedly gets in first. Consequently it is difficult if not impossible to recover R and D costs on a particular programme by including them in the supply prices of their products. The usual practice is to recover current R and D costs from current sales revenue, especially while a current 'winner' is protected by patents.

The pricing consequences give rise to problems for the firms themselves and for public policy. The 'right' level of R and D is determined only within very wide limits. Commercial success depends as much on being first as being right. So where there is serious competition among leaders, any general level of R and D expenditure tends to be near the minimum for all (like advertising and other promotions). An upper limit may be imposed by current sales revenue, minus current production costs and the minimum required return on capital. But the innovations are commonly patented, the patent holder deriving considerable if temporary monopoly. Prices and profits can be far in excess of reasonable returns, or of the R and D which actually produced the successful patent. Monopoly pricing can then lead to lavish and increasing R and D (a source of pride to many such firms) related only loosely to any real need or demand from the customers. This in turn can lead to highly promoted, 'improved' new products at still higher cost, thrust on a market showing no great dissatisfaction with the old ones.

The peculiar monopoly pricing arising from heavy R and D is well illustrated by the pharmaceutical industry. One customer, the Department of Health and Social Security (DHSS), buys on behalf of the National Health Service; this is a circumstance which might be expected to counterbalance monopoly pricing by the suppliers, as indeed it does; but only by administrative efforts. The DHSS is not the drug *consumer*, nor yet the drug *demander*; it merely pays the bills. The consumers (the patients) have very weak preferences; the demanders (the doctors) do not themselves pay (and frequently have vague or mistaken ideas about prices); so price elasticity is virtually nil. The Sainsbury Committee described it as product-competitive rather than price-competitive, a familiar if extreme example, characteristic of branding. Price awareness is the unhappy function of the DHSS, without much power of substitution. It undertakes 'counter-promotion', that is informing doctors of costs, and urging the prescription of generic (non-branded) drugs, but with limited success. However, though the market for major selling drugs is worldwide, the DHSS has some bargaining power in controlling a valuable part of it. Most UK-based companies have therefore joined the Voluntary Price Regulation Scheme, an anti-exploitation device in the form of an agreement between DHSS and the Association of the British Pharmaceutical Industry. Participating firms provide cost and profit returns to the Department, on which 'reasonable' prices are agreed, to cover costs (including R and D of course—on 'reasonable' levels) and adequate but not excessive profits.

Owing to the uncertainties of the lifetime sales of a new drug, it is usually priced high enough at first to cover a substantial allocation of the R and D costs already expended. As marginal manufacturing costs for on-going established lines are typically very low, a major success means that revenue eventually becomes largely profit. The normal pricing pattern for a particular drug therefore is a gradual fall. A similar lifetime pricing pattern occurs with 'speciality' dyes developed by one of the leading firms, sometimes patented, sometimes based on 'know-how'; research efforts are largely directed to such specialities. The NBPI found no less than a third of dyestuffs were of this kind. The fall in price of drugs also may be hastened by the end of the patent (after fifteen years under the Patents Act 1949, though with powers for the Comptroller to order compulsory licences to be given to other drug producers on payment of a royalty); or by the entry or threat of a competitor. 'Copying' firms commonly produce mass-selling drugs at less than half the price of a patented or branded version, a circumstance which increases DHSS's bargaining power.

Nevertheless, Roche Products (based in Switzerland) was found by the Monopolies Commission to have made profits 'far in excess of what is justifiable', even on a generous view of costs, on tranquillisers, mainly Librium and Valium. The company had recovered increasing contributions to its current expenditure on R and D, which it could use to develop future product innovations. It had exercised 'considerable market power without self-restraint', the power being manifested in excessive profits or excessive research expenditure.

The Monopolies Commission did not accept that there was no limit to the price and profit levels a manufacturer is justified in setting himself, as long as he uses the proceeds to expand his research. In other words, some R and D can become conspicuous consumption by firms, rather than necessary costs, or even a defensive barrier against competition. Prices are only limited then by administrative means: in this case, a combination of patient erosion by DHSS, followed by the Monopolies Commission investigation, and finally more negotiations by the Department of Prices, the whole episode lasting more than a decade.

Multi-national companies

Multi-national companies, whatever their product, can cost and price their output with more freedom than national level companies. The two extra dimensions are international price structures and transfer prices. An enterprise marketing in many countries maximises its profits by charging what the market will bear in each. Prices might then be different in each country. If price elasticities are different, because of different preferences, income structure or availability of substitutes, the most profitable average revenue is likely to be different. (There would also be differences due to import duties and other taxes, and possibly appreciating or depreciating currencies.)

However, many world markets are competitive enough to prevent much discrimination more than temporarily. Even where the producer is a monopolist, his high-priced market can still be undermined by his own customers in low-priced markets. If he sells to merchants or wholesalers in one country, and seeks a much higher margin in another, the merchants may find that the overseas price is high enough to cover the costs of reselling and leave them with extra profit. Such problems of international price structures arise where prices bear different relations to costs (perhaps because of controls). Mallory Batteries, for instance, wanted to raise UK prices of hearing-aid batteries in 1968, even though they were already profitable in the UK, in order to prevent their prices in other countries being undermined by UK wholesalers reselling. Even companies with loss-making products (not due for elimination) want to spread the loss, as Esso did for butyl (synthetic) rubber at about the same time.

International price structures can be competitively determined even where a few multi-national companies dominate the major markets, as demonstrated by dyestuffs and pigments. The range of products runs into thousands, each major producer offering part of the range, partly overlapping with the ranges of their competitors. As might be expected, the total market is not affected by price changes, being so small a part of the total costs of the products in which they are incorporated; but individual products are. Most large producers dominate their own home market, and act as price leader there, on price levels, and possibly also on price structures. Price competition is concealed by making widespread concessions to major customers from nominal listed prices, each major producer being wary of provoking overseas competitors into attacks on his leadership of his home market. The price leader, ICI in the UK, leads when the price level is generally raised; but this is followed by gradual erosion as price competition for separate products causes their prices to fall relative to the still protected 'specialities'. As the producers do not charge their various customers the same price for each product, changes in competitive pressure can quickly be reflected in prices, the process being halted temporarily by a further general change in price levels.

Integrated multi-national companies commonly buy and sell materials, components or goods for resale between subsidiaries in different countries. They can reduce taxation or increase their profits by charging their subsidiaries a non-market transfer price for inter-company sales. The market, or 'arm's length', price is that which would be charged by an independent firm; that is, it would be one sufficient to cover costs and a 'reasonable' (meaning perhaps market-determined locally) return on capital as would be charged by an independent firm. If *less* than the arm's length price for a material is charged, the income of the supplier is reduced, the costs of the customer company reduced and his income or sales increased. The parent company (or consolidated group) then escapes tax in the first country, and increases it in the second, or increases his income more than proportionately in the second, or increases his market share by reducing his price, thereby keeping off or driving out competitors. Transfer prices represent a transfer of resources between companies. If these do not correspond to the real resources actually employed in the different countries, sales and hence welfare will be lower somewhere than it would be with independent production. This alone is a reason for governments being very interested in transfer prices; and of course the revenue authorities have their own interests in tax-avoiding transfers (though they are notoriously difficult to track comprehensively through the accounts of a complex international operation).

Production may be specialised between countries; product development frequently is, because of the large fixed costs and difficulties of controlling expenditure. All subsidiaries use the results of R and D, and possibly other central services, and their cost should be included in the cost of production. Contributions to R and D and similar overheads from subsidiaries are often collected by including a charge for them in transfer prices. Exactly what these contributions should be can be doubtful, if only because of the difficulty of allocating R and D to its proper 'outputs'. But the transfers can be used as the vehicle for transferring profits back to the parent company, as Roche Products did in the opinion of the Monopolies Commission.

However, companies themselves often insist on transfers at arm's length prices in their own interests. Parent boards want to deploy their resources to the maximum effect; and devices that conceal or confuse relative resource costs in the various operating companies make investment appraisal and decision even more difficult than it need be.

Similar considerations apply to multi-plant or multi-company operations within one country. Transfer prices at less than arm's length can be used in a particularly profitable market to keep out competitors who must buy their inputs on the open market. Rists and Cables were suspected of doing this for the cable included in electrical wiring harnesses for cars, though the Monopolies Commission thought their costs were lower. British Plasterboard, however, took paper from its subsidiary at a deliberately low transfer price, a practice the NBPI wished to see ended, so that the management were fully aware of the costs they incurred (or gains made) by buying wholly within the company.

Industrial prices above all others relate to costs. When unit costs rise, prices tend to rise with them. This is not simply because monopoly gives rise to administered prices, relatively free from competitive pressure. In competitive industries neither material, labour nor capital costs are very flexible in the short term. All enterprises in the industrial sector are buying in materials and components they cannot easily alter, in very large proportions if they are the suppliers of parts to the big assemblers. The assemblers have large production lines or organisations not adaptable to other products, nor even to different methods very quickly. Their overheads are considerable and unit costs are very sensitive to levels of activity. A rise in input prices or rising or falling unit costs due to falling or rising capacity use are likely to be common experiences for the firms in a sector.

Where producers and customers have alternative channels of sale or purchase the bargaining is likely to be keen. The pressure on prices may be on particular items in a jointly produced range, resulting in changes in price structure, less in the average revenue. For custom-made and contract jobs prices virtually are costs, given accurate estimates and a market-related return on capital. For some of their many suppliers, the right product and capacity to deliver may be more important than price. For some off-the-shelf goods there are few competitors or strong price-leadership. Nevertheless the market in some sense determines prices. A survey of the effects of the Price Code (in mid-1976) found that firms in 'metals and engineering' had their prices restrained much more by the market than by the Code. No doubt their customers' incomes or prospective profits were the restraint, rather than competition from rivals. Whether prices relate to the costs of the more-or-less efficient firms depends on the sector. Where there is a dominant supplier or a strong price leader, it depends on standards of management there; where there is not, it depends on the attitude of the buyers.

Note on Further Reading
Prices of Bread and Flour, NBPI nos. 3, 17, 144 and 151.
Costs, Prices and Profits in the Brewing Industry, Beer Prices, NBPI nos. 13 and 136.
Beer, Monopolies Commission (1969).
Tea Prices, NBPI no. 154.
Costs, Prices and Profitability in the Ice-cream Manufacturing Industry, NBPI no. 160.

Costs and Prices of the Chocolate and Sugar Confectionery Industry, NBPI no. 75.

Margarine and Compound Cooking Fats, NBPI no. 147.

Frozen Foods, Monopolies Commission (1976).

Breakfast Cereals, Monopolies Commission (1975).

Starch, Glucose and Modified Starch, Monopolies Commission (1971).

Prices of Household and Toilet Soaps, Soap Powders and Soap Flakes, and Soapless Detergents, NBPI no. 4.

Manufacturers' Prices of Toilet Preparations, NBPI no. 113.

Arrangement regarding International Trade in Textiles, GATT, Geneva (1974).

Distributors' Costs and Margins on Furniture, Domestic Electrical Appliances and Footwear, NBPI no. 97.

Pay and Conditions in the Clothing Industry, NBPI no. 110.

Distributors' Margins on Paint, Childrens' Clothing, Household Textiles and Proprietary Medicines, NBPI no. 80.

Wire Harnesses, Clutch Mechanisms, Electrical Equipment for Cars, Asbestos Products, Monopolies Commission (1966-8).

Economic Theory and the Construction Industry, Hillebrandt, Chapter 13 (1974).

Aviation Contracts. Cmnd 2581 (1965).

Reports of the Review Board for Government Contracts (various dates beginning 1969).

Metal Containers, Monopolies Commission (1970).

Wire and Fibre Ropes, Monopolies Commission (1973).

Flat Glass, Monopolies Commission (1968).

Prices of Fletton and non-Fletton Bricks, Pay in the Fletton Brick Industry and the Prices Charged by the London Brick Company, NBPI nos. 47 and 150.

Building Bricks, Monopolies Commission (1976).

Portland Cement Prices, NBPI nos. 38 and 133.

Chlordiazepoxide and Diazepam, Monopolies Commission (1973).

Proposed Merger between Beechams and Glaxo, Monopolies Commission (1975).

Prices of Hoover Domestic Appliances, NBPI no. 73.

Price of Butyl Rubber, NBPI no. 66.

Synthetic Organic Dyestuffs and Organic Pigment Prices, NBPI no. 100.

Chapter 5

Distribution and Housing

DISTRIBUTION

A considerable proportion of the retail prices of goods is in fact the distribution margin, which only in a general sense corresponds to cost or price. Total distribution costs for a distinguishable trade, firm or department must be covered by the total margin. The *gross margin* is the difference between buying-in and selling prices, and it includes operating costs, advertising, head office or other administrative costs and the *net margin* or net profit on turnover. But it does not follow that product prices, as the customers understand them, include as much (or more, or less) than the distribution costs incurred for that product. Wholesale or retail *prices* are decided by conventions, habits, assumptions and enterprises' competitive strategy as much as by costing. Manufacturers usually sell to distributors at listed prices, often in terms of recommended retail prices with discounts for trade customers, probably supplemented by quantity rebates and settlement discounts. If trades are competitive, the more efficient or aggressive distributors sell at less than recommended prices, with costs or net margins less than the standard discounts cover; if they are not, the standard discounts are passed through into prices.

The distributors' buying prices can be totally inflexible where he buys from a virtual monopolist. But this is rare. Even glass merchants can buy imported horticultural glass to supplement Pilkington's range; and most distributors have rather more choice of sources of supply than this. More important is the size of the buyer relative to the seller. Most wholesalers of industrial products are small in relation to their main supplier; the leading retailers, however, are of comparable or larger size than their main supplier. Manufacturers or importers, themselves operating nationally, must use the national distributors to reach their final customers. The retailers can therefore bargain very strongly within the limits of what manufacturers can concede, and within whatever terms the manufacturers can get by playing one distributor against another.

Distribution margins as a proportion of prices vary greatly, depending partly on costs and turnover, partly on the degree of monopoly. On cost and revenue grounds, quick-turnover, frequent-purchase goods, such as food, cleaning materials and toilet necessities, are more likely to have low margins, and the larger, or high-value goods, such as consumer durables, high ones. But competition from new outlets, for instance mail order, discount warehouses, cash-and-carry wholesalers, alters relative margins considerably. On the other hand, branded goods from monopolies or price leaders often have higher margins than the nature of the product would otherwise suggest. Distributors of monopoly products can enjoy part of the monopoly profits while competition concerns product or service rather than price, and consumers are unresponsive to small price differences.

Wholesaling

Wholesaling essentially involves ordering from manufacturers (or importers) in quantities and sizes appropriate to minimising production costs, and selling to purchasers in quantities, size and assortment appropriate to their sales and revenue. Wholesalers' costs comprise administration and accounting, and usually storage and display. Sometimes processing is done, such as cutting to size (steel stockholders, glass merchants, timber and other builders' materials such as plasterboard) or repairs and fitting (such as car components).

For standard materials supplied to industrial firms, wholesalers' own margins are small in proportion to turnover and can add little in aggregate to final prices. Unit costs are reduced elsewhere, since producers have fewer, large accounts, more regular deliveries in larger loads and few risks of bad debts; and the wholesalers' customers have quicker supplies, easier access to a range of products and better service. In practice, the benefits can be diluted by inefficiencies or non-competitive behaviour. For bulky materials (metal sections and shapes, building materials) the producers often sell wholly or largely through merchants as a matter of policy, giving the merchants a discount off list prices, possibly varied according to the size of orders or turnover. But large consignments may be sent direct to the user, leaving the merchant with little but minimal accounting costs. The discount may or may not be shared with the customer. Builders' merchants rarely shared their discount on plasterboard with builders receiving direct delivery; but for bricks there was enough direct sale, including sales by LBC, to restrict merchants' margins; and the NBPI considered that the merchants' activities strengthened competition.

On the other hand, the NBPI concluded that distributors'

margins on goods sold to retailers were liable to be raised more than costs could justify when manufacturers' prices increased. Percentage margins are clearly more likely to have inflationary effects than cash margins; but even cash margins can add more to prices than cost increases. As merchants' buying prices rise, there are some costs that rise automatically, such as financing and insuring stocks, or allowances for loss or damage. For instance, when import prices rise, wholesale prices must rise somewhat for these reasons. However, the import content of distribution generally (as recorded in the input-output tables of the National Income) was only a quarter that of manufacturing when the NBPI advised on distribution margins (1967). Changes in the margin should take into account changes in the mix of trade as well as the wholesalers' own costs. For instance, a price reduction on car batteries (1964-5), due to competition from smaller firms, automatically reduced wholesalers' cash margins (as these were quoted in percentage terms by the manufacturers). At the same time, the cheaper batteries of the smaller firms were taking an increasing share of the market, also squeezing the wholesalers' margin. But their operating costs were virtually the same. Expanding total sales were thought to have offset this to some extent. With so many conflicting influences, the NBPI was unable to justify the margins on separate products in the light of the margins on the business. RPM-like habits persist in the car components field, the practices of which had been thoroughly documented by the Monopolies Commission a little earlier. Cash margins would damp down the repercussions of manufacturers' price increases considerably in trades where margins are as high as they were on batteries, about 50 per cent taking wholesale and retail together.

Wholesalers supplying consumer goods are generally subject to more competition than merchants handling bulk materials. More than half the trade goes direct from manufacturers to large retailers, so the remaining wholesalers in effect have to compete with direct sales from manufacturers. Yet margins are often a considerable proportion of selling prices. Wholesale margins on large electrical goods were down to 8 or 10 per cent on small ones to 10 to 15 per cent. After the Resale Prices Act put an end to RPM enabling the discount houses to move into the market, wholesale margins on electrical goods went down to 8-10 per cent, on smaller ones to 10-15 per cent. Footwear wholesalers made between 12 and 20 per cent, textile wholesalers mainly 20 per cent. In grocery, by contrast, with faster turnover and fiercer competition from direct sale, gross margins were less than 10 per cent for traditional wholesaling, and less than 5 per cent for cash-and-carry, with net margins not much more than one per cent.

It is rare for wholesalers of manufactured goods to have as deter-mining an influence on prices as the egg packers, marketing boards or wholesale markets have for fresh foods. The structure, size and profitability of wholesaling depends on the selling policies of the large manufacturers, or competition from retailers buying on wholesale terms, or the bargaining power of their larger customers. But where competition is not keen, RPM-like behaviour keeps gross margins above the costs of the more efficient, and encourages unnecessary handling of uneconomically wide ranges of goods.

Retailing

Retailers cannot fail to have the major influence on final prices since they are the firms which react directly to consumers' pur-chases. The larger retailers have the more positive role: they set the price level by seeking or bargaining for the lowest prices on their main lines, given the quality or tastes they aim to meet. They set the price range by the assortment of goods they stock. The wide assort-ment of goods sold means that shopkeepers can adjust margins on individual products, and therefore product prices, in various ways, either to meet competition on some lines or to earn their required revenue on the business as a whole.

The NBPI's study of margins and prices in food distribution led them to conclude that costs are borne by individual items on the basis of what the customers are prepared to pay, one of the major factors affecting prices being the competition between local super-markets. The differences in realised margins, the NBPI found, could not be explained by differences in the product. Margins recom-mended by manufacturers and wholesalers often seemed to be based on 'traditional concepts' and, worse still for price competition, they changed little with changing circumstances. The competition took the form of the more active retailers ignoring the recommenda-tions. Where the manufacturers priced in a non-competitive way, retailers to some extent rectified it by setting a market-determined price themselves, and increasingly used their bargaining power to force more competitive pricing on their suppliers.

But the dominant price leaders are relatively invulnerable to pressure from the retailers, since most retailers are as keen to stock the leading brands as the manufacturers are to have outlets; so price or margin cutting was less for the brand leaders.

For children's clothing and household textiles, the NBPI found ample competition to prevent excessive margins, the competition occurring through different combinations of margin, price and service in different types of outlet aiming at different strata of the market. In footwear, too, margins varied with the type of shop, the service offered, and the range and exact quality of product for higher- and lower-priced markets. The specialist shops with large ranges and relatively high prices have high margins, partly because of high costs, partly because of low price sensitivity among the customers.

For electrical appliances, margins were still very varied in 1968, soon after the end of RPM; but price competition was becoming keener, with prices falling below manufacturers' recommendations. By 1975 price cutting below the recommendations was more widespread, but margins had not fallen greatly on average.

Another means by which retailers have fostered price competition is through own label brands. As these are produced to order, with secure outlets and no promotion expenses, costs are lower; prices are lower than national brands, though they may well be in excess of costs. Even where price elasticity for the product generally appears low, consumers are sensitive to price differences in one shop or in neighbouring shops. The NBPI regarded own brands as a bulwark of competition as powerful as any, the advantage being greater choice for the consumer as well as a check on prices. Price competition among retailers was also necessary to force them to pass on their lower costs into lower prices. A spectacular example of the erosion of monopoly by an own brand was Boots marketing its own mercury batteries in competition with Mallorys, when a rival manufacturer (Varta) capable of making them appeared on the scene. On the other hand, own label ice-cream, welcomed by the NBPI in 1969 as a potential curb on the two dominant producers, had not made enough impact on the market to prevent the Office of Fair Trading (OFT) referring them to the Monopolies Commission in 1976.

Independent shops, especially in food retailing, have increased their bargaining power and reduced their costs and prices through the voluntary buying groups. A large wholesaler, trading with a national mark, buys in bulk. The retailers agree to take a regular minimum order to allow terms comparable with the large chains to be negotiated.

Retail co-operative societies have traditionally been a source of competition to other retailers. But the development of the national chains left them at a disadvantage since they were locally controlled. However, they have developed some of the features of the national chains by trading under a common mark, and taking own label products from the Co-operative Wholesale Society, jointly owned by the retail societies. The CWS is thus able to bargain as strongly as any chain, as well as producing its own lines. Though the local societies buy and set their prices independently, political loyalty to the Movement has added to the economic incentives to stock CWS goods. The better societies are local price leaders, especially in food, and the dividend stamps by which the profits are distributed add to their attractions.

Retailers' operating costs consist mainly of selling space and staff. Much retailing expertise relates to maximising sales per square metre. Above all, the capacity of the shop including its complement of staff needs to be matched to the trade. The biggest obstacle is the unevenness of demand. The huge peak of food shopping on Friday and Saturday morning determines capacity. For the rest of the week it is mostly under-used, unless promotional pricing can alter the pattern; for instance, the double and treble stamp days are a familiar Co-op method, and some butchers support a 'mid-week special' scheme. But the weekend trade is by far the most lucrative. The high-margin, expensive lines are sold when the families shop. Cutting the weekend trade peak may reduce costs, but it reduces profits more.

In spite of their efficiency, the national chains do not always have the lowest prices. It is more difficult to handle fresh or perishable foods on a large scale. The Price Commission's food panel repeatedly found fruit, vegetables and meat cheaper and better in specialist shops.

Active price competition depends on the retailers behaving as though the consumers are price sensitive. How near the retail price of a particular product is to its lowest can nevertheless still be obscure. Variations in price for the same goods in different outlets, from market stall to High Street shop, is a constant source of complaint. Differences due to varying trade discounts may be the result of bargaining power, or they may be administratively determined by monopolistic suppliers. A retailer's mark-up may be a fair reflection of his costs, or an ill-informed testing of an inactive market. So long as consumers have an effective choice of outlets, non-competitive pricing, remote from costs or consumers' preferences, is likely to lead to loss of business. Meanwhile, wide variations persist, some of which can only be explained by inherited conventions and habitual mark-ups, probably rationally determined at one time but long since overtaken by changes in costs or demand. Some retail prices are not so much determined currently, as enduring in gaps in competition, or while businesses run down.

HOUSING

By far the largest part of most household's expenditure goes on housing. Yet the pricing of housing is the most confused and under-researched section of the subject. It is an area where social costs and benefits are probably greatest, and where social needs compel major expenditure by local and central governments. Social policy and administration are paramount, but economic principles are not thereby made irrelevant. Housing is priced and marketed, though many prices and half the market is administered. But the relation between costs and prices or prices and demand influences supply throughout the market.

Houses, or permanently separate dwellings, including flats, bungalows, maisonettes, chalets, caravans and houseboats, have two special features. They last a great deal longer than most house-holds' possession of them; and they can be divided or amalgamated into a very different number of separate units of housing. Repair and maintenance or conversion may involve improvement or deterioration over a lifetime. The supply of housing can vary independently of a change in the supply of houses; and the supply of both changes as much with the demolition or rehabilitation of the old stock as with additions of new. New houses are usually under 5 per cent of the supply at any one time.

Supply
The market is supplied by three distinct streams: local authority housing for rent; private housing for sale; and private housing for rent, furnished and unfurnished. The first two are comparable in size, the third dwindling.

Because of the possibilities of conversion and the indeterminacy of 'unfit' dwellings, the supply of old (secondhand) housing responds to price as well as to government policy. Rising prices encourage subdivision, care of fit dwellings and rescue of the unfit. Government policy affects old housing by improvement grants, thus increasing the supply at a given price level; and by controlling rents and security of tenure for tenants, thus reducing the supply at a given price level. The part of the supply of old housing owned by local authorities is probably less responsive to prices, as the variable part mainly consists of older, privately built un-modernised houses, suitable for conversion to flats.

The supply of new houses from private builders responds to the difference between price and cost, and the probability of selling on completion. The supply of new houses from local authorities depends on their own policy, central government policy on housing subsidies, on the availability of land and on costs. Prospects of letting them are only in question in a few areas; but revised ideas about lower population growth have led more authorities to think in terms of satiable demand for tenancies. Some 'overspill' areas, due to receive tenants from congested cities with joint financing arrangements, have found themselves with unlet houses for an unusually and undesirably long time.

Central and local governments have been setting minimum housing standards for over a century. At first public health demanded some limit on overcrowding and improvement of services. Now amenity and general improvement of the environment dictate tighter control and rising minima. Building regulations determining minimum standards for construction, size and fittings, and planning regulations determining housing densities and location, have accumulated as a result. Rising mandatory standards mean rising minimum costs for 'basic units' of housing. The general effect is to reduce the supply (but increase its quality) at any given price level. But the improvement in building standards should lengthen average lives, so increasing the supply of old houses. Costs for both private builders and local authorities depend on the price and availability of land, building densities and standards, current operating costs for labour and materials, and rates of interest. But actual cost structures differ.

Building land

Building land carries a formidable surplus or economic rent, since its supply is restricted by planning regulations as well as by location. Among sites with planning permission there is a hierarchy of values, depending on suitability for building and particular position. Flat, well-drained land, empty of old buildings (for demolition), trees or other obstruction, near to town centres, trunk routes and prosperous employment centres commands the highest price, nearly all of which is the rent (*economic*, not contractual: contractual rents of buildings include management expenses, and rate of interest on the cost of the building and possibly local authority rates, as well as the pure economic rent on land and building). There is some price elasticity of supply if farmers or owners of large gardens are induced to sell for development by rising prices—if planning permission is forthcoming. Planning procedures can be lengthy, extending the production period, increasing the cost and reducing the flexibility of supply of houses.

Increasing demand pressing on restricted supply pushed up the economic rent and hence the price. Since the surplus is entirely due to society's needs and community policy, governments have tried to collect the 'betterment' element in land prices by means of various kinds of tax. None of them worked as intended and all were costly in administration. Where a monopolist's assets have value for his own use, or where continually expanding demand encourages him to expect higher prices in future, a market price reduced by taxes or levies below his own valuation or expectation merely dries up the supply. Taxes therefore have to be smaller than the betterment, or accompanied by non-market techniques to maintain the supply. Hence the Community Land Act (1976) giving local authorities the power and duty to acquire land for development at existing use value and then sell it to builders at its enhanced value with planning permission, thereby collecting the surplus for themselves. The most difficult point of the scheme is establishing this latter value without a market to test it. Selling to the highest bidder would push land prices up to the maximum, and increase the price or rents of houses and other buildings. So a market limit would have to be set by a market limit on house and building prices. If planning regulations are tight enough, or the CLA procedures cumbersome enough, to keep supply below demand anyway, the surplus will still be very high—and will be paid by the purchaser or tenant of the building rather than by the developer (in the private sector). Building land for local authorities is provided by CLA procedures at existing use value. All large-scale housebuilders use land acquired five or more years before, such are the delays involved in planning and preparation. Uncertainties over future demand, supply and regulations over such a period divorce land costs at the time of building from concurrently rational views on supply and demand.

Building construction
Private builders build on their own account, and by contract for local authorities. Input costs are largely labour and materials, for site preparation and building. But output costs depend on site management, especially the co-ordination of material supply and labour time, and the orderly sequence of specialised or subcontracted work (plastering, roofing, plumbing, glazing). Wasted time and wasted materials account for a measurable part of the cost. Prefabricated parts allow better co-ordination in the factory and on site; but the product is less valued, and many design and construction problems still make the actual cost or the risks attached to them relatively high. Builders frequently borrow their unusually high working capital. Interest charges add to their costs. Costs can be trimmed by reducing outgoings on finish and fittings, and on hidden qualitites of construction. Capital costs for the purchaser are kept down at the expense of much higher future maintenance or running costs. This is the rationale of detailed building regulations and the National Housebuilders' Registration Scheme, as purchasers are usually unable or unwilling to assess running expenses realistically.

Local authority building costs are either the contract terms or costs incurred by direct labour. Much the same cost problems occur for private housebuilders. But as the financing is different they have much more freedom in using unorthodox designs and methods of construction. Housing authorities (usually the district councils) are not planning authorities; planning powers for housing are delegated to them by the counties. So housing authorities control their own planning up to the level of estate planning.

New local authority housing (since 1974) is subsidised if it replaces slums, built on very costly city-centre land, or if it is part of an urban renewal scheme. Apart from this, the finance required for land and construction is borrowed. Few local authorities borrow on terms which match the life of the project. Housing is reckoned to have a life of forty to sixty years (the period for which subsidies were committed). Local authorities issue bonds which mature in periods from one to 40-60 years. Interest rates are fixed at the time of issue, roughly in line with current yields on equally secure assets. As loans are not linked to batches of housing, local authorities have to regard their whole inheritance of housing as needing a whole hierarchy of interest charges to finance its capital cost, ranging from nil for housing where loans have been paid off, up to the 12 to 15 per cent common in the inflationary 1970s.

The prices of new private sector houses are usually construction and other costs plus a profit; but as local markets are often active and the purchasers price conscious, competition sets limits to the range of prices even for so differentiated a product. The price of old houses is demand-determined if there is a shortage, as in conservation areas, national parks and green belts, or for irreplaceable antique properties, or for favoured sites. Otherwise they are influenced by the supply prices of new houses. If demand falls, the stock of empty houses increases, as well as prices falling; if demand rises faster than increases in supply, unsatisfied demand (a 'queue' of would-be purchasers searching longer) is part of the adjustment, as well as some rise in price.

Local authority rents
Local authority housing is almost all built to rent. If any is sold, the price is related to the market price of privately built houses. Authorities must by law balance their housing accounts. Hence their rent revenue must cover interest on the capital value, costs of repairs and maintenance and other management services, and rates. Housing of varying age, accommodation and condition clearly needs varying rent; so the structure must match quality differences. But how rents ought to reflect costs is not self-evident. Older

houses were built with loans already fully matured, or on terms far below current levels; maintenance costs are high, but do not counterbalance low interest charges. *Historic* cost rents would result in a variety of rents bearing little relation to perceived value, and felt to be unfair. Total rent revenue would probably be too low, as rent adjustments to take account of changing management expenses would probably lag behind outgoings. Interest rates and construction costs have both risen over the lifetime of the stock, not only because of inflation but also because of rising standards and higher relative prices for construction labour and materials. So although the newer the property the lower the management expenses, *replacement* cost rents would give rent revenues far in excess of current expenditure for a good many authorities. They would also give very varying surpluses to authorities, not related to housing need but rather to whether they were in a new fast-expanding area or an old declining one. Which method yields revenue nearer to balancing expenditure would depend on the age profile of an authority's stock. Which is logically preferable is arguable. Historic cost-based prices encourage queues or unsatisfied demand, since they are below current values, measured either by consumers' preferences or market prices of substitutes. Replacement cost-based rents follow the logic of marginal cost pricing; but in the sphere of housing, the biggest social necessity, with very many social costs and benefits attached ranging from crime to health and educational attainment, to impose market rents yielding a huge surplus to many authorities would be socially questionable and politically impossible.

In practice, a middle way is usually chosen. The interest charge is generally regarded as the average which the authority has to pay on all loans of all maturities, a definition exactly matching charges to outgoings. Basing rents on this 'pool rate' means that tenants of old housing are subsidising tenants of new, while interest rates and construction costs continue to rise. This arrangement means that tenants pay rents near but not necessarily up to current market values, so far as these can be assessed, especially in congested and prosperous areas.

Private rents

Private housing for rent has been a declining sector, largely due to long years of rent controls and rising construction and maintenance costs, finally killed by statutory security of tenure for tenants, first of unfurnished dwellings, then furnished. The existing stock dwindles as some are demolished, more sold to sitting tenants, or sold with vacant possession as tenants die or move. Rents are determined more by past costs than by anything else. 'Fair rents', administratively determined by rent tribunals where landlord and tenant cannot agree, are supposed to represent current market value. But with a shrinking, minor, inactive market there is often no definable current market value. The rule of thumb is then a multiple of the rateable value, a nice piece of circular reasoning, as the rating assessment is supposed to represent current market value also; but the capital value of a rented house would normally be a multiple of the rent, net of management costs.

The market for housing

Private housing for purchase is overwhelmingly bought with mortgages, from building societies, insurance companies, banks or local authorities. Building societies do most of it, financed by small deposits. Insurance companies support building societies by issuing endowment policies to cover a housing loan, attracting higher tax reliefs for middle to upper income borrowers. Banks extend overdraft facilities to their customers, for a much shorter term and higher charges, readily available, especially for second homes and major extensions. Banks also in effect support building society financing, by providing bridging loans to cover the gap between completing a purchase and receiving the money for a sale. Local authorities may mortgage housing, within their borrowing limits; they normally give priority to purchasers with similar claims to those who would get a place on housing lists for their own tenancies. Their loans are often a larger proportion of the purchase price (up to 100 per cent) than building societies (who normally lend 70 to 80 per cent only). Some local authorities also supplement building society finance, by 'topping up' loans, or by guaranteeing part of a loan building societies consider rather risky. The various institutions supply different needs, and complement one another as much as competing.

The demand for housing has many aspects. Long-term changes in demand are determined partly by demographic changes, partly by social changes, partly by rising real income. For instance, the increase in numbers of men and women of marriageable age, and longer survival of the healthy old, increases the number of separate households and hence the demand for housing. With a given population structure, demand also increases as more single people set up house for themselves, and more previously married couple households split up into separated or divorced single, or single-parent households. Rising real income increases the number of separate households actively seeking housing, and increases the quality (especially space) of housing demanded.

There is a series of separate housing markets in different regions or areas. Travel-to-work areas are clearly important boundaries. But not all households work; and some which do find work accessible to their chosen housing area, rather than vice versa. Travel-to-work areas overlap, especially in the conurbations; and changes in demand or supply can cause repercussions over wide areas. Nevertheless there are distinct differences between regions, with different independent balances between supply and demand. External and internal migration also add to or subtract from housing demand in various regions and areas, generally increasing disparities.

These long-term underlying shifts in demand are more important for housing than any other consumer good because of their extreme durability, and the long lead times for increasing supply. But short-term *effective* demand, consumers actually in the market with the money, borrowed or not, to complete a transaction, is much more complex. The basic unit, satisfactory housing for separate households, is a necessity which must have a very low price elasticity. At the same time, house-room and its quality is a rich-man's good with high income elasticity, and probably modest price elasticity also. Because of income constraints, those in the market for basic shelter, defined by current minimum standards, will probably have to be tenants, of local authorities if they can, of private landlords if not.

Potential tenants of local authorities need prescribed social characteristics more than money. The rent is paid for social security beneficiaries, and rents are also rebated by local authorities according to tenants' means. Qualifications for the housing list include previous residence in the area, designation as a 'key worker', unsatisfactory, unfit or overcrowded housing, residence in a development area, or special need such as large families or health problems. Once at the head of a list, the customers in some areas can choose reasonably freely among houses, locations, rents and facilities. In others, housing departments match housing to income and perceived need, leaving only the right of refusal to the tenants. Lists are so long in congested areas (so much demand frustrated by queues) that variations in supply or price in other markets do not in practice affect demand for tenancies. In others, lists of eligible tenants grow as the supply of loans or the number of houses for sale diminishes, or mortgage instalments increase elsewhere in relation to local authority rents, and shrink again as supply increases or price falls back. As rents are cost-based, and not adjusted up to reduce queues, or down to clear the market, the supply is shared administratively among socially acceptable customers. Even so-called 'economic rents' (non-subsidised) are cost-based (non-pooled, historic costs usually); so such properties may also have a waiting list.

Changes in local authority rents therefore depend on changes in costs, subsidies and renting conventions. Rents rise as costs go up, as accelerations in housebuilding increases the pool rate of interest, as subsidies go down (or fail to keep pace with costs) and as maintenance costs increase. Demand (short term) does not fall even if rents rise faster than incomes, as higher relative rents merely means that more tenants are eligible for rebates; in other words, the higher average price of local authority housing is automatically structured by cross-subsidisation of the poorer by the richer tenants. Longer term, the demand for local authority housing must be reduced if the unrebated rents rise faster than mortgage payments, provided the supply of mortgages and private sector housing is allowed to rise. But if local authority rents rise in line with mortgage payments on private sector housing (though faster than incomes), demand would probably increase; that is, local authority housing would be a poor man's good, with apparent positive price elasticity reflecting substantial income effects.

Effective demand for purchased housing largely depends on the availability and terms of mortgages rather than on house prices. The price elasticity of demand for the housing is low, and the fragmentation of the market makes it lower still. The higher the purchase price, the larger the repayments; but the mortgagee's outgoings depend as much on rates of interest and terms of loans building societies will lend. As interest rates increase instalments go up, or the term lengthens for past borrowers. If this deters potential purchasers, or if building societies do not extend their loans to match the higher repayments required, house prices may tend to fall. On the other hand, with an expanding market, if building societies provide loans faster than the supply of acceptable housing for sale (whether new, secondhand or improved), prices go up. A rise in interest rates or house prices relative to income chokes off demand, primarily because building societies operate so that it should. When incomes rise relatively, bringing more effective demand into the market than current supply can accommodate, building societies can still choke it off by requiring a higher percentage deposit. If demand is still excessive, as it is periodically as in 1966-8 and 1971-3, mortgages are rationed, the clients having to wait longer than they wish (form a queue).

Effective demand for housing is therefore indirectly responsive to price, via the size of mortgage obtainable, the deposit required and the size of repayments out of given incomes. Changes in tax liabilities and reliefs, or changes in building societies' or local authorities' lending ceilings, also influence demand. The cash purchasers, many of whom will be erstwhile mortgagees surviving long enough to take full possession of their property, might be more responsive to price changes. But housing prices naturally tend to rise in step, since those on offer include very close substitutes within an area, and often satisfactory substitutes on a regional scale. The higher the asking price, the higher the likely price obtainable for owned property. Buyers are probably sensitive to price differences; but investigating price elasticities with any accuracy would be a formidable task, given all the other possible determinants of demand at any one time.

The income elasticity of demand is obviously more important, and clearly relatively high. An important part of the difference in life styles and in the social characteristics of income groups stems from housing standards. The most critical point is the one which brings potential first-time purchasers into or out of eligibility for building society or local authority rules. Housing prices moving more slowly or faster than incomes will have just this effect. Once in the market, a sufficient number of owners move up the market during their lifetime to maintain an active demand for higher quality. At the same time, minimum standards administratively maintained (but dependent on 'public opinion') push up the quality of new down-market housing and reduce its supply.

In short, effective demand for housing can be very unstable from year to year, depending as it does on so many other changes (and second-order effects). This is in spite of the much more stable and, in the end, stronger determinants of demand in the long run. The price of housing is determined by the short-run effective market, and also shows considerable instability, on a rising trend.

Commercial building

Commercial building responds to price and cost changes in different ways because it is less subject to minimum standards. As construction costs rise, houses must still meet the minimum standards, though different materials or methods of work may be substituted. Commercial buildings, however, may be smaller, less durable or less elaborately fitted. If the market is so imperfect that rents rise to cover the extra costs of construction or interest rates, no substitution of factors or variation in the quality of the product will occur. This seemed to be the case in the 1960s and early 1970s, the era of town-centre commercial development and speculative expansion of demand. But the recession of 1974-6 (mercifully) disabused such optimism. Speculative demand in a boom for so long-lived a product causes waste of resources at least as serious as unused capacity in slumps, by making the market so effervescent that market prices lose their function of matching demand and supply at levels of output within the capacity of the industry and the incomes of the customers. The loss can only be temporary: income constraints become effective again through potential occupants of new commercial buildings staying in old ones (so long as planners allow them to remain), reducing their demand for space, moving to lower-cost locations or going out of business.

Market pressures are as strong in the public sector as in the private. They do not operate in the same way, since governments restrict or regulate the behaviour of the enterprises more. Nevertheless, changes in supply and supply prices are determined as much by changing factor costs and methods of costing and operation even in the activities such as housing or water, nearest to social services. Few public sector prices could be predominantly demand-determined, in the nature of the industries; but demand responds to changing prices, especially relative to incomes (real price changes) in much the same way in any sector. Marginal cost pricing is relevant to much of the public sector because of the large scale of production and low level of competition; but its relevance is that of a useful logical rule that can (sometimes) indicate in which direction prices or price structures need to be changed to achieve certain objectives. Other objectives may indicate other logical solutions: the market may, and often does, dictate or induce other policies no less in the public interest.

Note on Further Reading

Economics of the Distributive Trades, McAnally (1971).
Prices, Profits and Costs in Food Distribution, NBPI no. 165.
Distributors' Margins on Paint, Children's Clothing, Household Textiles and Proprietary Medicines, NBPI no. 80.
Distributors' Costs and Margins on Furniture, Domestic Electrical Appliances and Footwear, NBPI no. 97.
Food Prices in Outlying Areas, Price Commission no. 10.
Prices of Commonly-purchased Diabetic Foods, Price Commission no. 8.
Economic Theory and the Construction Industry, Hillebrandt, Chapter 4 (1974).
Government of Housing, Donnison (1967).
Rents in Local Authority Housing, NBPI no. 62.

Part Three

THE PUBLIC SECTOR

Chapter 6

Pricing in the Nationalised Industries

Public corporations market their output at a price, with varying emphasis on other commercial objectives. The nationalised industries are the core of the group. These are the subject of the next three chapters which begin with general questions and then examine energy and transport and communications more particularly.

The National Enterprise Board (NEB) owns and controls a number of nationally owned firms. It is itself a nationalised enterprise, expected to behave commercially in terms of a return on its capital, and to secure good commercial behaviour in its subsidiaries. As it is solely a holding company it does not have a pricing policy. Its subsidiaries are subject to the Companies Acts and the Fair Trading Act, rather than to a specific statute as are the nationalised industries. Their pricing practices are therefore no different from those of other industrial enterprises.

The British Steel Corporation (BSC), the British National Oil Corporation (BNOC) and British Airways (BA) operate in international markets, and government policy could not influence their pricing policies as much as it influences those of other nationalised industries.

The public utilities

Many nationalised industries are public utilities: gas, electricity, postal services and telephones, public transport. These all provide a service on demand from consumers, with the consequent peaks and troughs of calls made on an expensive, inflexible system. Managing supplies and pricing the services to produce a tolerable load factor (the relation of peak to average demand), so that unit costs do not rise because of poor capacity use, as well as rising prices of inputs, is at once crucial and difficult to achieve. Where markets expand faster than incomes or prices (as for gas and electricity) the task is easier than in cases where they do not (as for public transport).

The public utilities are mainly 'natural' monopolies: that is, as physical distribution involves a link between suppliers and customers, competition is impossible and even a duopoly wasteful of capital. Moreover, all the services are essential to households' welfare and enterprises' needs. There is no market constraint on the industries exploiting their market to the full. Monopolistic weaknesses, whether inefficiency, disregard of the customers, exorbitant prices or extravagant investment, would be particularly damaging in these sectors. Consequently public supervision, if not ownership, is almost universal. Some of the concern over nationalised industry pricing in the UK arises from the problems of public utility pricing, rather than simply from their being nationalised industries.

Another characteristic of the public utilities is that they carry substantial social costs and benefits. The real cost to the community of most industrial enterprises is little more than the cost of the items in their accounts for inputs. Where there are other costs, such as smoke, fumes, pollution, noise, spoliation or danger, governments increasingly aim to suppress them by legislation rather than to account for them in prices. Similarly, real benefits to the community are usually not far from the market value of the output. But for the public utilities, social costs are far more important relatively to their own outgoings or income. The social benefits are subsumed in their being called public utilities: they are the services by which an industrial society lives. The social costs partly consist of the same kind of environmental damage writ large, partly of the special problems arising from congestion and demands on land. Active government policy towards public utilities is a consequence of the large social costs and benefits. Both governments and the industries find great difficulty in deciding on the right principles for pricing.

None of the public utilities are pure monopolies, in the sense of a sole supplier of services with no substitutes. Prices or sales of each are to some extent, for some purposes, constrained by their rivals. Nevertheless, all have a considerable degree of working monopoly, both for specific uses and for consumers who have become captive for the time being by complementary investment decisions. Consumers of gas or electricity (or solid fuel) have to install suitable equipment. Freight consignors may need railway sidings or yards with good road access. Use of public transport may be determined by choice of residence, job or school. The monopoly is very real to individual households, though it may appear less stark viewed nationally, or over a long period, allowing more freedom to respond to price changes.

The abuse of monopoly by public sector utilities can only be prevented by political constraint (apart from the good sense of management). Rules are laid down, either in the statute creating them, or in White Papers, ostensibly explaining the rules. The first pricing rule is fairness. Monopolies, especially public utilities, can impose discriminating prices on consumers; therefore they are statutorily obliged not to discriminate between customers or groups of customers. Innocuous as it may seem, this rule alone has consequences of some importance. The public utilities have to demonstrate non-discrimination by sticking to published price lists or tariffs. But prices are an important bargaining weapon when monopoly supplier negotiates with monopoly or oligopoly customers. Unpublished rebates or discounts are important weapons in the private sector; public corporations can be at a disadvantage competing against private enterprises (as happens in the energy sector). Non-discrimination has also been interpreted as pricing according to costs, to avoid the subsidisation of one group of consumers by another.

Their second obligation is to behave 'commercially': that is, trading revenues should cover costs. But in spite of continual efforts by officials and politicians to devise means which will actually bring this about in a satisfactory way, it has only been achieved by some of the corporations some of the time; and when it has been achieved, there is suspicion of high costs as well as ample revenue.

Revenue cannot be expected to cover costs contemporaneously with any accuracy. Even if it were administratively possible, letting prices follow short-term fluctuations in cost is not a sensible commercial policy when consumers need to make some long-term commitment to their choice. Hence the balance is only required 'taking one year with another', as the statutes had it. But if the period is left undefined, so is the state of the balance. Even a persistent series of deficits can be explained as a prelude to a new era of better performance or widening markets. If the industries could be set in balance (or in surplus), maintaining this over a period would be easier than many have found it, having either started in deficit or got into deficit. An industry in deficit (for good reasons or bad), when input prices are rising, has to raise revenue to cover the cost increases (net of productivity gains), and to correct the imbalance of the past. Unusually steep price increases (most probably steeper than other prices or incomes) dislocate the trend of demand, perhaps making it even more difficult to get rid of the deficit.

Investment and prices

Valuing the assets employed in the nationalised industries is particularly difficult, especially for the energy and transport enterprises.

A corporation's inheritance of assets may be considerably different from up-dated or new generation equipment, sometimes with increasing capital-output ratios, sometimes with decreasing ratios. Freight trains with vacuum brakes move much faster than old wagons could; modern signalling systems allow more frequent and faster trains over the same track. Both increase the capacity of track and rolling stock, and are capital-saving. A new power station has radically different fuel consumption and performance from the average installed capacity; it may be capital-using (like nuclear plants) or capital-saving (like some large fossil-fuel plant).

The value put on the capital affects prices in two ways: first, the capital has to be depreciated, depreciation being a cost; secondly, an 'adequate' return on capital employed has to be earned. The capital to be depreciated should be that necessary to carry on the business. But what is necessary to carry on depends on a view of how the system is to be run, in relation to demand. The capital properly employed to satisfy expected demand is no easier to determine; it depends partly on the performance of the system, and on the capacity in use of both replacements and new equipment. Naturally, the difference between historic cost and replacement cost in such capital-intensive industries is also considerable. Agreeing the figures for assets employed involves almost as much negotiation as the proper returns to be made on them. Only after agreement can the required revenue, and therefore prices, be decided.

The right return on capital, average (historical) or marginal (forward-looking, for new projects), is arguable. On the one hand, as natural monopolies the nationalised industries are subject to far less than the normal commercial risks; on the other hand, they should make a 'normal' return on their capital in order to prevent too much being invested in them where there are better alternatives elsewhere. But what this rate is, and the extent to which there is substitution between investment in public and private sectors, are things which are never clear in an economy subject to fluctuations and distortions, as likely to be out of equilibrium as in it. Nevertheless, the return required can have a substantial influence on prices; and generally the greater the monopoly, the greater the price effect of the returns on capital.

Nationalised industries' investment programmes are extremely costly. As they commonly account for a major part of national investment, and as they usually need government funds to supplement their own reserves to finance the investment, governments inevitably control them. But the financing of investment affects prices, and price changes affect demand, if only through income effects, which justifies the investment. Whether they wish it or not (and on the whole they have not), governments are concerned with nationalised industries' pricing.

The source of funds for investment affects the distribution of welfare, and is therefore a political-type choice, whoever makes it. If the total reserve, made up of depreciation, contribution to replacement cost and surplus, is not enough to finance an approved investment programme, either taxpayers must find it or consumers must pay through higher prices. It is possible to argue reasonably for either. Because the public utilities provide basic necessities the average consumer may be poorer than the average taxpayer, though there is considerable difference between the proportion of the output bought by rich and poor among the different industries. On the other hand, there is no economic reason for taxpayers to finance an expansion (or modernisation) of a service which is supposed to sell its output commercially, that is, allowing potential consumers to choose how much to use in relation to the costs properly incurred. Though the present consumers may not be representative of the future (marginal) ones, marginal taxpayers may be less so, especially when inflation pushes the threshold of direct taxation lower down the real income scale. Governments have usually preferred to build up the industries' reserves, by making the present consumers pay for the expansion of capacity as far as their willingness (or ability) to pay allows.

Governments feel compelled to support this policy to alleviate public sector financing problems. But it is not a painless solution, especially with accelerating inflation. As construction and equipment costs rise financing requirements grow, on top of the increases needed for expansion and new technology. Self-financing means increasing prices, unless very considerable improvements in operating efficiency or capacity use can be made. If the industries (or the government) aims to increase the degree of self-financing, as well as covering rising operating costs, and possibly eliminating past deficits (as happened in 1974-6), some formidable price increases may be reflected in the RPI—and even more heavily in the consciousness of the hapless consumers. Governments may be hard-faced about financing, but they are bound to agonise over the consequent price increases, if only for the consequences in trying to control the price level. Hence governments have intervened more and more in pricing practices, sometimes to prevent even cost-based increases being made (1971-3), more often to urge marginal cost pricing on the industries.

MARGINAL COST PRICING

Marginal cost pricing is logically a method of getting the balance of resources between industries and products right. The marginal cost is the extra cost involved in producing one more unit (or batch) of product, or in going into another line of business. Whether or not it is worthwhile for an enterprise to accept an extra order, or maintain or increase particular lines, depends on the extra revenue compared with the extra costs otherwise avoided. But the possible extra revenue depends on the market structure. If price competition is strong enough for the market to set a definite limit to the producer's price, the extra revenue is the market price times the extra output. Marginal revenue per unit is the same as price, which is closely related to average revenue. Moreover the market price, determined as it is by aggregate demand, represents the value consumers put on the extra supply, within the limits of their income.

From the community's point of view, if such behaviour prevails everywhere the economy is making the best use it can with its limited resources. The extra costs represent the inputs which have to be bought for that purpose. If those inputs were used elsewhere, they would be represented by other marginal costs for other products. If *those* marginal costs were less than the price of their product, this would indicate that consumers valued this product of their work more highly than the first, and the resources should clearly be transferred. Conversely, if marginal cost was above price in the alternative use, this would show that consumers did not value the alternative product enough to make the transfer as good as the first use. Transfers of resources from uses with marginal costs more than price to uses with marginal cost less than price would be desirable until it could not be done further, that is, until marginal cost was equal to price everywhere. Then resources would be allocated among firms and products to best advantage.

So much is straightforward, and little more than encapsulated commonsense. But the conclusions do depend critically on a number of conditions, each of them dubious. *If* price competition prevails everywhere, market price represents consumers' valuation and the extra revenue available to any producer; marginal cost then represents the best combination of inputs for the consumers. But price competition clearly does not prevail everywhere, especially not in the public sector. *If* consumers do choose purchases according to their own preferences, their valuation of what they buy represents contributions to their welfare. But consumers do not always have any choice, especially over the short periods in which changes of price and pricing policy have occurred, and especially in relation to public services. Where they do, the eternally busy, well-informed consumer with all the time in the world to observe the tariffs and charges of public sector enterprises is well-nigh a figment of the economists' imagination. *If* the economy remained stable enough for the transfers out of less valued uses to be completed before new cost structures or new consumption patterns are established, market-induced changes might be in the right direction. Above all, price-competitive markets and price-responsive customers only combine to maximise the general welfare *if* there is no greater benefit than making the best use of *present* resources, with present technology, present consumption patterns and present income distribution.

The public utilities and some other nationalised industries have considerable monopoly, with weak market constraints on prices. Moreover all have complex cost structures, for which it is extremely difficult to distinguish marginal cost. Extra capacity or radical changes in operating techniques take years to mature, over which period all the costs, and demand too, have to be predicted in an uncertain and badly predicted economic system. The producers are only too likely to over- or under-extend their systems. In either case, costs would be higher than predicted; but prices are more dependent on costs than in the competitive sector. The customers pay for mistakes in the public sector; and if over-extension there deprives them of some of the products of another sector, they will collectively suffer also by being deprived of more-valued products. Under-extension of capacity in energy, steel, air transport or manufacturing generally, usually increases imports, which imposes its own penalties through governments' responses to weak balances of payments.

Getting the right allocation of resources between industries in the energy or transport sectors, and between nationalised industries and others is peculiarly important because of the concentration of investment in the basic services. It is also peculiarly difficult, because of the social cost-benefit considerations, as well as their monopoly. Any help to be derived from a pricing rule is politically welcome and administratively easier and cheaper than allocation based on forecasting and planning decisions. Marginal cost pricing is supposed to serve that purpose, by providing a logical proxy for competitive-market prices.

Marginal cost pricing in nationalised industries

Marginal cost pricing would get resource allocation in nationalised industries right on four conditions: that consumers can and do order their purchases as supposed; that all enterprise competing for resources use the same pricing principles; that resources are scarce in total; and that their scarcity is represented by marginal cost. None of these conditions holds without qualification. Consumers react to public utility prices in a variety of ways. Where use of the product requires investment by the consumer, active choice is infrequent. Once having decided to install central heating, most of us are committed to the decision for a long time—because we do not move house, or because we are struggling to pay off the debt incurred in the transaction (to say nothing of wanting to forget the appalling domestic trauma of arranging and enduring the installation). Many consumers never actively choose as individuals at all. Fuel systems are part of housing, chosen or allocated for different reasons, and endured through poverty, ignorance or lack of will. (Consequently, some of the poorest households use the dearest fuel; the equipment, though grossly inefficient, is the cheapest to buy.) There is an active minority of consumers choosing houseroom and incurring commitments to fuel and transport, if no other services. Choice of transport may be equally patchy. Travellers far from a railway or in rural areas with rudimentary bus services have no choice. Even in towns, times and destination may determine the mode used.

However, commercial or industrial consumers are much more likely to make careful choices, based on capital and running costs of alternatives, though the rationality can be exaggerated even here. Where a service is a small but entirely necessary element of costs, such as water, fuel or transport, purchases and contracts made long ago may well be repeated from habit, long after relative costs have changed. Unusually steep price increases may induce a new 'choice'; extraneous crises, like the oil crisis (1973) or the drought (1976), are much more effective stimulants of economy than normal price relativities in a good many firms.

There is an actively choosing, rational fringe to domestic and industrial markets, but the core of inertia is considerable in both. Consequently price responses are normally slow. The right allocation of resources cannot be made until the demand responses and shifts have settled down. The delay makes it all the more likely that real costs will shift again, before responses to the last shift are complete.

The second required condition is that marginal cost pricing be consistently applied. Many nationalised industries sell in competition with private sector alternatives: coal, gas and electricity with oil, steel with imported steel, public sector freight transport with private hauliers. If oil is priced above marginal cost, and public sector fuels are priced at marginal cost, too little oil and too much of the rest will be used. If imported steel sells at less than marginal cost, marginal cost pricing by BSC would ruin an economic industry. Some public sector enterprises sell a service with complementary private sector products, as gas, electricity or coal needing cookers, heaters and so on. To get optimum welfare, the price of the total package bought by the consumer should represent the marginal cost of all the resources. Overpricing in the private sector should then be matched by underpricing in the public sector.

Thirdly, resources have to be scarce in alternative uses. A coalpit or waterworks put out of use because prices do not cover its costs will not contribute to welfare elsewhere; the resources are too specific. Asset values and costs do not always reflect this. Labour is in general a scarce resource. In practice, at particular times and places it may be superabundant. Though the enterprise has to meet a money cost equal to the price of the labour elsewhere, the social cost of using it, where it would otherwise be unemployed, is far less.

Obstacles to marginal cost pricing

Marginal cost pricing is far from straightforward, even as a principle. It is made even more esoteric by the need to assess social costs and benefits. It is clear that, for instance, congestion, noise and air pollution are among the costs of transport, wider horizons for leisure and greater opportunities for earning among the benefits. Electricity generation imposes nuclear hazards (or the costs of applying the stringent regulations to avoid them), distributes waste heat and fumes where they are not wanted and spoils the view. But it makes possible release from domestic and much other hard labour, and from subjection to the seasons for food. Consequently, it is important to amend marginal cost pricing to marginal *social* cost pricing for such services. Calculating the internal average costs of the various services for various purposes is difficult enough. (The Post Office has thousands of separate items to cost, as does British Rail.) Calculating marginal social cost is even more so.

Marginal cost is concerned with the future. The extra cost that *would* be incurred for extra output depends on the unit of output and the period being considered. The extra cost of a temporary addition to the load of an underused system is a great deal lower than a permanent addition to capacity or peak load. Extra peak load for a fully loaded system is potentially very costly, but how costly depends on development plans already being implemented and the forecast performance of new techniques, not yet tried.

The White Paper on the *Financial and Economic Objectives of*

Nationalised Industries, for nearly a decade the principles on which
the nationalised industries were supposed to price, tried to
overcome some of the complexities by distinguishing long-run
marginal cost from short-run marginal cost, the long run allowing
for changes in capacity, the short only changes in the level of
output. But capacity is constantly being adapted through up-dated
replacements and gradual removal of technical constraints on performance. The concept is clarified somewhat when price is related
to *system* marginal cost, meaning the extra resources cost on the
whole system, given whatever adjustments are made or are going
on, of accepting an increment of load now rather than, say, one
year hence. But the calculation is still difficult: the variables are so
numerous, with complex technical or operating relations between
them, that a computer simulation is the least that will provide the
necessary figures. It is partly for this reason that few of the
industries have found the idea of any practical use (except for
electricity, discussed further below). A National Economic
Development Office (NEDO) Study reported on pricing practices,
as well as other policies pursued by the nationalised industries, and
found reasons mainly specific to the particular enterprise why they
had never in fact carried out the ostensibly official principle.

There are other reasons why the principle has remained a matter
of continual controversy, in spite of its apparent logic. As other
official investigators have frequently observed, the calculation of
marginal social cost is difficult or questionable because of the
uncertainties involved in quantifying social values, especially time
or life. Most of this kind of work has been done in connection with
roads, using standard values for time saved. Yet when the
Transport Policy Consultation Document (1976) was published
the officials themselves drew attention to the deficiencies of the
formula. With so much powerful criticism, official clinging to
the principle begins to look like obstinate or desperate attachment
to a cerebral principle by people who cannot or will not get to grips
with the untidy and kaleidoscopic facts of life. However, the
strength of the principle is that other principles appear to be worse.

Fourthly, marginal cost must represent the real value of the
scarce resources. For this, they must have a market price in
alternative uses. But many nationalised industries are the sole users
of some factors—coalminers, mining engineers, railway signalmen
being a few. At some stage, usually juvenile recruitment, there are
alternative uses, and choice according to relative price. The price
bears some relation to the value of the recruits in various sectors
(provided there are enough jobs to go round). But once recruited,
trained and settled, most stay in their sector, at pay rates

increasingly remote from value in alternative uses, and hence from an independent market value to influence the price of their product. If the price of their product is a determinant of the pay, which itself partly determines price, unless the product price is market-determined the price and the pay is indeterminate. It is no wonder public sector pay rises, and nationalised industries' prices only too clearly following them, are so often political problems, politically settled.

Other input prices can be as remote from market valuation. Nationalised industries are sole or dominant purchasers of a great deal of their equipment. International markets, or a number of independent home suppliers, can establish a proper price for the resources they employ; but this does not always apply. Nationalised industries sometimes share out their orders among suppliers in order to preserve competition, an imperfect substitute for market pricing. Again, political problems reveal the market indeterminacy, in the form of requests for support from the government for the equipment makers, or pressure to advance orders, or share them in a particular way.

GOVERNMENT PRICING AND INVESTMENT RULES

The government's rules for pricing and investment, as laid out in the 1967 White Paper (by a Labour government, but neither amended nor withdrawn by its Conservative successor of 1970-4), are based on three interdependent principles: marginal cost pricing; appraisal of new investment with a standard rate of discount; and 'target' returns on capital employed. They are based on the following arguments.

If prices are *higher* than marginal costs (as those of monopolies setting out to maximise profits by charging what the market will bear would be), the customers have to sacrifice alternatives more valuable to them than the resources employed; some entirely economic opportunities would be wasted. If prices are *lower* than marginal costs, the customers are not paying for the resources employed fully. Someone else then must, if only in the form of extra finance for new investment. Therefore prices should be set in line with marginal costs (taking the trend of long-run costs). Generally speaking, public utility prices higher than they need be impoverish consumers to whom they are a basic necessity. Prices lower than they should be encourage wasteful use of services in the more optional, luxury uses; and equipment will be badly designed. There is good reason for proper pricing, both to give consumers the right signals, where they exercise choice, and to provide a reasonable service where they do not. Proper pricing leads logically to marginal cost pricing.

Price, marginal cost and demand are linked to investment. Marginal cost depends on the investment to be made; the necessary investment depends on demand; demand depends on the price (at the margin); and price depends on marginal cost. Hence a standard for worthwhile investment consistent with marginal cost pricing is needed. New projects are to be appraised according to a test rate of discount, representing the community's preference for present income over future income. As there is no way of knowing this (the so-called 'social time preference rate'), it has to be judged by officials with what evidence there is from market rates of interest (though the market rates are clearly not themselves *social* preference rates, influenced as they are by risk, government policy and the expectations of a relatively few capital market operators). Thirdly, the industries need to earn a proper return on the capital employed in the businesses. This is intended to be analogous to the return earned in other industries, and is a market rate. This makes prices include capital charges, and should provide some of the finance needed for the new investment properly appraised (though there is no reason why it leads to complete self-financing).

The target rates of return on capital employed bear no simple logical relation to the return on future investment, properly appraised, as they apply to the whole inheritance of capital from the past. But the three rules together, marginal cost pricing, investment according to the test rate of discount, and the target returns, can be interpreted so that reserves are built up to cover estimated investment needs, or part of them. But for this to be achieved, demand and costs have to turn out exactly as estimated, and investment programmes have to proceed on time. It hardly needs to be said that the events are seldom very near the estimates. The industries need a fourth rule: which of the other three to abandon when things go wrong. The logic undoubtedly requires the pricing rule to be put first (if it were practicable), the appraisal rule next and the returns on capital employed to be treated as the residual. In fact, governments are concerned with financing first (and hence the target returns), investment appraisal perhaps, pricing very much last.

The government's apparent concern for marginal cost pricing arises because some prices are often below marginal cost. Emphasising the virtues of marginal cost pricing is equivalent to getting in more revenue. Decisions have to be taken about how much prices ought to *change*, since operating and investment costs rise, and ideas about investment programmes are revised, appraisal rules or no. The technicalities make the appraisal rules seem more determinate than they usually are. When the estimates are mainly a matter of judgment (even extrapolating a past trend is a judgment about the future), there is considerable latitude for doctoring the appraisals to make them come out as expected or required.

Unit and marginal costs rise for inflationary reasons. Higher output from new capacity to meet fresh demand can only appear as new plant comes into commission or new methods can be applied. Inflation pushes costs up, while new plant or other equipment brings them down. Whether the result is rising or falling costs depends on the rate of change of each. The faster the inflation, the more likely that frequent price increases will be needed to keep revenue in line with costs. Consequently, marginal cost pricing usually involves raising prices. The real reason is to improve revenue, especially to increase reserves to finance new investment. When the three rules are incompatible, the real horror is not wrong pricing but inadequate revenue. The industries (other than electricity) clearly take the same view for they do not practise marginal cost pricing.

The NEDO solution to the pricing problem was to suggest that targets and pricing should be decided for each industry, in the light of its own particular structure, market and history. This is probably a recognition of what has to happen anyway. But it does not provide a principle for pricing in place of marginal cost pricing. There may not be one for monopolies, taking into account in one rule all the considerations with which governments do concern themselves. Nevertheless, the defects of marginal costing do not undermine the principle that revenue ought to cover total costs, where the consumers' choice is supposed to guide enterprises into increasing or reducing supply at a socially justifiable rate. Incurring costs in excess of revenue gives a welfare bonus to heavy consumers, which may or may not be socially desirable. Setting revenue in excess of costs in effect taxes the consumers who cannot switch to substitutes. These distributional effects are bound to keep governments or Parliament closely interested in the pricing practices of the public utilities among the nationalised industries, quite apart from questions of efficiency.

Note on Further Reading

Financial and Economic Objectives of Nationalised Industries, Cmnd 1337 (1961).

Nationalised Industries: a Review of Financial and Economic Objectives, Cmnd 3437 (1967).

A Study of UK Nationalised Industries, NEDO (1976).

Ministerial Control of Nationalised Industries, SCNI (1968).

Chapter 7

The Energy Industries

Until recently three nationalised energy industries, the National Coal Board (NCB), the British Gas Corporation (BGC) and the Central Electricity Generating Board (CEGB), competed with a fourth private sector industry, oil. But since 1975 the oil industry too has been partly nationalised, in the British National Oil Corporation (BNOC). However, there is still a world price of oil, hardly influenced by BNOC policy, to which all must to some extent adapt. All supply some users under monopoly conditions, with coal having the least market strength and electricity (for power) the most. Electricity's competitiveness (for heating) depends critically on the prices of other fuels. While oil was cheap, electricity was relatively cheap enough to compete in the heating market; though using a fuel with no possibility of storage, for a load as uneven as heating is not on the face of it an efficient way to use resources. Relatively dear oil, after the end of 1973, has curtailed its potential market, as coal (the close substitute for oil in generation) edges its prices upwards under the ceiling set by fuel oil. Gas became relatively a great deal cheaper as North Sea fields came on stream; but it is not certain how far or how fast successive fields will cost more to develop, or how yields will compare.

The markets for electricity and gas have been expanding, faster than the growth of GNP. Demand for oil also expanded, especially for transport, up to 1973, and is expected to keep pace with GNP into the 1980s. Coal has been in declining demand for fifteen years or more, a trend perhaps halted by the oil crisis and the discovery of hitherto unknown new reserves.

ELECTRICITY

Electricity is generated by the CEGB in England and Wales, and the South of Scotland Electricity Board and the Hydro-electricity Board in Scotland. The CEGB distributes to twelve Area Boards through the national high voltage grid. The Area Boards transform it to lower voltages, control the low voltage distribution system, market the current and set the tariffs, independently of the CEGB.

The Electricity Council (for England and Wales) consists of an independent chairman, together with the chairmen of the CEGB and the Area Boards; but though it provides certain common services and negotiates pay agreements for the whole industry, it has no management responsibility for generation or distribution.

Generation and distribution is a technically integrated system, with three distinct blocks of costs: the production costs of the energy, distribution, and consumer services, all including capital or overhead costs as well as operating expenses. Supplies have to face a fluctuating demand, with a peak load considerably above average or night-time loads, and little possibility of deflecting peak demand at short notice. Consequently, different units of consumption make different demands on the system. If it is fully used, or planned for full use when current plans mature (given a generous safety margin to cover extreme weather and other hazards), extra units demanded at peak times require extra investment. Units demanded at off-peak times require little more than the direct cost of the fuel input. Consumer services vary hardly at all with consumption.

There are therefore three kinds of costs to be recovered: *consumer*-related costs (which do not vary with demand); *consumption*-related costs (which vary directly with consumption); and capacity costs (varying with peak load demand, called confusingly by the industry *demand*-related costs). The suppliers are in a good position to recover their different costs, and make sure that the customers contribute to the fixed costs. Two-part tariffs, consisting of standing charge and a commodity rate, are used for domestic consumers, and similarly structured tariffs for industrial users.

The Bulk Supply Tariff
The CEGB supplies Area Boards with the current they require, charging by means of the Bulk Supply Tariff (BST). The BST is a complex affair, albeit a simplified reflection of the structure of generating costs. First, there are certain fixed costs, independent of consumption or capacity; secondly, there are operating costs of a given capacity; thirdly, there are capacity costs. Operating costs vary between types and ages of generators; nuclear and hydro-electric stations have very low running costs, gas turbines very high; new coal or oil-fired stations have much lower costs than old ones. Generators are run in merit order, that is, in ascending order of operating cost. So peak demand is more costly, not only because extra capacity has to be used, but also because the plant has higher unit cost. At off-peak times the cost of extra supply is very low indeed, since the industry is able to escape the start-up costs

invariably involved after even an efficient plant has been shut down. Capital costs are spread from peak to trough somewhat by the merit order working, since the low operating-cost generators usually have high capital costs and vice versa.

The BST is designed to reflect the marginal cost of distinguishable increments of demand. The principle is that the extra costs imposed by each Board depend on the level of demand at which the system is working (as though the CEGB supplied a market in which no one of the customers is large enough to determine demand). Average unit costs can be reduced by filling in the trough in the 'deep night' hours, thus reducing shutting-down and starting-up costs; flattening the daily peaks, thus avoiding the higher costs of running efficient plant flat out; or using high-cost plant for short periods; or to flatten the costly sharp build-up of demand after 6 a.m.

There are four basic elements: a fixed service (standing) charge; commodity rates; capacity charge; and a peak demand charge. The *service* charge is relatively small. It consists partly of a cash sum divided among the Boards to cover overheads, partly of a service charge for each bulk supply point. The *commodity* rates (since 1975-6) include a standard unit rate, a low minimum night rate, a higher non-minimum night rate, and a peak rate. The minimum night rate applies to the off-take at the system minimum (the lowest demand recorded in half-hours during the eight hours after midnight), multiplied by all the night hours. Demand in the remaining night hours is then surcharged at the non-minimum night rate (the surcharge for 1975-6 being half the minimum night rate, making the non-minimum rate 150 per cent of the minimum).

Consequently Boards have an incentive to increase the minimum off-take, since they get seven-and-a-half times the difference between the minimum and non-minimum rate off their charges for extra units in the lowest half-hour. The peak rate applies to the whole of the off-take during the four half-hours of peak system demand each day. There is incentive for the Boards to lop off the system peaks if they can predict when they will occur. But as their own peak does not necessarily coincide with system peak, attempts to cut it down are not certain of success.

All the commodity rates are subject to the 'fuel cost adjustment', whereby they are *automatically* raised pro rata with increases in the 'national fuel cost per ton', a statistical amalgam of expenditure on coal, oil and gas. The CEGB in effect accepts no responsibility for offsetting such increases by reducing its net revenue, though it absorbs it eventually by developing more fuel-efficient stations. The commodity rates thus reflect, broadly, the varying costs of the daily pattern of demand.

The *capacity* charges relate to the seasonal pattern of demand, the peak of which determines the capacity of the system, given the industry's obligation to supply. Given capacity, it is increasingly costly to bring it into operation, as the CEGB moves down the merit order and drives the more meritorious stations harder.

A *peak capacity* charge (in £ per KW) is levied for the two peak half-hours for the system. The peaks charged for can occur on any day between November and February, provided the CEGB has given warning before 17.00 hours the previous day of a 'potential peak'; not more than sixty hours may be the subject of warnings in one season. On the face of it, this looks rather like the CEGB defining the peak as any time it chooses to declare one. But some warning is necessary to give the Boards an opportunity to moderate it, which is the object of the tariff (as well as to collect enough revenue).

A *basic capacity* charge (also in £ per KW, nearly twice as much as the peak capacity charge) relates to Boards' off-take when the system is at 90 per cent of the two peaks, as defined for the peak capacity charge.

As costs vary, revenue varies with them; and the Boards are given a financial incentive to improve the load factor. The load factor did improve fairly steadily during the fifteen years from 1960; but this could have been due to the consultations at the Electricity Council as much as to the subtleties of the BST. The changes in the market, particularly the declining relative importance of the very peaked heating load, must have helped. The Boards can only modify load patterns by passing on the cost 'messages' in their own tariffs.

Retail electricity tariffs

Domestic and industrial supplies can be distinguished as they are sent out at different voltages. The tariffs for the two classes of consumers are also distinct.

Domestic tariffs apply to household or commercial users supplied at low voltages, in small amounts. In general, the *consumer*-related costs are recovered by the standing charge, and the *consumption*-related costs through commodity rates. This leaves capacity costs apparently uncovered. However, the industry considers that maximum demand is correlated reasonably closely with consumption; therefore capacity costs are appropriately charged in the commodity rate.

There are three domestic tariffs: the standard tariff, the day/night tariff (promoted as the 'white meter' tariff), and the tariff for pre-payment meters. The standard tariff includes a fixed standing charge, and a constant commodity (or running) rate applying to all units whenever used. The day/night tariff also includes a fixed standing charge; but there are two commodity rates, for day- and night-time consumption. The standing charge is about 50 per cent higher than on the standard tariff, to cover the extra metering and time switches. The day commodity rate is also higher than the standard rate, to allow, it is said, for the extra costs of reinforcing the network for higher demands. Considerable night-time consumption is necessary for consumers to offset the penalties of higher charges elsewhere, thus making it possible for the Boards to escape theirs by filling in the night-time trough. But a penalty on day-time consumption, which is presumably lower than it otherwise would be, is an odd reward for contributing to a better load factor. Cost-based it might be; though it is somewhat surprising that distribution costs can be so specifically allocated to the day/night tariff customers. But the electricity industry has sufficient monopoly to collect its revenue as it will, governments permitting.

The *pre-payment* (coin-in-the-slot) tariff is in principle the same as the standard domestic tariff. But the charges are somewhat higher, to cover the higher cost of metering and money collection. The standing charge is collected by the meters being set to deliver a lower amount of current than the running rate implies. The customer then gets a rebate on units used in excess of enough to collect the standing charge. There is also an overall limit on the average charge per unit, so that in effect the standard charge is reduced for very small consumption.

The fuel-cost-adjustment was introduced into domestic tariffs in 1974, after the steep oil and coal price rise left the industry in urgent need of more funds. An 'adjustment', or unannounced price increase, was added to bills each quarter. Thus the delay in collecting revenue to match cost increases was reduced; but consumers were faced with considerable price increases—long after the decisions to consume were taken. Cost-based pricing can hardly be taken to greater extremes for domestic consumers.

Industrial consumers make more demands on capacity at peak times, and there is more variation in demand between firms. Maximum demand is not closely related to consumption, as heavy consumption for power or process heating may nevertheless be an even load. Hence it is worth the industry's while to incur extra metering cost in order to collect extra revenue for maximum demand.

The *maximum demand* charge relates to consumers' own maxima, not to their own consumption at the system maximum. It is not therefore strictly cost-based, but an incentive to reduce the consumer's peak, intended on average to modify peaks and troughs. Maximum charges can be annual or monthly. The monthly charges reflect system demand, being very much higher in winter than summer. They do not, however, vary with actual peak demands.

The *unit* (or *commodity*) rates are charged on all consumption. Night-time demand may attract lower rates. Industrial rates are on average considerably lower than domestic rates, though some day-time industrial rates are higher than domestic night rates. All industrial consumers also pay a *service charge* related to installed capacity. A fuel-cost-adjustment clause has been included in industrial tariffs for many years.

Consumers, particularly domestic and commercial users, need tariffs simple enough for them to understand how the totals are constructed. This alone means that many costs must continue to be averaged over large classes of consumers, and among regions (for instance, lumping urban and rural areas together). As crude as the tariffs are in relation to costs, they are already too complex or remote from consumption decisions for some consumers to respond (where they have enough choice to make any response).

The relation between the BST and retail tariffs eluded the Select Committee on Nationalised Industries (SCNI) when they reviewed the matter, diligently though they pursued it. The Boards have to recover costs of their own, including the fixed consumer-related costs. Nevertheless the BST is the largest part of their costs. But retail domestic tariffs could not possibly reflect the BST accurately. (The mind boggles at consumers' reaction to such signals.) The SCNI found the 'translation' of the BST's cost signals into the retail tariffs 'extremely crude and obscure'. It also noted the evidence from welfare and consumer organisations: both criticised the tariffs for being too complicated, rather than too remote from costs.

The SCNI recommended the abandonment of the fuel-cost-adjustment, but felt unable to recommend any other change. It had received no positive evidence of distortion, nor suggestions for a better system. The Department of Energy, it thought, should take a more independent view of the proper allocation of costs, and hence of the appropriateness of the tariffs.

As the electricity industry is the only one which has systematically applied marginal cost pricing, the electricity tariffs are the best evidence we have of how the method works, where it can be applied at all. The industry has been among the more successful in keeping revenue above costs, and in containing costs by improving capacity use. However, problems remain. The CEGB has effectively insulated itself from any risk, by a carefully designed cost-based tariff. So strong a monopoly is only more deeply entrenched. Whether it incurs the right costs is probably a more important resource allocation question than whether it charges the right prices. But this is partly a matter of investment at the right time, in the right form, partly of the management of the system. Pricing hardly influences either of these.

GAS

Gas is also an integrated system, with the three blocks of costs similar to electricity, consumer-related, consumption-related and capacity costs. The BGC negotiates with the producing companies for North Sea gas, and operates the main transmission system. Twelve areas control further distribution, market the gas and service consumers. Their tariffs are set under guidance from the BGC.

Demand and supply

Consumption of gas is subject to daily and seasonal peaks, the seasonal peaks growing more pronounced as the industry has penetrated the heating market. Cost control depends on incurring the minimum total cost for distribution and storage combined, to link fluctuating demand with supply fluctuating under different constraints.

North Sea gas becomes available intermittently in large quantities as different fields are tapped. Once on stream, the supply needs to be fed into the distribution system as evenly as possible, to make the best use of capacity. Variation in daily off-take is matched to more even supply by line-packing (forcing gas into the mains under pressure, releasing it as required). Some seasonal variation can be met by storage, using underground cavities. But long-term storage to offset completely seasonal variation is not feasible; and all storage has high marginal cost. Hence, for the BGC to supply gas as required to its 'premium' markets, where it has a natural advantage in cleanliness or controllability, at reasonable cost and price, it has had to find a market for intermittent surpluses.

The Gas Act (1972) gave the BGC powers to supply in negotiated quantities at particular times, as well as its usual open-ended obligation to supply all-comers within reasonable reach of the mains. Industrial supplies therefore can be 'interruptible'; that is, contracts provide for the interruption of supply at times of high system demand. The users have installed plant capable of using other fuels, usually oil, the extra cost being offset by the lower cost of heat while gas is supplied, usually during the summer. Other industrial contracts have been made for low-priced supplies with a very even load factor, such as the gas sold to ICI for feedstock to produce fertilisers and other chemicals, a contract much criticised by the SCNI, though they were eventually satisfied that it was justified. Such contracts are often in a 'take or pay' form, that is, the customers are committed to paying for minimum supplies, whether they draw them or not, the main purpose being to provide a cash flow to match the constant costs of servicing the bulk transmission system, as well as to reduce the total average cost by improving the load factor.

The Gas Act also gave the BGC the duty to provide a safe and economical supply, and to operate in a 'commercially sound' way, which is interpreted in the usual way, as an obligation to cover costs and maintain 'adequate' reserves. This is the foundation of its pricing policy. But it is constrained by competition from other fuels in almost all markets. The premium markets allow considerably higher prices than the much more competitive bulk heat market, so much so that the former are far more profitable to supply, in spite of their poor load factor. Consequently the BGC aims to supply the premium markets first, the non-premium market being treated like a by-product. The least-cost match between demand and supply, after allowing for premium demands, indicates availability for the non-premium market, the price being set by the nearest alternative fuel, usually fuel oil. The economic match depends on three factors: the relative costs of supplying low-load-factor, high-load-factor or interruptible customers; the extra average revenue in the premium market; and the desirable rate of depletion of a wasting asset.

Fluctuations in the daily load do not involve such marked cost differences as in electricity, since the marginal costs of line-packing and release are relatively small. There is no point, therefore, in price differences for peak and off-peak supplies, as the cost-based differences would be too small for customers to respond. Gas tariffs are simpler than electricity, and considerably less dominated by marginal cost calculations. No doubt because of greater market pressures on prices, the industry shows a more sceptical attitude to the niceties of costing.

Gas tariffs

The BGC has much more control over the areas than the Electricity Council or the CEGB has over the electricity Area Boards. Hence, matching demand and supply is an important part of its own activity, and does not have to be indirectly induced by means of a complex tariff like the CEGB uses. The BGC sells to the largest industrial customers itself. For the rest, it controls the tariffs to a large extent. There is, however, a BST for gas sold to the areas, roughly on marginal cost principles.

The BST is set to cover the cost of the gas, the cost of the bulk transmission system and all the BGC's own expenses, including the provisions for writing off obsolete coal- and oil-based gas-making plant. There is a capacity charge and a commodity rate, determined by what the industry regards as guidelines to marginal cost. The costs are themselves produced in the BGC's corporate plan, which is in turn used to forecast and plan sales.

The *retail tariffs* are designed nationally to recover the costs of the gas, its transmission and the distribution, marketing and servicing costs of the areas. They are not directly related to the BST and are not intended to be so. Their principles were summarised in the NEDO Study (1976) in this way: 'prices for contract sales to large industrial and commercial users are market related while tariffs for domestic and other small users are based on average costs'.

There are four sets of tariffs in four zones, representing different cost levels. In each zone three tariffs are available, a general credit tariff, the 'Gold Star' tariff and the prepayment tariff.

Both the *credit tariffs* consist of a standing charge and a commodity rate. The standing charge is meant to cover consumer-related costs, although the industry admits it is none too clear what these are. Its main purpose in practice is to deter customers from keeping or requiring unwanted meters; but almost any charge would achieve this. The costs are estimated differently according to the way the concept is formulated. Taking a consumer off the network saves billing, meter reading and servicing and some future need to replace service pipes; and the meter becomes available for others. Putting a new consumer on requires a new meter and service pipe, and the addition of the usual services. The latter concept gives an estimate considerably higher than the former. 'No precision', as the BGC put it to the SCNI, attaches to the estimate of amounts to be put in the standing charge; indeed, the BGC suggested that part of capacity costs might logically be added, though it did not do so. The commodity rate is then left to cover the commodity costs, capacity costs and any consumer-related costs not in the standing charge, and BGC costs not allocated.

The Gold Star tariff is the gas industry's equivalent to electricity's White Meter tariff, in that it carries a higher standing charge and a lower commodity rate than the general tariff and is designed for consumers with space heating. But the gas industry's space heaters have a *worse* load factor than average (in contrast to electricity); so their more-than-proportionate use of capacity justifies a higher standing charge.

North Sea gas is clearly a wasting asset; and costing and prices ought to reflect its limited life. But how fast the waste, and how expensive the replacement (whether other gas fields or coal or oil gasification), requires guesswork about a very uncertain future. Setting prices according to current low costs would lead consumers to install gas-burning equipment which would soon turn out to be unexpectedly expensive to run. Prices ought in principle to be based on a smoothed trend of long-run marginal costs, for whatever the supply will be; the extraction rate would then be adjusted to demand at that price. But with the alternatives doubtful, the price is doubtful; and the extraction rate has to be decided as a matter of policy. The policy could have a substantial effect on prices. The gas available for industrial contracts would be influenced, and hence the revenue to be collected from premium markets. Prices based on long-run marginal cost would need to be considerably higher with a pessimistic view of the future than an optimistic one.

COMPETITION BETWEEN GAS AND ELECTRICITY

Competition is fierce between gas and electricity for domestic cooking, water heating and, to a lesser extent, space heating. But both industries enjoy considerable monopoly once consumers are joined to their network. Electricity Boards at one time exploited their monopoly in ways which penalised consumers long after the abuses were stopped. Housing developers can limit choice of fuels by the system they install. In the days of the industry's dominance, before the oil crisis, Electricity Boards were able to persuade some estate developers, including local authorities, to install electric wiring only, by reducing the connection charges providing no gas was installed. Some Gas Boards responded by offering to pay the electricity charges provided gas *was* installed. Complaints led to a Monopolies Commission investigation, though not before a good many all-electric schemes were built. The Monopolies Commission reported, as expected, that the practice should cease. The only fair remedy seemed to be for each to charge according to costs. However, although this prevents blatant abuse, it does not entirely settle the problem. The relationship between capital and running costs in the two industries is different. Gas fitting costs more than electric wiring, though the running costs of gas, especially for heating, is lower. Private developers have to add connection charges to house prices, local authorities have to add them to the rent. The gas industry has to persuade householders to prefer gas strongly enough to seek out gas-equipped houses, to overcome the disadvantage to the builders in installing it.

Pricing problems

The impact of steeply rising electricity prices on poorer tenants in electrically heated flats or houses led to a plethora of official reports through 1975 and 1976, including the SCNI. As a result the philosophy behind domestic tariffs was made more explicit, but in principle little changed. The issue was whether the tariff structure should be changed. Cost-based tariffs make smaller consumers pay a higher average charge (taking into account the standing charge) than larger consumers. As poorer consumers spend far more of their income on fuel than the richer ones, and the majority of poor consumers use less than average amounts, the distributional effect of cost-based increases was regressive, the standing charge being, it was thought, further below cost than the commodity rates. An official committee was against tariff adjustment, because charging customers the cost, distinguishing consumer from consumption cost, was economically sound; because the industries have a statutory obligation not to discriminate between classes of consumers; and because the Consumer Councils wanted no change. But the emphasis of the report was on the harm that would be done to the poor consumers exceptionally dependent on one fuel (hence above-average consumers), especially the unfortunate tenants of the all-electric flats. The SCNI were obviously uneasy about this, and criticised the report for its lack of quantitative information on the total effects of restructuring, including the general economic effect of moving away from cost-based pricing. But they felt that the case for a change had not been made.

Electricity and gas seem to be the most suitable industries for the application of marginal cost pricing; but even here there are problems. Coal and oil compete with them in a number of uses, and are inputs for electricity generation; so the socially desirable allocation of resources through pricing requires that these also should price according to marginal cost. Marginal costing of coal and oil is difficult in itself, and not in fact practised. In the gas and electricity industries, a compromise has to be reached between the extra cost and complexity of accurate cost-based tariffs and the possible benefits in improving the load factors or revenue.

The benefits can only accrue if consumers respond to the signals, avoiding the costlier supplies unless their value is particularly great. As it is, one wonders who in their senses would turn down the heating in the middle of a cold spell in winter (the costliest time), rather than at off-peak times or seasons. The 'signals' ought to induce better insulation of buildings, and may well do so for some marginal consumers with new houses or with resources to finance structural improvements. But this applies to a small minority of householders at any one time. Direct propaganda in favour of insulation, or government support for its installation (though there might be objections to this on other grounds), might be more effective more quickly than waiting for responses to price signals. Domestic consumers are not prepared to devote much effort to following a complex tariff; simple uniform tariffs, even flat-rate tariffs, are their primary request. So two-part tariffs with night rates for electricity are a crude compromise, far from accurate in terms of costs, but reasonably efficient revenue-gathering devices nevertheless.

Energy costs are relatively more important for industrial consumers; and with all the resources at their command they can exercise more discretion. But some resource allocation questions are still unsolved. Charges and conditions of supply from the industry influence the amount of private generation. The electricity industry naturally wants to reduce it; the consumers' interest or even the national interest might be to increase it. Consumers on maximum demand tariff can be required to shed load when the system approaches capacity. The maximum demand charges are still levied; that is, the *customers* are made to pay for the suppliers' inability to supply, on top of the cost of own plant. Yet the industry is reluctant to accept privately generated current into its system. The social benefits of a unified system are great; but there may still be a good case for supplementing supplies.

Rising (or falling) relative energy prices impoverish (or enrich) domestic and small industrial users. For this reason alone, energy prices are not likely to disappear far beneath the surface of economic or commercial rectitude. Gas and electricity prices are based on costs and current government policy about prices generally and target returns for nationalised industries. But the costs are based on planning decisions about capacity, loads and demand taken years before, some of which may turn out to be seriously wrong, such as the surplus capacity for electricity generation, the charges for which burdened consumers from the late 1960s onwards. The BGC could plan to distribute gas too fast or too slowly, if they misforecast demand or future costs. Policy judgments cannot be eliminated from the management of public utilities by marginal cost pricing principles.

COAL

Costs

The coal industry produces a storable commodity, with no special distribution links with its customers. Its revenue is determined by gas and electricity prices for domestic uses, and mainly oil for industrial uses, especially electricity generation, its largest market. Though it is highly capital-intensive, productivity depends on labour performance. The key to minimum unit production costs is to keep the machinery working the maximum number of hours. Actual working times are well below theoretical working times, in some places less than half as long. Some of the shortfall is due to difficult conditions, some to breakdowns; but much is the result of absenteeism and avoidable lost time.

Mining is among the least congenial and most dangerous of occupations; problems stemming from conditions of work are entirely predictable. The means of improving output from a given amount of equipment, in given natural conditions, include appropriate pay determination. But this is elusive.

Before systematic mechanisation, the main system of pay for coal-getting was piece-rates, settled at pit level. Miners' pay was more dependent on local agreements about payment by results than on national agreements on basic rates. Local disputes were endemic, and district union officers more powerful than national ones. With mechanisation, piece-rates became unfair and ineffective; both the pay principles and the unrest were unpopular with labour and management. National day-rates were substituted (in the 1960s). At first these were a great success in stopping disputes, and allowing the benefits of mechanisation to come through in steadily improving productivity. The improvements then tailed off, and even went into reverse. After the disastrous strike of early 1974 the NCB wanted to reintroduce productivity bonuses, relating pay partly to output pit by pit. But the union was emphatically against it. A more remote productivity scheme was brought in, but it proved ineffective. The dilemma remained. With no close relationship between increments of pay and production, productivity slumped; with a close relationship, the interest of different pits or areas conflict, national union control over pay is weakened, and the possibility of local disputes grows.

Unit costs differ widely with different geological conditions, ages of pits and methods of extraction. Marginal cost pricing has been much discussed in relation to coal. The difference between average and marginal cost for the whole industry is so great that national or even regional average cost-based prices leave the marginal pits making huge losses. But marginal cost pricing would make the consumers pay considerably more, part of the extra revenue being substantial profits on the intra-marginal pits. The surpluses built up would not necessarily correspond to finance required to carry out the current policy on re-equipment or development of new seams or pits.

Prices
Coking or smokeless coal commands a 'premium' (partial monopoly) price. Some is produced in high-cost pits; some sells at high margins, especially as coking coal tends to be in short supply in international markets. But most coal is suitable for a number of markets, with further preparation. The price of domestic coal depends on the price of other fuels, coal being cheaper (in terms of heat content) to balance its disadvantages of inconvenience, dirt and poor efficiency in old equipment. Industrial coal for heating and steam-raising has to compete with oil mainly. While oil was growing relatively cheaper, industrial coal could not be sold at prices high enough to cover even average costs, and the industry contracted rapidly with persistent deficits. The NCB became more dependent on the CEGB as its main customer.

Pricing coal either in relation to markets, or in relation to cost is a complicated exercise, with much trial and error to get a required amount of revenue. Given anticipated average revenue, set by the maximum increase in price consistent with no worse a trend towards rival fuels, many grades have to be priced, and supplies of the grades from the various sources planned. The quality variables, apart from size, include ash content; sulphur content; coalfield 'additions' (to reflect the extra value of supplies from fields near valuable markets); and selective supplements for coal with special carbonisation properties, such as coking coal. All of these have influenced price structures from time to time, modifying the pattern given by uniform pro rata increases to get the required average percentage increase. Most of these relate to value to the market. Size and preparation relates to extra cost for the screening and washing, as well as to market value.

Pricing according to cost, especially marginal cost, is a conundrum solved by a model simulating conditions in various areas. Demand has to be forecast for each category of demand, distinguishing coal qualities with separable costs, rather than customers. Then minimum costs are worked out, distinguishing areas of supply, and taking transport costs into account. Even to do this, which is a summarised version of full marginal costs, forecasts of planned output and costs for five years ahead had to be made. It does not follow that these costs can in fact be charged, because of market pressures, nor that more could not be earned where the market was less competitive. In practice, commercial judgment must be exercised.

With the very long lead times for new production, allowing resources to follow market responses to marginal cost pricing is likely to leave capacity out of line with requirements in one direction or the other. The oil crisis improved the industry's prospects; oil and gas from the North Sea depressed them. Speculation about the exhaustion of North Sea gas improved them again. Miners' pay relative to other input prices, and to coal output, is a critical part of the estimates. New capacity approved one year will affect supplies and costs five or ten years away, and for a generation after that. Plans can be modified or postponed, conceivably speeded up; but major investments may be no worse as political decisions than notional responses to notional costs.

Coal and steel prices are governed by the European Coal and Steel Community (ECSC) set up by the Treaty of Paris (1953), of which the UK industries became members on accession to the EEC (1972). The principle is to establish a common competitive market. Price or market-sharing agreements among member enterprises are forbidden. Prices must cover costs, and the Authority (of ECSC) can set maximum or minimum prices. All prices and discounts must be published and strictly observed. Member governments cannot overrule the ECSC, for instance by applying price control to their industries. However, prices may be reduced below cost to meet competition from imports. Consequently, coal and steel have been excluded from UK prices policy since 1973. Normally, enterprises are expected to raise their prices in line with costs, including a return on capital, to stop competition at loss-making prices, culminating in further concentration. Neither NCB nor the BSC have managed to cover their costs consistently; but their obligations to ECSC give them support for raising prices on occasions when the UK government might have adopted a different policy.

Note on Further Reading
Gas and Electricity Prices, SCNI (1976).
Gas and Electricity Tariffs, NBPI no. 7.
Gas Prices, NBPI no. 57.
The Bulk Supply Tariff, NBPI no. 59.
Gas Prices, NBPI no. 102.
Coal Prices, NBPI no. 138.
Coal Prices (Second Report and Supplements), NBPI no. 153.

Costs and Efficiency in the Gas Industry, NBPI no. 155.

Fuel Policy, Posner, Chapter 9 (1974).

Connection Charges for Gas and Electricity, Monopolies Commission (1972).

Annual Reports of BGC, CEGB, Area Electricity Boards, NCB.

See also references on North Sea Gas and Oil given for Chapter 3.

Chapter 8

Transport and Communications

Public sector transport undertakings operate with more severe market pressures than any other nationalised industries. The Post Office operates with more monopoly than any other. The nationalised industry pricing rules are not applied in either.

TRANSPORT

Modes and Markets
There is scarcely a more baffling sector in which to apply pricing principles, or work out satisfactory practices. The public corporations have been reorganised, the functions of public sector and private sector, central and local government redefined, the laws and regulations revised. The problems persist, merely changing in circumstantial detail from one reform to the next. There are three main peculiarities accounting for the problems. Different *modes* of transport do not correspond to different *markets*; social costs and benefits are too important to be ignored in policy making; and the cost structures of competing modes are complex and radically different.

None of the nationalised corporations covers a whole mode or market. *British Rail* (BR) covers all rail services, except for containerised freight (covered by Freightliners, a jointly owned subsidiary), and parcels carried by National Carriers Ltd (NCL). In its passenger market it competes with cars or buses for commuter traffic, cars, coaches or airways for long-distance travel. In its freight market it competes with road or shipping. The *National Freight Corporation* (NFC) has subsidiaries with interests mainly in road and rail. Freightliners is one, jointly owned by BR and NFC; NCL is another, also jointly owned. British Road Services and its subsidiaries is the other important constituent. The *National Bus Company* is a holding company for thirty bus undertakings providing intercity or local, rural services, sometimes overlapping the areas of the Passenger Transport Executives (PTEs), which run town buses in six metropolitan counties; and fifty district councils run other urban services. The PTEs also control commuter rail services. London Transport (LT) is owned by the Greater London Council and runs passenger services, closely competing with BR on some routes; on others LT's buses and its own Underground compete more closely. The British Waterways Board controls canal and river transport, but not sea transport, and is as much concerned with leisure travel as freight journeys. The British Airports Authority (BAA) controls most of the larger civil airports, local authorities the rest. British Airways (BA) provides air transport, with much competition. Most ports are publicly owned by the National Ports Council, the Dock Labour Board and Ports Authorities. Coastal shipping is largely privately owned.

Private sector transport undertakings are mostly more compact, mainly devoted to one mode, and often to one market. Road haulage is the most varied in size and range of business. Private passenger undertakings mainly provide coaches for contract or custom hire. Private airlines are more closely controlled than other private sector transport. Public and private surface transport firms all compete with the private car and user-owned commercial transport.

Social costs
Transport generally brings social cost and benefits as no other activity, apart from housing. The costs of congestion, air pollution and noise are obvious to us all. Yet reliable, speedy and cheap freight transport is an increasingly important condition for competing in world markets or passing on the benefits of efficient, concentrated production to household consumers. Passenger transport is increasingly an important ingredient of the more comfortable and stimulating life to which most of us aspire as incomes rise. Contact with family and friends, access to services and entertainment, and relief from the confinement of narrow surroundings all require mobility.

All transport modes have problems related to the uneven utilisation of their services over time, with pronounced daily peak loads. But they are also subject to congestion, a phenomenon with no parallel in gas or electricity. A traveller or purveyor of goods who chooses to use road or rail at peak times on busy routes endures a poor service himself, but also imposes costs on others. Journey costs are greatly increased. On the roads the distance covered by each vehicle is reduced, increasing the fixed costs per mile; and running costs per mile are increasing through the inefficiencies of slow speeds. On the railways, speeds are less and stopping times greater. In the air, aircraft circle round airports wasting fuel, and eventually deposit passengers in overcrowded terminals.

The peak load problem often results in congestion; but both contribute to extra costs. Congestion arises from too much transport in restricted space, peak loads from disproportionate concentration at particular times. Both are connected with capacity: congestion when the system is overloaded, peak loads when vehicle capacity is used at its fullest. Peaked demand increases operators' costs by increasing capacity costs and also operating costs. Congestion imposes costs on society, partly in the extra costs of traffic control, partly in the general reduction of the efficiency of all vehicles. The peak demand determines the capacity needed by the undertaking, the costs of which have to be recovered.

Marginal cost pricing would mean charging more at peak times than off-peak. The case for piling costs on to peak users is that consumers should pay the costs it is worth their while to incur. But competition may prevent such a policy; or the customers may revolt by political action.

A social cost can either be avoided or paid for. Avoiding congestion involves planning action: regulating parking, altering traffic flows, designating bus lanes and lorry routes, controlling landing and taking-off for aircraft. Congestion can be paid for in two ways: travellers or consignments contributing to congestion can pay more; or more can be spent on removing particular causes, like badly sited road junctions, narrow roads and bridges. Higher prices for peak-hour travel or travel over congested routes might alter the pattern of demand, if it were sufficiently responsive to price (if other journeys are near-substitutes for the peak journeys). Costs would thereby be reduced, rather than providing more revenue to cover higher costs. Generally, the various methods are directed to increasing the effective capacity of track or terminals, whether by increasing the flow or the space available.

Flattening peaks or preventing congestion by discriminatory pricing can only succeed if consumers respond. The idea that consumers choose their journeys freely is somewhat misleading. Some consumers, some of the time can choose between alternative modes of transport. Some consumers choose passenger journeys when they need not make a journey at all. But a growing proportion of public transport journeys are to and from work, and most freight journeys are incurred as an incidental cost of marketing. Some choose to live near their work, or work where they live, to avoid commuting; but other determinants of work or residence are more important than transport prices. If consumers have no real choice, price serves no allocation function, though it might in a stable world eventually affect the pattern of supplies. It merely enables enterprises to pay their way, if they can. Choice lies between modes of transport in urban areas, but surprisingly often there is none among public modes; the practical choice is between public and personal transport. In rural areas, poor, unreliable and costly services are no real alternative to personal transport.

Cost structures

Cost structures relate mainly to the modes, while prices relate to the markets. Transport costs are made up of some combination of vehicle, track and terminal costs. Rail and inland waterways own and maintain the track and terminals. Bus and coach undertakings usually own the terminals but not the track. Sea and air firms own neither track nor terminals, though both pay for the terminal facilities provided by harbour or airport authorities. Roads are provided by central or local government but no direct charge is made to users. Private transport cannot own its track, but may use private terminals.

Track and terminal costs are heavy for both road and rail. Road is an expanding system, with heavy outgoings for both new track and maintenance. Rail is contracting, with much of its track written off; but signalling and track maintenance are both costly. It is often thought that competition between road and rail is 'unfair' because rail bears its own track costs whereas road does not. However, road vehicles are taxed, by Vehicle Excise Duty (VED), fuel tax, Value Added Tax (VAT), and car tax on cars and taxis. Road transport as a whole fully covers its track costs by the tax revenue; though classes of road vehicles do not always cover the avoidable costs properly attributable to them. Buses do not; taxes are intentionally light, as an element of the subsidies they enjoy. Heavy lorries did not pay enough to cover their estimated track costs at the time of the Transport Policy Consultation Document (1976), probably unintentionally, as licences had not been increased in line with inflation.

Changes in the structure of taxation might be needed, to relate use more closely to cost. For instance, the tax on petrol or diesel fuel is a better proxy for road costs than VED, as track cost clearly varies with mileage more than the number and class of vehicle.

Terminal costs vary a great deal between modes. Rail, sea and air terminals are relatively costly. Road terminal costs are usually small, though bus stations sometimes occupy valuable city centre land. One of the most difficult problems is costing the parking of road vehicles. Money outlays on parking are zero on unrestricted roads or lay-bys. The real costs may also be negligible where the space has no other use; but increasing density of traffic makes this less and less likely. Meters could be set to collect charges equivalent to estimated cost (including social cost), but they seldom are. Off-street parking charges are more likely to relate to the proprietors' operating costs than to the value of the space. But charges determined by the full social cost would not necessarily bring about a better use of resources. Charges imposed on commercial vehicles, including cars, might well be added to the firms' output costs, with no change in the demand for the space. Such charges are usually so small a part of total costs that it is not worth organising the required change of behaviour. Where firms use their own or customers' premises, it is doubtful if they would cost transport so exactly that the costs of space were allocated to it. Loading bays and parking space would be just another overhead to be recovered where markets allow. Once again the unresponsiveness of consumers casts doubt on the wisdom of marginal cost pricing, a practical move towards which would merely raise the price level.

Operating costs vary with modes. Most vehicles need a relatively inflexible crew and maintenance service. Vehicle costs are therefore sensitive to increasing fuel prices or pay rates. Unit costs of traffic depend on capacity use. Pricing can influence capacity use, by both passenger and freight traffic. Non-peak passenger traffic may be attracted, at lower unit cost. Freight can be matched to vehicle capacity by prices discriminating in favour of full loads, return loads or off-peak times or routes.

Railways

BR has to meet the cost of track capacity larger than the business really needs. Track and signalling costs are not entirely fixed; the density of traffic and speed influence standards of maintenance and cost in use. Nevertheless, track and terminal costs vary much less than proportionately to passengers or freight carried; the costs have to be shared between the services.

In the *freight* market BR competes with hauliers' or consignors' vehicles. The customers are discriminating, the more so as transport costs rise relative to other things. But they are as much product- as price-sensitive; speed, reliability, safety and care in handling influence preferences. Containerisation has helped rail as well as road to restrain handling costs and prevent damage and loss. But rail is still at a disadvantage for much traffic, in having to deliver by road at destination, a costly operation. It is also socially costly, in increasing traffic in congested town centres.

Over long distances, the cost per mile begins to compare more favourably with road; though customers' own transport or contract hire may still have the advantage for flexibility, to fit in with production or delivery timetables. The railways' freight market is thus mainly for bulk consignments, usually over long distances (200 miles or more), or for delivery into customers' sidings. Because of the reduction in social cost through keeping heavy traffic off the roads, the government provided grants for sidings to be constructed, as an indirect and cost-effective subsidy to rail transport. BR's business has been increasingly concentrated on trainload traffic from a few dozen customers. Coal, oil, cement and steel account for a large proportion. This brings more problems, as all of these are vulnerable to general recessions; cyclical or secular reductions in demand from these alone are enough to push BR into deficit, even if it could break even on the rest.

For *passenger* traffic there are a number of linked but separate markets. Commuter traffic into the conurbations is carried by rail in competition with cars or buses. Business travel over intercity routes is carried by rail in competition with cars, or airways. Holiday and leisure traffic competes with coaches as well.

The more captive markets, from which BR might expect to recover its fixed costs in a self-supporting enterprise, are commuter passengers, especially into London, and intercity passengers. But this had never been achieved over any significant period; it remains to be demonstrated, therefore, whether it is possible. A significant part of total traffic (over 40 per cent) is commuter travel in and out of central London. The peak is exceptionally steep, with rolling stock, terminals and other facilities being grossly underused between peaks. Piling the costs of this and system overheads on to fares either drives more passengers on to the roads or gives rise to unacceptable hostility. A change from subsidised to unsubsidised fares is also inflationary, at least to the extent that London allowances in pay rates reflect extra costs in London, a large part of which is transport fares.

Intercity passengers are far less sensitive to fare increases, no doubt because many of them pay with someone else's money. In the fifteen months between January 1975 and March 1976 intercity fares were raised four times, by over 80 per cent on average; yet revenue continued to increase. Family rates, weekend rates, special cards for pensioners or students (on certain trains, out of the summer season), reductions for booking in advance, day returns (excluding peak services) and party rates (where competition from coaches is keen) allow varying discounts below standard fares. Though designed to attract different groups of passengers with different demand characteristics, these techniques of increasing revenue can only succeed where full-fare passengers cannot take advantage of them. Hence the complexities and conditions. But this has disadvantages; too few potential passengers know what fares are. When the railways enjoyed their monopoly, fares were mainly based on mileage; the idea of a standard fare for a journey dies hard.

Fares and freight charges can only be decided in the light of political decisions. If the railways are to be maintained at a level which keeps more traffic off the roads than a market system would achieve, they must be subsidised. Then the aim of pricing should be to maximise revenue, or minimise losses on the socially desirable system. Maximising revenue would imply an open-ended subsidy, since avoidable costs of extra traffic might be above marginal revenue, even on a system with spare capacity. Minimising losses, given whatever specific subsidies there are (for keeping open particular routes, for instance), requires that avoidable costs are covered. But on a system with so many joint costs, with so many services to offer, matching fares or charges to avoidable cost is a perplexing task in itself. In an integrated system there are many ways of varying the traffic over different time scales, from running extra trains to redesigning timetables, routes and stopping places, to altering the capacity by technical improvement of vehicles or track. Working out a rule book for salesmen to set an appropriate charge for additional freight business is a complex matter, which has to be based on some assumptions about the future system. The joint costs of track and terminals should then be recovered where and to the extent that markets would allow.

The Transport Act (1968) attempted to solve the pricing problems by making subsidies specific to certain routes or services. The rest of the system was then to cover its costs, by whatever prices BR chose to impose. But these proposals were never really implemented. Setting the subsidies requires detailed and sophisticated costing; before this could be provided fully, BR was in such urgent need of more support that a new Act on different principles was passed. The Railways Act (1974) was based on a political decision that passenger services should be maintained at their then level, with a revenue subsidy to cover the difference between revenue from fares and costs, including the joint costs. Rail freight would be run as a 'commercial business', defined as covering avoidable costs. But even that arrangement was overtaken by events. Almost as soon as the Act was passed, the recession so reduced traffic that freight revenues were very far from covering avoidable costs. Nor did passenger revenue achieve this. It is difficult to believe that more efficient marketing or increased charges, given the competition and income constraints, can raise enough revenue to cover costs of a system anything like the present one, save intermittently in boom years. 'Commercial' or 'economic' pricing may be an impossibility—while costs remain broadly as they are.

The Transport Policy Review Consultation Document (1976) again exposed the problems, the emphasis being on the need to limit the subsidies. But no new pricing rules emerged. As the NEDO Study pointed out, the prices of all rail services are limited by the competition. Though marginal cost principles should mean that a loss-making system is reduced until revenue at least covers marginal cost, BR's investment programmes, a large part of which are replacement or required to maintain a competitive standard of service, are decided on quite different grounds, in essence to preserve the system in an imperfectly articulated national interest.

Road passenger transport

Road passenger transport consists mainly of public sector buses fighting a losing battle with private cars. But bus costs are high and inflexible, with about 70 per cent being the pay of crews and maintenance staff. As split shifts have mostly been eliminated during collective bargaining, labour costs cannot be escaped at off-peak times. The trend of demand is downwards, more and more concentrated on the rush hours, and towards steadily fewer passengers. In the 1970s 4 per cent less passengers each year were carried, though bus mileage declined only by 2 per cent a year.

Costs being spread over fewer journeys, average costs have risen steeply. So have fares. The Transport Policy Consultation Document reported that fares rose 13 per cent faster than the RPI from 1970 to 1975. Marginal costs where capacity is fully used (as it is in London and most other cities) is astronomical, partly because of the rising cost of vehicles, partly because of increased operating cost due to congestion. Pricing according to the costs incurred would mean loading formidable increases on to peak-hour travellers. But the decline in demand can hardly be halted by charging monopoly prices at the very time most passengers need to travel. Not surprisingly, the Ministry of Transport has found that bus passengers are damagingly responsive to relative fare increases (a 10 per cent increase losing 3 per cent of passengers). They transfer to cars, bicycles or mopeds—whose drivers are not paid. Peak pricing 'spreads the load' to other modes, as well as, or rather than, to other times.

The task of pricing bus journeys competitively is difficult because the perceived cost of car journeys can be very much lower than bus fares. The obvious cost is petrol, oil, and wear and tear on tyres and engine. Accountants and the public transport lobby urge the motorist to cost his motoring 'fully' or 'properly', including taxation, insurance, depreciation and interest on capital. But decisions are rarely taken on this basis (apart from convenience). The standing costs of the car may cover a whole family's journeys for many purposes. For one or more of these purposes there may be no acceptable alternative. The *marginal* cost of the rest is then relevant. Moreover, with persistent inflation pushing up the value of secondhand as well as new cars, they do not depreciate very fast. However, the overwhelming difference between private and public transport is that the driver of the car is not paid. Since the driver as often as not derives positive pleasure from driving, there is no real cost to add in. Few people lead such bustling lives that minutes or even hours spent sitting in a car is a loss of welfare, especially if the alternative is half the time standing in wind or rain, waiting for bus or train, carrying cases, baskets or babies. The cost not properly accounted for is the social cost of increasing congestion, and pre-emption of land for motor roads. Market demand is an impossible determinant for new roads; space is limited and increasingly valuable. Land use must be administratively controlled; this alone means that transport modes must be to some extent administratively controlled.

The great convenience of own transport for passengers or freight is the main obstacle to making public transport enterprises viable by refinements of costing or pricing. So long as the main competitors were all public carriers for hire, a desirable allocation of resources might conceivably be achieved by pricing according to marginal cost, provided the costs could be reasonably assessed. When private transport became the chief competitor to the public carriers, the principle lost its validity. Once a substantial proportion of traffic goes in own transport, the peaking problems of public transport become much worse. At the same time, the enterprises have to struggle with surplus capacity as demand falls in total, and with increasing unit costs due to under-used capacity at off-peak times. Pricing according to cost makes matters worse. Fares go up, tipping the comparison between public and private transport more towards private even for commuter journeys, limited only by the capacity of the roads. So far, traffic engineering (controlling the flow, with minor improvements in the roads) has increased the capacity of apparently fully used road systems. Public undertakings cannot raise more revenue by raising prices, so they cut costs by reducing the service, giving an even bigger advantage to private transport, and the downward spiral takes another twist.

Bus fares are fixed by Traffic Commissioners, an arrangement dating back more than forty years. The Commissioners are primarily licensing authorities for stage services, the original purpose of which was to safeguard public transport and the public. Competition in such special circumstances resulted in too many insufficiently financed firms; a good service requires both continuity and safety, both of them expensive. Licensing was the method chosen to control standards of service and safety. The licence holders had a high degree of monopoly; in consequence, their fares were also made the subject of the Traffic Commissioners' approval. But their existence makes it difficult for either central governments or local authorities to pursue properly co-ordinated price and investment policies, since the Commissioners are independent, and need give no reason for their decisions. The NBPI had to review LT bus fares, after a previous recommendation had been thwarted by a different view taken by the Commissioners. The Transport Policy Document suggested transferring the licensing powers to local authorities, to give them more effective control.

Road freight transport

In the road freight market, the private sector road hauliers set the level of charges. It is a highly competitive sector, with an array of firms of all sizes. A few private enterprises with national coverage compete directly with the nationalised carriers; but both are in competition with smaller firms specialising on routes or traffic. The NFC accounts for only 10 per cent of road freight (excluding own-vehicle transport), with 40 per cent parcels, 40 per cent containers, and 20 per cent specialised haulage, which is the fastest growing market.

Firms specialise by types of transport (tankers, tippers, coal or ore carriers); by route or areas; connection with container ports; contracted to particular firms or industries. Costs vary appreciably within each class. Operating costs for vehicles, crews, fuel and taxes are augmented by quite heavy overheads for depots and administration in large firms, spread over more or less turnover according to their success in organising return loads and continuous working for the vehicles.

Charges are naturally variable as well, with intermittent complaints from the Road Haulage Association (RHA), representing mainly the larger firms, that smaller 'sub-marginal' firms cut prices below costs to the detriment of the whole trade. There is indeed an unstable fringe of near-marginal firms; though whether they do any damage to the national interest is doubtful. Large customers want service and continuity as well as a keen price. If a small haulier can get the business, he is probably not sub-marginal. As so often, the more usual situation is that the small supplier deals with the small customer, possibly to their own and the national benefit; though they may also pre-empt resources in inefficient uses too long.

Road freight is a prime example of a highly competitive market where the great range of services and prices is a sign of competition. In the mid-1960s the NBPI found that the biggest impediment to competitive pricing was the indifference of the customers. Too many transport managers were prepared to accept whatever price increase their usual firm, advised by the RHA, demanded. After the publicity given to the report, in which it was proposed that the RHA should cease recommending increases, customers have certainly become more discriminating. No doubt the NBPI had some effect; the higher standards of operation imposed by the Transport Act (1968) had more, as transport costs began to rise relatively. More specialised management in retailing and manufacturing has also increased the cost- and price-consciousness of the main customers.

The public sector hauliers have had to adapt their methods to meet the competition of firms with lower overheads, not being committed to so wide a coverage of freight, with so large a network of depots. When market-determined prices press on such enterprises, the only solution is reorganisation to reduce overheads, and a change of marketing to increase capacity use. Depots have been concentrated, contract hire business expanded and specialised operating units formed (like NCL's 'Fashion-flair' for clothing). With prices market-determined, costs adapt to them. Increases in the level of prices follow cost increases common to all firms.

Air transport
Commercial air transport is a natural oligopoly, competition being severely restricted by airport capacity and air-lanes with navigational support services. Considerable economies of scale enjoyed by airlines working major routes have restricted it more. Domestic air travel in a country the size of the UK is subject to competition from rail and even road. Consequently, it is difficult to make airlines profitable based on domestic traffic; the revenue of British airlines of any size comes from international services. This introduces yet another factor reducing competition: international travel requires pairs of countries to grant one another rights for landing and over-flying. As might be expected from an essentially political process, the agreements are market-sharing bargains. The revenue as well as the traffic is pooled. If one party has only one

airline, it grants rights to one of the others, unless traffic is unusually heavy. Each government is responsible for safety and noise control; broadly equivalent standards are agreed. Licensing of operators is universal; space at airports would not in any case allow a large number of operators to have their own terminal offices, passenger-receiving or maintenance facilities. Many countries have one airline on international routes; the UK has two, British Airways (BA, a nationalised industry) and British Caledonian (BCAL, a private enterprise).

The industry has all the characteristics of an oligopoly writ large. Competition is overtly fierce, but concentrated on marketing and service, with some surreptitious price cutting. But an international cartel with the support of governments, the International Air Transport Association (IATA), fixes most prices for international traffic (including freight rates). Neither the industry nor governments have yet found an acceptable alternative. In the absence of IATA, no doubt prices would be part of the maze of bilateral Air Services Agreements between countries. But international supervision of some kind in the interest of consumers seems highly desirable. The perennial problem is surplus capacity of aircraft, characteristic of both oligopolies and public transport.

Domestic services incur heavy costs per passenger- or package-mile, partly due to surplus capacity at provincial airports. The relatively short hops also mean either relatively inefficient operation of large aircraft, or a separate short-haul fleet. Some specialised firms exist, but scheduled services are still often unprofitable because of low load factors.

Two public corporations, The British Airports Authority (BAA) and the Civil Aviation Authority (CAA), provide between them the terminals and track. The BAA owns the international and some other airports. It charges enough to cover its costs, and is supposed to earn an adequate return on its capital. Since it is a monopoly supplier there is no market reason to impedè it. Charges made by the BAA and other airport owners are supervised by the CAA.

Domestic air fares are controlled (in the UK) by the CAA; and it licenses operators, the power which enables it to fix or approve fares and other conditions. Licences are renewed or granted for economic competence as well as compliance with safety standards. The CAA also provides civil air traffic controls and the UK's share of en-route navigational aids. Its costs must in principle be recovered by charges for services and licences. But charges for en-route navigational aids are subject to international agreement and are not due to cover costs until 1978.

Operators on both international and domestic routes look to

charter services and holiday 'packages' for incremental revenue far in excess of incremental costs. Charter flights naturally have a much better load factor than all but the busiest scheduled services. Fares can be reduced drastically and still leave higher margins. But charter business competes as keenly with scheduled air services as with other modes for the marginal business, the weak-preference, lower-income travellers. Hence, IATA sets minimum prices and conditions for charter flights also, to prevent the cartel prices being eroded.

The passenger market is divided between business, holiday, personal and 'affinity group' travel. The holiday and affinity group travellers go mainly on charter flights, the business and personal travellers on scheduled flights. The business travellers respond to regularity, convenience and comfort rather than price, the rest more to price. Customers can be attracted by frequent services at convenient times; the result is too many half-filled planes on rival lines. The quality of the product has been improved mainly by increasing speed; but as this depends on the design of the aircraft, major airlines can gain only short-lived superiority in this way. Marketing the incidental services remains the chief competitive technique.

Substantial economies of scale are derived from using a large fleet of standard aircraft. They are so large a part of the capital in such expensive units that idle time adds appreciably to overall unit operating cost. High utilisation depends on flying many routes. The constraints set by daily or seasonal peaks, restrictions on night flying, and different route lengths cancel out for a comprehensive world service. High utilisation also depends on having the aircraft available for flying for the maximum time. Servicing can be scheduled more economically with increasing numbers, and engineering costs reduced by specialisation. Marketing on a world scale can reduce the unit costs of the expensive city centre premises airlines maintain.

The price-fixing procedure of IATA is subject to considerable tension. Demand is both price- and income-elastic. Incomes the airlines cannot control; prices they can. The more profitable airlines do not necessarily have the lowest costs; they may have favourable routes or good marketing techniques. The lower-cost operators have every reason to want low prices. But IATA, being a cartel, must reach some compromise between the high- and low-cost members, by which the less efficient members have some hope of continuing in business, with whatever subsidies they get. The result is something near average price covering costs somewhere between high- and low-cost lines. In the long run, IATA fares depend on costs, and costs depend in part on the growth of demand in relation to capacity. But the connection between prices and efficiency is too remote to induce operation at minimum cost. Reductions in average costs have been made by using larger aircraft. Least-cost performance requires possession of the latest aircraft. But the aircraft and the routes at the disposal of an airline can make so much difference to costs and revenue that inefficient operation with the right aircraft and routes is more profitable than efficient operation with the wrong ones. This, plus the inevitable cushion in IATA fares, leaves the long run in which the reward goes to the efficient a very long way away.

The official remedy is to price more selectively according to costs. This would mean that if one aircraft has lower seat-mile costs than another it should be priced accordingly. But this ignores the market. The customer may not have a choice, or may be indifferent, so long as flight times are not changed. Similarly, peak and off-peak costs cannot always be reflected very closely in fares.

The UK government rules for civil aviation were renewed in 1976, in the form of the guidance to the CAA. Tariffs should be 'rational, simple and enforceable'. The rationality consists of the principle that 'each charge should be related to costs at a level that will yield sufficient revenue to cover the costs of efficient operators'. A literal interpretation would give a tariff anything but simple. Some averaging and cross-subsidisation is inevitable. Moreover, an efficient operator aiming at 'sufficient revenue' to earn a return on capital in an industry vulnerable to cycles of demand would match his tariff to his market, in particular to the strengths and weaknesses of price responses rather than to costs. For all its apparent precision, the guidance gives little but the most general advice. The CAA is also left with the problem of distinguishing efficient operators. As so often with administrative pricing rules, the effect is to rule out some undesired policies rather than to prescribe positive ones.

THE POST OFFICE

The Post Office (PO) covers two distinct communications services, the postal services and telecommunications, the former being labour-intensive in a relatively declining market, the latter capital-intensive in a growing market. Each is a complex integrated system; costs and standards of service depend on the design of the system, and how the variable load impinges on it at different times and places. Designing a better system, improving its use and matching unit or marginal costs to it requires a vast piece of operational research.

Postal services

The postal service comprises letter post, parcel post and money transmission, using common staff and premises. The letter post accounts for two-thirds of the revenue, parcel post providing the only other strictly postal service.

Prices for letters vary with weight, but not with distance travelled. For any one weight, a first or second class service is available at a considerable difference in price, relating to priority in sorting and delivery. The distinction is intended to reflect the difference in sorting costs. As most mail is collected towards the end of the working day, and postal staff work the same standard hours as their customers, immediate sorting and despatch requires overtime or night working at higher rates of pay. A slower service also allows the work to be spread more evenly. Demand does not always allow a difference equal to the avoidable cost of the faster service. Customers might substitute phone calls; or a smaller than intended proportion of mail might be sent first class. Both would reduce revenue below the estimate; costs could not be reduced so quickly. Too small a difference in price would induce more first class mail than the staff could handle, the service would deteriorate and this would discourage its use.

Costs vary in many other ways than by speed of delivery. Transport costs vary with the distance travelled; other costs depend on the number of sortings. Differences between low-cost local delivery around one main sorting office, or from one main office to another, and high-cost delivery between one rural area and another are considerable. The more extreme differences must be much greater than those involved in speed of sorting; but they cannot be reflected in prices if the post remains a national service. The more costly deliveries are supported by relatively minor cross-subsidisation from the bulk of the intercity mail. Commercial and residential location is stable enough for most of the sorting network to be efficiently used; but as the business rises less than GNP, or declines, capacity is not reorganised fast enough to contain costs.

Letter prices are further adapted to costs by the offering of special rates for bulk postings. Mail already franked, or already faced, sorted and bundled has lower handling costs and keeps capacity employed more regularly. But in general the mail prices cannot be very closely related to costs because of the variations in transport and handling costs between easy and difficult journeys.

The parcel post has close competitors in the public sector: BR, BRS and NCL all carry parcels. There are also commercial carriers in the private sector; but the public sector parcel services have been losing ground most to own transport. The costs of conveying parcels vary with the journey and some combination of weight and volume. Volume must mainly determine the transport capacity required, and probably speed of sorting. PO prices vary with weight, but neither with journey nor volume.

If the PO tries to recover its total costs by setting its average price to cover average costs, price for a short or easy journey is well in excess of the costs, while for the expensive journeys the price does not cover costs. Where PO prices are high in relation to costs, it is most likely to lose business to its other public sector rivals (because their prices are journey-related) or to own transport (because their costs are journey-related). It is not surprising that the PO service suffers chronic losses, in spite of expensive cost-saving schemes. The PO has improved its situation somewhat by bargaining on price for low-cost business, with special bulk rates to large users, such as the mail order houses. Operating costs have been contained by concentration on a few purpose-designed and better equipped sorting depots, which reduce the range of journey costs. But success in reducing total costs enough to be competitive for profitable business seems to elude it.

The PO's main asset is the chain of offices serving the public in more localities than any other public authority. It is well placed therefore to act as agent in cash transactions, for which it charges an agency fee. Pensions and social security benefits are paid, TV licence fees and vehicle duty are collected. In some remote areas gas and electricity payments are collected. As the PO in principle recovers fully allocated costs for agency services, they help to reduce the average cost of postal services; but the agency income is only one-eighth of the total revenue.

Few of the PO's costs are variable on the same time scale as governments expect nationalised industries to balance their accounts. It is especially vulnerable to labour cost increases, and the cost-inflationary years after 1973 saw it revising estimated costs and revenue more than once in a year. But such frequent price changes may not be feasible, and are certainly unpopular. Reductions in service (fewer collections) have been used as an alternative to price increases, mistakenly called cost-saving.

The proper level of a monopoly service is not easy to decide. Most improvements are costly; most reductions to eliminate costs are feasible. The market remedy would be to allow those customers who valued the costly services as highly as their marginal costs to pay the appropriate price. But it is impossible to relate variations in service corresponding to variations in cost, to variations in price. Sunday or bank holiday collections are no doubt valuable to some customers intermittently; but such a service cannot be provided for some intermittently. Marginal collections and deliveries are financed out of normal revenue, leaving no indication of the customers' preferences. What service at what price has to be decided by a mixture of trial and error and direct consultation through the Post Office Users' National Council. What costs ought to be has to be left to management.

Telecommunications

The telephone service is another integrated system with a peak load problem. There are the customer-related costs (for lines, receivers, metering and billing), call operating costs and capacity costs. As with gas and electricity, its customers are physically attached to it, so it is able to charge a rent as well as the call charges. As with transport, congestion at peak times reduces the service as well as increasing costs; frustrated callers, all no doubt listening to the engaged signals, actually prevent other callers either reaching them or getting a call on the overloaded line or exchange. Long term, extra capacity is needed, much of which may be underused outside the peak.

However, cost-based pricing can serve a more useful purpose than it may in transport. Most telephone calls are rather more flexible as to time than commuter journeys. Consumers can be deflected from the peak, either by failure to connect or by price discrimination. The tariff structure is designed to deter avoidable calls at peak times. Automatic metering at exchanges makes time-of-day metering less expensive than it would be for gas and electricity. There are therefore three rates, for peak, standard and off-peak times. But even this incurs costs, since domestic consumers need to be reminded constantly of the differences by advertising.

Peak prices have to be considerably above off-peak to induce a shift in demand; costs are not always as far apart as the charges. The principles of allocation require that the peak calls contribute enough extra revenue to cover the return on capacity installed to accommodate them. But this is formidably difficult to achieve, given that the demand for phones increases year by year anyway (apart from the recession years), and that new capacity is installed as the design of the system is improved. Attempting to price in line with system marginal cost suggests desirable changes in the tariff structure; but consumers' behaviour when charges increase is not consistent with optimisation of resource use through price signals.

Domestic consumers respond to an increase in the rent by making fewer calls (as this is the only way open to them to control the size of the bill). This both makes the customers' perceived average call charge higher and puts the PO's unit costs up, as capacity use deteriorates. With technological improvements at the exchanges, call costs, especially subscriber-connecting costs, fall in relation to capacity and consumer-servicing costs. Call charges have fallen in proportion to rents, but not in line with the costs. When inflation is rapid, so that prices have to rise in spite of increasing efficiency, average costs and prices per call are higher than they need be if consumers were less income-responsive and more price-responsive.

Telephone connection charges are analogous to connection charges for gas and electricity. Connection costs are appreciable, for the receiver and its installation, and the capital cost of other equipment committed to a subscriber. Old subscribers gain by having more subscribers on the system in a general way; but there is no reason to charge old subscribers the connection costs of a particular new one. The PO has therefore to try to attract new customers, when it has spare lines, but deters them by a considerable charge to join the system. The alternative would be to charge a higher rent until the connection costs were covered, allowing it to fall thereafter. But this is considered by the PO to be unfair or confusing; so the cost-based charges remain.

As the telephone service is one of the strongest monopolies, even in the public sector, marginal cost pricing might be an appropriate policy. However, it prices according to average cost, on the grounds that collecting the necessary data for marginal cost pricing would be costly; and that the results would not be significantly different from average cost pricing. The biggest difference would be to make trunk calls cheaper in relation to rents, and possibly in relation to short distance calls as well. As it is, rents account for rather less income than call charges.

A more significant influence on prices is the investment programme, variations in which can violently alter the extra revenue required, either to provide funds for the investment or to service the capital when it is installed. Forecasts of demand are related more to presumed secular trends, based on uncertain forecasts of national real income, than to demand revealed by price changes. New exchanges and techniques of operation have to be planned much further ahead than consumers' decisions to install phones.

In the whole transport and communications field, there is no section where prices are decided on the basis of marginal costs. Moreover, there are good reasons why they should not be, or cannot be. The *concept* is a useful one for planning purposes, as a notion to suggest improvements in price structures, when average revenue has to be raised. But pricing in practice has to be done with other considerations in mind: investment programmes, government forecasts and policies, and the reactions of consumers.

Note on Further Reading

Road Haulage Rates, Road Haulage Charges, Charges, Costs and Wages in the Road Haulage Industry, NBPI nos. 1, 14 and 48.

Productivity Agreements in the Bus Industry, NBPI no. 50.

Proposals by the London Transport Board for fare increases, NBPI nos. 56, 112 and 159.

Pay of Municipal Busmen, NBPI no. 63.

Proposed Increases by British Railways Board in fares and charges, NBPI no. 72.

Transport Policy Review, vols. 1 and 2, HMSO (1976).

Civil Aviation Policy. Cmnd 4213 (1969).

Future Civil Aviation Policy. Cmnd 6400 (1976).

Post Office Charges, NBPI nos. 58 and 121.

Annual Reports of BR, NFC, NBC, BAA, CAA, BA, PO.

Part Four

PRICES AND SOCIETY

Chapter 9

Prices Policies

THE CAUSES OF INFLATION

Prices policy is largely concerned with stabilising the price level. How it works, if indeed it does work, depends on how changes in the price level are supposed to occur. The orthodox view of market economies has produced two explanations, a market one and a monetary one, neither satisfactory in themselves. Prices rise because either demand rises or supply falls. Demand changes when the conditions change. New purchasers come into the market, or more affluent or eager purchasers are willing to pay more to avoid waiting or making do with substitutes. Alternatively, supply may fall at a given price, because costs have risen, or new, more profitable markets have opened up elsewhere, or natural or commercial accidents have reduced output below expectations. As the price rises, some purchasers will be discouraged, or unable to afford more, while suppliers will be attracted back, or encouraged to sell their stocks. Allowing time for buyers and sellers to rearrange their plans in the light of the higher price, the new market-clearing price will be somewhat higher than originally, and supply somewhat larger. The price rise itself causes responses which are partially deflationary.

If the price level rises unacceptably fast, the remedy would then be either to stimulate supply or to restrain demand. But stimulating supply without raising the price level involves reducing factor cost of output. This depends on raising productivity, which takes time, or reducing factor prices, which is, mostly impracticable (for labour) or impossible (for imported raw materials).

Price rises no longer choke off demand generally (if they ever did). *Relative* price changes alter the pattern of demand quite readily among near substitutes; but demand for product groups is income-sensitive rather than price-sensitive. Indeed price rises are as likely to be a signal of more rises to come, or impending shortage. The response to widespread price increases is to seek more income. Both households (through pay and other contractual income) and enterprises are able to do so, in an economy of large organisations.

The second explanation of general price rises is a monetary one. The price level rises if money supply times the velocity of circulation permits. In a sense, this must be true. If the price level rises, the extra money for transactions is in circulation. If it were possible to control all sources of credit, the rate of increase in money supply might be restricted for long enough to demonstrate a link with the price level. But governments have great difficulty in imposing control; when they do interest rates rise. This in itself increases some costs, which are mostly passed on in higher prices. It also discourages investment, and reduces the level of activity. This should, it was argued, reduce demand and hence the price level. But it now merely increases unemployment, without much effect on the price level. Reducing activity actually increases unit costs in most industries, as fixed costs are spread more thickly over smaller output. Prices rise, as much as demand will allow, and profits fall. Credit restriction, especially with rising costs and prices, reduces the cash flow of large enterprises; the level of activity falls as stocks are reduced. Prices continue to rise.

Government economic management through the Budget is largely directed to balancing estimated national demand against national supply, making due allowance for exports and imports and other overseas income. If aggregate demand is less than capacity output, it can increase in volume faster than technology and managerial skill allows capacity to increase. Once demand is up to capacity output, further increases at a rate faster than the underlying trend of productivity (that is, the increase in capacity) can only cause shortages and queues—and a rising price level. Periods of buoyant and fast-rising demand have indeed been periods of rising prices. But unfortunately it does not follow that suppressing the demand suppresses the inflation. Failing to control demand allows inflation to worsen; but other measures have proved necessary to improve it.

An explanation of the persistence of inflation in face of repeated efforts to control it by monetary or fiscal means runs broadly as follows. In a market economy, it is supposed that wages are determined by the market value of the particular product of the labour involved. Employers decide how much they can afford to pay, given the techniques of production by reference to the price of the product, where products are marketed in the normal way between willing buyers and sellers.

There are two reasons why this does not happen: product markets do not determine prices fully (even with willing buyers and sellers); and the units effectively making decisions on pay and prices do not correspond.

The first point has long been familiar: product differentiation, concentration and economies of scale in manufacturing have all encouraged monopolistic pricing, leaving competition to be carried by marketing techniques or development strategy. *Changes* in price are largely determined by changes in average production cost, subject only to keeping within a range set by potential competition or more-or-less rival products. There is no longer an independently determined market value of a product, to set an upper limit to wage cost per unit of output, and therefore (given techniques of production, and minimum returns on capital) no upper limit to the commercially possible increase in wage rates to the individual enterprise.

Multi-product firms supplying different markets with different degrees of competition would in any case have great difficulty in working out a market-determined maximum price (average revenue) to guide their representatives in pay negotiations. There must logically be such a limit, provided there is still some competition for all the lines produced. But it is very doubtful whether firms can really know what this is before they actually market the goods. After pay increases have been negotiated unit costs may rise. Some of these may make continued production unprofitable at prices which the competition will allow. The firm's response is to cease production of the unprofitable lines, rather than negotiate less generous wage increases. Employment is a variable whose adjustment helps to restore full market equilibrium when wage rates change. But this part of the adjustment fails to limit wage increases when the response comes more slowly than the pay claims. For the sake of good relations with its staff, firms find jobs for those redundant workers who want them in other parts of the enterprise; and if that is not enough, they slow down recruitment.

Since there is no longer a market restraint on wage increases, agreement has to be reached on other principles. A generally accepted principle is increased cost of living. Thus, the combination of imperfect competition and multi-product firms opens the way for real wages to be maintained or increased via cost of living claims and settlements.

However, even where price competition is still strong, the way pay settlements are organised prevents product price increases having much influence on pay increases. Single product firms in competition often face one principal union, or a group of unions organising various occupations throughout the industry. The employers know that others are subject to like increases in pay bills, and therefore roughly similar immediate increases in labour and staff costs per unit of product. Raising prices to the extent of the increase in labour costs is therefore a policy expected and followed by all. The price competition continues, at a higher level all round. The more times such a policy is followed, the more habitual it becomes.

Some support for this account can be derived from the experience of controlling prices. Different industries found themselves constrained to reduce prices by the Price Code to different degrees. From time to time, markets imposed a stricter limit than the Price Code. Two industries above all others were much more seriously and more continuously handicapped by their market than by the Price Code, which would have allowed them far higher prices than they had: textiles and clothing, and chemicals and oil. Both these industries are competitive; but so are many others. These particular two are subject more to international competition, from producers with radically different input costs determined in different ways.

Prices no longer feed back into the economic system as a restraint on pay; but pay pushes on prices with little resistance. Market pressure on the price range or level of competing products has to come from consumers. Competition from rival suppliers forms the differences within the ranges, and helps to settle market shares. Consumer resistance comes mainly through limited income. Even then it is patchy: we must all eat, and continue to live in the same houses, with the same services (financed as necessary by the social services). But income, especially corporate income, is limited mainly by inadequate total demand, which involves unemployment and idle capacity. Governments cannot allow recession to go too far before trying to correct it, which inevitably means restoring income levels and, as soon as possible, rates of increase. So general pressure on price levels has to be politically applied.

Relating prices and incomes policies
As the price level rises too fast because pay increases are too high, governments have been tempted to conclude that incomes policy will itself restrain price increases. This is probable in general, and seemed to be borne out in 1948-9 and 1961-2, when a short period of incomes restraint was accompanied by rates of price increase lower than before. But other causes, especially rising sterling prices for imported materials, can start a burst of inflation. Moreover, lower rates of pay increase may be wholly or partly balanced by higher profit margins. Both can quickly destroy an incomes policy. Rising import prices, duly passed on into retail prices, reduce the purchasing power of incomes more than intended. Incomes

restraint is no longer politically acceptable. Higher profit margins (from whatever inadequate or excessive level) as a result of pay restraint is felt to be unfair. They also keep prices higher than intended, and the feedback into higher pay, via cost of living agreements or arguments, is not cut as intended. Incomes policy as a means to prices policy has not been effective, nor politically acceptable.

Prices policy, in the positive sense of direct restraint of prices, can be regarded as safeguarding social justice, by preventing profits rising proportionately to pay, or as a contribution to counter-inflation, by limiting prices more and sooner than pay restraint alone would achieve. Trade unions, whose toleration of the incomes policy is essential, lean to social justice aims; officials lean to counter-inflationary aims. Systematic prices policies must as far as possible achieve both, a necessity which imposes growing strains on policies the longer they last. To further social justice, total profits or returns on capital employed need to be restrained; for counter-inflation, cost control might be enough.

Apart from leaning towards cost or profit control, various types of prices policies can be flexible and applied selectively, or codified and applied comprehensively. The 1965-70 UK policy was an example of the first, the Counter-inflation Act 1972-7 an example of the second.

WHITE PAPER PLUS NBPI: FLEXIBLE-SELECTIVE POLICY

The first policy was actually designed to be voluntary, without statutory powers of any kind to support it. The general rules were merely published in a White Paper, *Prices and Incomes*. It was to be given support indirectly by the NBPI.

The NBPI was a virtually autonomous body, representative of industrialists, trade union officials and relevant professions. It had its own staff, including a much higher proportion of professional advisers (accountants, economists, statisticians and industrial relations experts) than government departments usually have. Its function was to investigate cases referred to it by the government. It could approve, disapprove or modify price increases put to it, according to the rules. But it recommended action to the government, which then had to accept and apply the advice as it saw fit or had power to do. Its impact was to be via public opinion. In particular, as it covered both prices and incomes, it could examine the link between them, and suggest counter-inflationary ways of weakening it.

But the completely voluntary government prices policy was quite unworkable. The immediate practical weakness was administrative rather than political. Departments have to discover potentially offending price increases as best they can, sometimes merely by the volume of public complaints. Cases usually had to be referred after the event, except in the public sector. Rolling back price increases weeks after the event is usually difficult, even with back-up powers. New price lists are printed; commercial customers adjust their own costs and prices, and make new contracts. Some customers will have paid the excessive prices; whether they should be compensated, and if so by whom, would have to be faced. Without powers it is scarcely possible. Advice to reduce prices relating to a hypothetical next time loses much of its impact.

The first White Paper prices policy soon gained statutory support. Proposals to increase prices had to be notified, by 'early warning' to departments. Notification was naturally required for the second Price Code policy too. The notifiers for the first policy were mainly manufacturers or nationalised industries. Fresh food prices are subject to such marked seasonal variation, with so many grades and outlets, that specifying 'the' price, or significant price changes, is a statistical problem of some complexity. They were therefore subjected to 'constant watch' by the Ministry of Agriculture, Fisheries and Food. For the rest (detailed in Schedules to the various Prices and Incomes White Papers), proposals to increase prices were reported to sponsoring government departments. They either approved the increase, negotiated a reduction themselves, or referred contentious cases to the NBPI. Statutory powers to delay or modify price increases, following recommendation from the NBPI, were soon added, after the 'standstill' or freeze on prices and incomes (July 1966) made a more effective policy imperative.

Institutionally it was a tidy enough arrangement, and worked harmoniously and economically. But a permissive policy, as the selective type essentially is, is only as strong as the government's will to apply it. The cases referred have to be sufficient in number and influence on the price level to have some general and continuous effect. Without strong ministerial guidance, industrial sponsoring departments may be indifferent or reluctant to get too involved with a policy not their own, especially when it runs counter to the friendly relations between themselves and the firms or associations they cultivate to implement their own policies. Moreover, in order to assess whether thorough investigation is justified one often needs actually to start the investigation. Departments did not then, and probably never do have, spare professional capacity to review accounts or question costs and profits rigorously, as specialist agencies like NBPI, the Price Commission or the Monopolies Commission are equipped to do. In principle, the NBPI was to be given a selection of 'shopping basket' goods; those where competition seemed to be ineffective; or where general issues of public policy were likely to be involved. But the Board was left complaining of lack of price cases after the initial political impetus disappeared.

The general rule was price stability with various exceptional circumstances to justify increases. The four criteria for the exceptions were: to allow pay increases themselves consistent with the incomes policy (where they could not be financed otherwise); to accommodate unavoidable cost increases in other inputs, notably materials, fuel or taxation; to accommodate unavoidable increases in capital costs; or to allow higher revenue to finance new investment (where demand justified it).

For general guidance, with no legal force, these were admirably drafted. They made sense in almost all sectors, and explained tolerably clearly what the aim was. But they proved extraordinarily difficult to apply. With such rules, nearly every price case should have had pay referred as well. Some did, but not enough. Costs need detailed examination for quantification of what is avoidable or unavoidable in a particular time scale. What did emerge was that to estimate prospective costs assuming inflationary pay settlements before they were negotiated merely exacerbated the inflation: only known pay settlements should affect the calculation of unit labour costs.

NBPI interpretations

Changes in costs relate partly to input price changes, partly to techniques of production or methods of work and hence to output costs. A good many bought-in input prices were accepted as 'unavoidable'. In other cases (margarine and cooking fats, tea, ice-cream) and a few other manufactured consumer goods (soap, Hoover products), the NBPI examined methods of controlling the mix of raw materials as relative prices changed. It usually carried out the same type of inquiry as management consultants should do, with the added discipline and purpose of making a specific recommendation about a price change.

Few generalisations about unavoidable costs are possible. Even taxes are not always unavoidable. For instance, Selective Employment Tax (SET, 1966-70) was effectively a tax on employment in services. Some trades tried to pass the whole tax (on their existing labour force) into charges, by adding a percentage 'surcharge'. Public complaints about laundries and dry cleaners, and a barely concealed dispute among wholesale fruit and vegetable traders led to costs and prices being referred to the NBPI. Competition would probably not have allowed such practices to endure for long, the NBPI thought; clearly they should not do so. Both trades were in the process of concentrating on lower-cost firms. Higher turnover per firm also meant higher turnover per head; unit costs were being reduced enough to offset some or all of SET.

Accommodating capital costs and funds for new investment in prices was a perennial problem, as it always is. With consumers' interests in mind, prices ought to include a return on capital sufficient to cover the costs incurred. Alternatively, the total revenue on a product or jointly supplied group of products should exceed total costs by an amount sufficient to finance extensions of capacity, where prospective demand showed a need. In either case, 'required' or 'adequate' profits have to be quantified. The NBPI did its not inconsiderable best to produce general principles and philosophy. The Monopolies Commission has never done so in general terms, though it has to make very similar judgments. But few incontrovertibly 'right' figures result in particular cases; the value of the analysis lies rather in its producing justifiable figures, taking the public interest into account.

The Monopolies Commission compiles an index of average returns earned on capital employed. Its standard of adequate, excessive or inadequate profits, or the net average cost of capital, relates firmly to actual returns. It has the great advantage of a statistical base though this is purely relative. The NBPI's practice was to relate adequacy primarily to the needs of the particular firm. The main function of the profit was to provide investment finance; shareholders' interests would be served indirectly in a general way, since the return on existing shares had to be 'adequate' to persuade potential lenders that further investment was worthwhile (illogical though such a judgment may be). The various sources of finance had different costs, and therefore required different returns to cover them. The tax laws made mortgages (for firms like breweries with much property), debentures or bank loans cheap, as the interest on them is defined as a cost, paid out of pre-tax income. In contrast, dividends or interest on preference shares are distributions from income, and therefore bear tax (on the extra revenue which has to be earned to pay them). Firms should not therefore seek price increases to restore their profits to adequacy before they had exhausted the possibilities of loan financing. There is a limit to the gearing (with loans) companies can stand, as it severely limits their flexibility or capacity to endure unexpected periods of poor trade or profits.

When the gearing was high enough, taking into account the nature of the assets and the business, 'adequate' returns would have to be higher to attract less secure finance. What a particular firm needed depended on how much extra investment was necessary over the planning period. An 'adequate' profit on this, to be allowed for in prices, was an average of the estimated cost of each source, weighted by the amounts of each that could prudently be added to the firms' existing liabilities. An element of judgment was still needed, since all the variables are to some degree uncertain. In spite of its inclination to reason from first principles, the NBPI frequently used the Monopoly Commission statistics to indicate the average cost of capital.

The NBPI standard sets firms on broadly the same path as the average of others experienced. It does not secure adequate or normal profits related to future investment needs; nor does it relate to stabilising the capital employed in an industry. In this instance, the NBPI preferred the average to the marginal price (of capital), the average being an indicator of the marginal, in the absence of other data.

The Price Code of the second policy adopted a different approach. In principle, each firm was tied to its own past record (with obviously necessary exceptions for new or reconstructed firms). Profit margins were limited to an average of the best two out of a previous five years (actually 1968 to 1972, immediately before the Counter-inflation Act), which for a good many firms was a generous view of adequacy. But this was supplemented by a fall-back in the shape of a minimum profit on capital (variously 5 to 8 per cent at different stages) or on turnover (1 to 2 per cent). Up to these levels, the question as to whether or not new investment was necessary, or indeed whether there was any at all, did not arise. But new investment requiring revenue increases beyond the level allowed by the normal rules did have to be justified to the Price Commission. The justification was similar to the evidence usually demanded by the NBPI, an investment programme quantified and ready for implementation.

The NBPI version of adequate profit would prevent monopoly profits being earned; the Price Code rules would not, except where major new investment was involved. The NBPI and the White Pper policy was intended to deal with monopolies, as price reductions were to be made in cases of 'excessive market power'. A number were referred, a few trying to charge excessively. Courtaulds (also a Monopolies Commission case) had been overpricing acetate yarns; but by the time the NBPI reported costs had caught up with them, so no reduction emerged. This was only shortly before the value of

Courtaulds' undoubted monopoly was undermined by recession and international competition. Prices of Mallory hearing-aid batteries had been increased too much, with excessive profits. The firm were aligning UK prices with European prices (though UK costs were much lower), to stop Mallory's customers underselling their own supplies in European markets. The NBPI recommended a restrictive covenant to prevent resale. But again Mallory's monopoly was drastically eroded, this time by countervailing action from the biggest UK distributor-customer (Boots). IBM and TV rental companies both tried to exploit their captive customers already renting old equipment, by raising the rents when the costs of new equipment rose. But vociferous protests from the customers, both enterprise (for the IBM computers and equipment) and household, led to the references—and some reductions. The NBPI turned to 'countervailing power'-type administrative action, where the market did not provide a remedy; IBM customers should organise, and the company consult them. The TV *rental* companies should behave competitively in anticipation of what competition would eventually enforce; but *relay* companies (then providing services by wire by means of a monopoly distribution network) should be supervised by the local authorities with powers to grant the monopoly. British Plasterboard (also later a 'client' of the Monopolies Commission) was neither making excessive profit, nor operating inefficiently. Esso's butyl rubber plant and Orkney and Shetland Shipping were struggling with losses.

The NBPI demonstrated how varied pricing practices were, and how unpredictable market behaviour was in relation to statistical data on structures. If its contribution to pricing principles and standards for profit were less than it hoped or intended, it at least increased official understanding of pricing problems in many sectors.

PRICE CODE PLUS PRICE COMMISSION:
CODIFIED COMPREHENSIVE POLICY

The essence of a comprehensive policy is a closely defined code, statutorily enforced. The Price Code regime (introduced in 1973) was enacted in the Counter-inflation Act (1973), and administered by the Price Commission. The Price Commission, like the NBPI, was an autonomous body, with its own staff and powers to publish, its members appointed by government appointment. Though designed to be representative of trade unions as well as industry and professions, as is highly desirable, the Price Commission did not have a trade union member. Its function was quite different from that of the NBPI, mainly consisting of administration to enforce the Code. The Commission may be required to report on general matters concerning prices, and has added to the sectors or products subjected to official scrutiny by the NBPI and the Monopolies Commission. The Price Commission was also separate from the Pay Board, and could not therefore consider prices in the light of pay, labour costs and productivity, as the NBPI did. When the Pay Board was abolished in 1974, the Price Commission was left to carry on with the statutory Price Code.

The Price Code

The Price Code was designed to modify price increases, rather than setting general aims for pricing practice. The main principle was to relate price increases to cost increases. Overriding profit controls reinforce the cost controls, mainly for distributional reasons.

All price increases were limited to a demonstrated increase in 'allowable' costs. Allowable costs include the main production costs for most enterprises: labour, materials, components, energy, rent and rates, interest, specified bought-in services (such as transport, insurance, storage, maintenance). Allowable costs excluded selling costs, royalties and licence fees, and at first even depreciation (which in 1972-3 would have reduced allowable cost increases since turnover was increasing). Depreciation was soon included, when declining turnover made increase in average depreciation costs a burden.

The intention of the Code was not only to tie price increases to cost increases, but, like the White Paper policy, to induce greater productivity. But inducing productivity generally with a detailed statutory Code is not so easy. The original Code solution was a 'productivity deduction'. Part of labour cost increases (50 per cent, later 20 per cent, before its complete abolition in 1976) were to be disallowed in price increases (with a lower level for labour-intensive firms) so that the presumed gains in productivity induced thereby would be passed on to the customers. First increases in allowable costs per unit of product since a base date had to be calculated; then the productivity deduction applied; then the remaining percentage increase in unit allowable costs divided by total unit costs at the base date; and this applied to the selling price (or average revenue) at the base date. The result was the permitted maximum percentage increase in average revenue for a given period (three months usually).

This meant that if turnover *increased*, the benefit went to consumers. Unit allowable costs would be lower to the extent that fixed costs were spread over higher sales, and only the net increase resulting from increases in other costs could be added to prices. If turnover *decreased*, unit allowable costs would rise by the spreading of fixed costs over smaller sales, and would add to cost increases due to direct labour and materials. Both these increases could then be added to prices—if the market would allow. The allowable cost rule was a fairly effective machine for limiting profits, as well as the productivity deduction and the profit control.

The profit control applied to profit *margins*. Net profits per unit of turnover were limited to 'reference levels', namely, the average of the best two years out of the results for the pre-policy five years (1968-72). Any firm exceeding its reference level had to reduce its selling prices, or modify increases otherwise justified by allowable cost increases. Where there was competition, especially among a few firms, if the price leader was forced to restrain or reduce prices to keep within his own reference levels there was strong constraint on the rest, whatever their costs or profit margins. Profits could be eroded so that loss-making or meagrely profitable production was dropped earlier than would have been done otherwise. The codified policy made price control and stable employment compatible only while demand was increasing steadily and generally.

A valuable innovation in the Price Code, and a lesson learned from the experience of the White Paper policy, was to cover distribution explicitly. The NBPI had had no terms of reference to deal with the few distribution margin cases it had, in the absence of White Paper rules. It advised cash margins, rather than percentage margins, but could contribute no more.

Distributors' additions to prices cannot be controlled directly, since they cannot cost separate products; the margin covers the costs of trading units, with individual prices and margins shaved to meet competition. The Code controlled distributors' gross percentage margins, as well as, like manufacturers, the net profit margins. No allowable costs were specified, so there were no productivity deductions. Actual gross margins in the base period were taken as the reference margin levels. Net profit margins were established in the same way as for manufacturing. Where firms exceeded either reference level, selling prices had to be reduced until the excess disappeared, in a 'reasonable' time, as interpreted by the Price Commission. A rash of special offers was a usual way for retailers to get back within their reference levels.

Any control based on performance in a past period works rough justice between firms or industries, as the Price Code undoubtedly did (in spite of a provision for reviewing reference levels). No past period is ever 'normal' for all trades, let alone firms. The first three of the five permitted years for profit control were years of credit restriction, near-static home markets, even recession for some. The last two certainly saw a boom developing, with some very buoyant consumer markets; but some companies were not showing the effects until the last months of the five years. The price initiative applied to the eighteen months in the middle, and although reference levels could be adjusted to imputed normal levels for this period, some of the larger companies still showed smaller profit margins than they might otherwise have shown. Any firms with relatively poor results reflected in reference levels could build few reserves for surviving a trade recession, or for expanding—except by buying in someone else's reference level, that is, by mergers.

The productivity deduction was designed to induce better performance, and to pass the benefit through to consumers, as competition is supposed to do. It could operate most severely on firms that had little slack to remove; whereas those with easy improvements to come were not so hard pressed at first. Labour-saving investment was liable to be discouraged (as industry often complained), since the productivity deduction forced firms to pass on some of the extra return. What remained could be insufficient to justify the investment, or pay the charges on external finance.

Apart from the unevenness of a price code's bite on various firms and sectors, such rigid rules gave rise to more problems the further the code was carried on from the base period (as had happened with war and post-war allocations and cost and price controls based on past performance). Passing on a maximum of allowable unit cost increases only, if competition or consumer resistance permitted, could drive firms rapidly down from reasonable profitability when turnover started to fall. On the other hand, large firms have had to be allowed to split themselves into 'reporting units' corresponding to their product or operating groups, which *gives* many of them unintended high margins. Splitting too freely *gives* reference levels up to the best two years' profit, for each split-off unit separately. These and many other anomalies had to be corrected by frequent revisions to the Code, each revision making it more complex. Some were protective of firms, some tightened control.

Safeguards in the Code set minimum profit levels, and limited the rate at which profits could be reduced. Net margin reference levels could be raised to given absolute levels: 5 per cent on capital or 1 per cent on turnover, subsequently raised to 8 per cent and 1½ per cent, then 10 per cent and 2 per cent. Loss-making companies could raise prices enough to eliminate further losses. Another safeguard was added limiting the rate at which profit margins could be reduced. If net margins for the *enterprise* had been reduced by more than one-tenth since the base date, due to the Code (not the growing recession), firms were allowed to add a sufficient amount to price rises to bring the margin back to nine-tenths of the base date level, when raising prices under the normal allowable cost rules. Alternatively, firms could raise profit margins on separate *products* to 70 per cent of the level at the base date (with the general minimum of 2 per cent). But none of the safeguards could justify the net profit margin reference level (for the *enterprise*) to be exceeded.

Though similar in intention, the safeguards for distributors' profits had to relate to the gross margins instead of allowable costs. As turnover stopped rising, the ceiling on gross margin reference levels could drive firms into very low net profits, or losses, as relatively inflexible operating costs rose faster than turnover. So *gross* margins were allowed to rise to 105 per cent of reference levels (but no more), if this was necessary to bring *net* margins up to 80 per cent of their reference levels. Earnest readers of successive Price Codes or the Price Commission reports will find more contortions than this, all designed to preserve control while doing justice to the more important groups of sufferers.

The investment problem also had to be met through suitable codified rules, whereas the NBPI could always relate its particular recommendations to the case in hand, notwithstanding its own quest for general rules. The Price Code allowed either allowable cost increases or profit margins to be modified (by the Commission) to provide an adequate return on new investment. But this turned out not to be much use to firms wanting to increase their cash flow (though some important cases were among the steady trickle of successful applications). In the depths of the depression of 1975, a new 'investment relief' was put in. In any period of twelve months (chosen by the firm) prices and profits could be raised enough to cover in revenue a percentage of expenditure on specified investment items (plant and machinery, commercial vehicles, new buildings and warehouses—but not cars or shops). The Price Commission checked that the expenditure had actually been made, and that prices had not been raised more than enough to earn the extra revenue agreed. This relief was much more effective, bringing in several hundred cases, though the extra revenue claimed was less than expected. The general effect was to allow prices to rise nearer to the levels demand would permit, but only if profits were quickly absorbed in new investment.

Technically, the variously amended versions of the Price Code were statutory orders. The descriptions of the provisions summarised above give some idea of the documents. Having statutory force, the Code had to be in lawyers' language, and to provide explicitly for many different types of case. For instance, the 1976 Code ran to over a hundred paragraphs, all of them necessary to cover specific points.

Administration and application
The administration of the flexible-selective policy was controlled by government departments, which monitored price increases generally, prepared the references and implemented recommendations. The NBPI was entirely devoted to inquiry and report, on cases referred first by the short-lived Department of Economic Affairs (DEA), later by the Department of Employment and Productivity. After the demise of the DEA, there was no appropriately staffed or instructed department to pursue the policy with purpose; if governments have no specific instrument to impose a political will, the will is inevitably lacking. The division of function between departments and the NBPI follows from the element of selection and discretion over recommendations. These lie better in the UK system with departments directly accountable through ministers than with a more independent agency.

Administration of the codified policy is an essentially legalistic process, requiring the minimum of discretion and interpretation. The burden more appropriately falls on the special agency, with direct involvement of government departments only in the Code, not in the cases.

Both policies applied in principle to all firms; but monitoring down to the smallest requires administrative arrangements on the scale of the Inland Revenue. With a selective policy, deploying the resources committed to the policy with worthwhile if not maximum effect is part of the selection process. With the codified policy, the administration also needs codification, since the coding itself requires special returns from firms and a routine for processing them.

The checking of accounts involved the Price Commission in detailed work such as the NBPI never had. The volume of work, for firms as well as the Price Commission, was limited through firms being distinguished by size: only the larger, relatively few firms had frequent, regular contact with the Price Commission.

Category I included the largest firms (over £50 million annual turnover for manufacturing, mining, most nationalised industries; £20 million for services other than distribution). Category II was the largest distributors (over £10 million annual turnover); the medium-sized industrial firms (£5-50 or £5-20 million turnover); the largest construction firms (over £10 million turnover), professions (over £0.5 million) and banks and finance houses (over

£200 million gross deposits). Category III was the next size range for all groups, going down to £1 million turnover for industry, £¼ million for distributors and services and as low as £100,000 for professions. Category I, 200 or so in number, were the pre-notifiers, obliged to report each quarter, with proposals, and supporting calculations for any price increases. Category II (well *over* 1,000) reported each quarter, but only reported and justified price increases after the event. Category III, in tens of thousands, were obliged to keep records in an appropriate form and produce them for inspection when requested by the Price Commission. The distinction between Categories I and II was soon found to be untenable, and all were made pre-notifiers.

At its largest, the Price Commission employed 700 (including regional offices), compared with 400 employed by the NBPI. The Price Commission needed Regional Offices to do sample checks on Category III and lower. These were also useful points of contact with the public, who were encouraged to complain. It was thus possible to follow up all individual complaints. The firms complained of, however small, were visited, offences against the Code were corrected, and often other dubious practices as well, an exercise impossible with a permissive or selective policy.

A comprehensive code still cannot apply to all firms or activities. For instance, exclusions from the Price Code were exports and imports; prices subject to international agreements; auction sales; commodity markets; secondhand sales; international transport and communications; 'ethical' medicines; defence contracts if non-competitive; insurance premiums; taxi fares; non-profit-making organisations; and fresh food. The national interest required export prices to be as high as possible to earn foreign currency, and the higher profits on them an incentive to export rather than supply the controlled home market. Commodity markets are also foreign exchange earners; it is difficult to see how the Price Code could be made to apply to them in any case. International transport is a foreign currency earner as well as being subject to many international agreements. Auction and secondhand sales are impossible to control by a price code. The rest are administratively controlled otherwise; medicines by the VPRS; defence contracts in the contracts themselves; taxi-fares statutorily (as a condition of licences) by the Home Secretary or Secretary of State for Scotland; insurance premiums by the Secretary of State for Trade.

Fresh food posed the same intractable problems to prices policy through the Code as to the selective policy. A similar remedy was adopted: fresh food prices were permanently referred to keep under constant review. The Price Commission's regional officer collected fortnightly information, and provided data for a series of studies on costs, prices and profits in particular food trades. An early success was a number of reductions in retail bacon prices, the margins having been increased excessively when import and wholesale prices increased.

A voluntary prices policy would have the advantage of avoiding administrative costs, in firms as well as government agencies. However, as we have seen, the first voluntary phase of the 1965 policy was unworkable. Without prior warning of proposed increases, monitoring or investigation tends to be ineffective. The only voluntary policy to work was the price initiative of 1971-2, with no monitoring agency and no government participation. The relatively few participating enterprises were left to decide themselves whether to keep the agreement, and how to interpret it. The circumstances were at that time relatively favourable, demand was being reflated and unit costs stabilising as turnover increased. Few firms were seriously handicapped, as it then seemed, by the initiative. Also the rules were extremely simple (not more than 5 per cent increase in average revenue for one year); at once simple enough to be clear, but too simple (or crude) to last long without amendment or qualification.

Voluntary restraint is effective while it lasts, if it is clear and limited in time and scope. A policy meant to apply more widely than the initiative, especially if it was intended to apply to retail prices, could hardly be voluntary for long. Some firms would be unwilling to volunteer at all. Either their prices would stay in line with the volunteers (because competition was holding prices), or they would move ahead to their advantage. The volunteers would want statutory powers to make the policy fair (just as conforming unions do for incomes policy). It is difficult to see how a prices policy could be effective without some statutory backing.

PRICES POLICY APPLIED TO NATIONALISED INDUSTRIES

Price increases by nationalised industries are a political problem for any government: more so when general prices policy prevails. The principle is that the policy applies to the public sector as to the private. But it cannot work in practice so neatly. As the rules by which nationalised industries normally work are different, so the impact of policy is different. Even the 'price initiative' affected them differently. For a variety of reasons, many of their unit costs were increasing much faster than average revenue, in spite of reflation. They were then persuaded by government to go into deficit with compensation from government funds. Such an arrangement would be impossible or intolerable for private sector firms.

With a prices policy in operation, even the flexible-selective kind, *not* referring (or refusing) a public sector price increase is interpreted as the government not taking its own policy seriously. Hence, all considerable increases had to be referred to the NBPI, which was also told to conduct efficiency studies as appropriate. It emerged only subsequently how limited the NBPI's terms of reference were to be. Each separate reference was made subject to an overriding requirement that the industries should meet their financial obligations whatever they might be. (They actually varied from break-even to 2 per cent on turnover or fixed target rates of return.) Only in the very broadest sense is this equivalent to 'adequate profits'. The long shadow of a chronic problem was falling. If nationalised industries' revenue falls short of their requirements for current expenditure or approved investment programmes, the difference must be borrowed, and according to UK laws and conventions this borrowing added to public sector financing requirements. National *financial* desiderata so often have to take precedence over conflicting objectives, even of prices and counter-inflation policy.

The efficiency studies could clearly not be comprehensive every time. The NBPI picked out particular themes, not duplicated elsewhere, often relating to corporate planning or forecasting. But it could have little of effect to say on current proposals to increase prices, within the inflexible targets. Price structures were criticised, for instance, Post Office charges, and some were postponed for a few months. The British Steel Corporation price structure was criticised to its great indignation—on the grounds that it must be left to exercise its commercial judgment. The National Coal Board *was* left to exercise its commercial judgment on its price structure; the complexity of the specifications, costings and market differences defeated even the NBPI in the time it was given. But almost always the need to earn more revenue to meet the financial target was already urgent before it got to work.

The Price Code applied to most nationalised industries and to water authorities. Coal and steel were included, only so far as any action was consistent with the ECSC rules through the Treaty of Paris. However, as usual, their circumstances were so different from most of the private sector that some supplementary rules had to be added. Allowable costs applied, and in principle average revenue was not supposed to be increased more than costs in any period. But as most of the industries started the period with massive deficits, this alone might have kept them there. They were therefore allowed to raise revenue fast enough to eliminate the deficits. The period over which the deficit should be phased out then had to be decided. As the government wanted a very short period, and as there is no principle on which a logical answer could be based, the Code was drafted accordingly. Without special provision the Code would have taken the power to decide particular price increases from ministers. Ministers were therefore given powers overriding the Price Commission's interpretation of the Code; but only within limits, namely, allowable cost increases, and similar minimum returns on capital turnover as applied to the private sector. A special addition relating to the peculiar pricing problems of public utilities was added; namely, where increased consumption on multi-part tariffs reduced average revenue, the tariff could be increased to restore average revenue. A comprehensive prices policy could be a way for nationalised industries to escape government control over particular increases; but so long as ministers want control over their investment programmes, it is difficult for them to relinquish control over prices linked with it.

POLICY PROBLEMS AND CONFLICTS

All prices policies apply to *products*, but have to be carried out by *enterprises*. As retail prices (the final measure of the policy) relate so remotely or incoherently to producers' costs and profits, there is a difficult hiatus to be overcome between controlling and monitoring prices or controlling and monitoring enterprises. The White Paper policy was not designed to resolve this. Where prices were referred, the structure and practices of whole industries or trades needed examination. At the distribution stage it was difficult to make specific recommendations at all. Competition and concentration, with opportunity for new firms with new methods to enter, was often all that could be commended. In manufacturing, the product (like 'standard' bread) might be only one among a range (other bakery products, rolls, buns, fancy breads, possibly cakes and pastry as well), jointly making or breaking the fortunes of the firm, especially where the firms (like the plant bakers) were also subsidiaries of a larger integrated group covering earlier (flour milling) or later (retail bakers' shops and rounds) stages of production. The examined influences on prices and profits of the referred product could be too narrow. On the other hand, referring a firm (Hoover, Ever Ready batteries) allowed something less than a full analysis of real competitive pressures on costs and prices of the product, as defined by consumers.

As prices policies have developed, conflicts have appeared

between them and other government policies. There is also some overlapping of function between the price-monitoring agencies and others. Two outstanding conflicts of policy concern taxation and prices policy, and industrial policy and prices policy.

Indirect taxation adds to prices and is quickly reflected by an increase in the RPI; prices policy aims to moderate increases in the RPI. Taxes on sales (VAT, excise duties and car tax) are mostly passed straight into final prices, with very little absorption by way of lower profits or costs. The taxes usually apply to a wide range of alternative goods or services, and the whole spectrum of competing firms; there is little reason for firms to expect their competitors will do anything but add the tax, the least avoidable of costs, to prices. Neither do the taxes much deter potential buyers; if they did, they would be less valuable revenue raisers than they are. So increases appear in the RPI with little modification; and the weights derived from consumers' expenditure shift very little from taxed to untaxed goods. (A large, or merely rumoured, tax increase changes the time profile of expenditure; but lasting effects are usually much smaller than the impact effects.) Much the same applies to taxes on factors of production (vehicle duties, employers' NI and other contributions, and rates); though rather more increases are absorbed by reductions in costs or profits, or altering the proportions of factors used. All firms are affected by the taxes, but to different degrees; so competition can modify the reflection in final prices.

But raising indirect taxes has been a valuable counter-inflationary policy, by absorbing excess demand on fewer goods at higher prices. This is achieved only if the higher prices do not themselves cause higher incomes; either by automatic cost of living supplements to pay rates, or by fresh pay claims more successfully achieved. Yet governments can hardly abandon one of their main sources of revenue. The problem stems partly from using the RPI as the sole measure of inflation or welfare. Price increases for candy-floss, beer and skittles (but not gambling) count, in proportion to the expenditure weights, as much as increases for bread, housing or fuel. Some of the conflict was avoided during the Second World War simply because the then cost of living index did not reflect all expenditure. The basic conflict remains.

Industrial policy is often designed to encourage 'rationalisation', that is, concentration of industries to improve efficiency of production or marketing, especially overseas. Also, as we have seen, the R and D-based industries competing in world markets need to be able to spread their risks, and finance research into the next generation products from current income. But in a country the size of the UK, concentration increases monopolistic or oligopolistic structures.

Prices policy requires more competition, preferably price competition, to restrain price increases consistently with consumers' preferences.

There was also overlapping in the field of competition policy, between the NBPI or Prices Commission and the Monopolies Commission or Office of Fair Trading (OFT). The NBPI had a number of cases where the industries were also currently or subsequently referred to the Monopolies Commission, (detergents, beer, batteries, London Brick Co.). The Prices Commission reported on manufacturers' recommended prices (in connection with small electrical appliances) in 1976, taking a different view from the Monopolies Commission which reported generally on recommended prices in 1970. Either the Prices Commission or the OFT could be used to keep a potentially damaging monopoly under review, or to monitor prices thought to be higher than competitive market prices ought to be.

Since there has been a separate Department of Prices (1974), the conflicts have been considered more systematically in relation to government counter-inflation policy. The same department being responsible for prices policy and the Price Commission's general references, and for competition policy, and for the OFT and the Monopolies Commission, also enables the overlapping functions to be reasonably managed. This is perhaps an alternative to the then government's proposal to merge the NBPI and the Monopolies Commission into a Commission for Industry and Manpower (CIM). The CIM would have taken over the functions of the NBPI, the Monopolies Commission, the Restrictive Practices Court and the Commission for Industrial Relations (advising on ways of improving industrial relations to get higher productivity, with pay determination and structures being important ingredients).

Finally, there is the special problem of import prices. When import prices rise, either because world prices rise or because sterling depreciates, there is a real resource cost to UK consumers. The easiest and most rational way of meeting the cost is through price increases for products using the imports. Price control ought to prevent the desirable increase from being multiplied by the time it gets to retail prices, either by monopolistic pricing, or by percentage mark-ups in distribution. the NBPI recommended cash margins; the Price Code enforced them.

The effect of prices policies
The NBPI and the Price Commission both reported regularly on their activities, and had their own views about what effect they had, and what would generally help price restraint.

The NBPI tried to establish general or sectoral principles of price determination to have less inflationary effects. Behaviour about profits, taxes and cost formation were its continual preoccupations. Changes of behaviour affecting performance, or changes of market strategy or structure were things it continually sought.

In the private sector, the NBPI's experience of reviewing consumer prices was that 'as a general rule the greater the degree of competition the less the need for a reference to the Board'; though it hastened to add that 'apparent competition does not necessarily lead to a low level of prices in relation to costs'. Furthermore, to emphasise the point, for private or public sector 'the primary need is to devise a substitute for competition where the latter is lacking or insufficiently effective or cannot be restored'. Where monopoly could not be replaced, the answer was an efficiency study—such as the NBPI was equipped to carry out.

All this was as much part of industrial or competition policy as it was of prices policy. It was quite in line with the NBPI's view of prices policy that the CIM should be created from a merger of all the related institutions.

The Price Commission, on the other hand, was at pains to emphasise its subordination to the Price Code. The Commission's role was 'not in any sense of the term deciding whether proposed increases in prices are reasonable or unreasonable. It cannot reject an application because it thinks that in social or economic terms it would be wrong for the price in question to be increased. The Code gives the Commission no general discretionary powers.'

Nevertheless, it too was persuaded of the virtues of competition. 'The resistance of buyers and consumers to price increases is one of the greatest protections against inflation. The Commission is determined that nothing it does should erode that resistance.'

The NBPI tried to measure the impact of its activities by comparing the actual increase in the price level with what past trends suggested would have happened otherwise. The conclusion was that *incomes* policy, a condition of which was the prices policy, had moderated the increase in earnings by about 1 per cent a year (a figure supported by some other calculations). This looks a derisory enough figure. But on the scale of the 1960s, and sustained over a period, it was useful enough. The government's own estimate of the gap between the UK and its competitors' labour costs was about this amount, the amount, that is, which had led to the devaluation of 1967—and all the structural operations that followed. The NBPI's own estimate was that the 1 per cent gain would be worth £100 million annually on the balance of payments; alternatively, the slower pay increase would have been worth 100,000 jobs.

The Price Commission had altogether more information about its activities. All firms of any size were obliged to report, and all the pre-notifiers had to work out a sum of money, namely, the extra allowable costs or profit margin the Code permitted them to recover by price increases. If the Commission rejected or modified this it could claim to have saved the customers the appropriate sums of money. This sum varied from £100 to £200 million a quarter. This was a narrow view of the effect of the policy. Had it not been for the Code, firms might have passed more than current cost increases through into prices, especially during the prosperous days of 1972 and 1973. How far they could have done so with the low levels of domestic demand in 1974 onwards is more doubtful.

However, the government eventually commissioned an inquiry into the impact of the prices policy, having been faced with unsupported assertions on either its total ineffectiveness, or its crippling effects on profits, investment, product or enterprise development, and so on. A small sample of large firms reported that the Price Code did indeed alter their behaviour and policy. The most general effect was a highly desirable one. Cost figures had to be more carefully compiled and scrutinised. Pricing decisions were taken at a higher level, were more centralised, or more systematically discussed. Relating prices more closely to cost changes, and to the general policy of enterprises, must improve their quality if only from the enterprise's point of view.

The Price Code had its greatest impact when demand was buoyant, as might be expected. But even when demand was generally very slack (mid-1976) there were firms who felt themselves to be effectively restrained by the Code, firms concentrated in food and 'other' manufactures (a group containing building materials, as well as a miscellany of consumer goods other than textiles, vehicles or metal goods). Predictably also, the indirect effects of the constraint were many and varied. Profits were directly squeezed by the profit control, indirectly by the price control. The level or character of investment could be changed, though whether by weakening incentives or reducing reserves is unclear, and no doubt varied from firm to firm. In most cases the change was for the worse. Unexpectedly, some of the same groups which seemed to be restrained by the Code even in bad times also reported that the Code had actually reduced their incentive (or capacity) to reduce costs. Sales and marketing activities could also be altered. Price differentials were changed in some cases, but not so widely as expected. Some manufacturers also thought that price leadership had been strengthened, a possibility that the NBPI was aware of and tried to avoid by refusing to name a price increase which might have been more readily imposed for being 'approved' officially. Probably the more significant result was that only a minority of respondents considered the Code rather than commercial considerations had influenced their day-to-day management of prices and sales at all.

Price controls are usually alleged to divert output to non-controlled goods. The Price Code left exports uncontrolled. A minority of the sample firms had actually devoted more resources to exports, though export prices had risen more than domestic prices in the majority of cases. In the longer term the effect of continuing control might be more damaging. A few firms reported that restrictions on profitability made investment in the UK less attractive to their foreign parent companies.

Predictably also, a large majority of firms preferred complete abolition of prices policies; and if that was not possible, then *profit* control should be substituted for *price* control. The case for this is partly to be rid of the reporting and pleading that price policies involve. It is partly also for the very reason that governments are reluctant to do it: because profit is too remote from prices to impinge much on price decisions at all.

Whatever the econometrics show, prices policy evidently does affect and mostly constrain prices. Even the comprehensive Price Code, however, cannot constrain them much in general recession or sectoral depression. Both profits and price increases are depressed then anyway, both awaiting a revival to restore them—if prices policies allow.

A significant warning about indirect reactions also came out of the review. A minority of firms considered that the Price Code type of policy had actually speeded up price increases. Because of the delay imposed by statutory notification (up to twenty-eight days), and the uncertain future effect of the rules, applications went in as soon as cost or profit figures justified it. What would have happened otherwise depends on the industry. Firms might be waiting for signs of a general increase; whereas the Price Commission acted as a go-between to satisfy each of an oligopoly about the intentions of the others, as notifications to the Price Commission frequently appeared in the press. Alternatively, the question might just have been dealt with by managers in a less purposeful way. In spite of the price agencies' commitment to competitive behaviour, the rules they administer may actually make them an instrument of more collusive or oligopolistic behaviour. But this was clearly not generally, still less universally true; it is a possibility for which some evidence exists.

Pros and cons of price control

Price controls are intended to come between market demand and suppliers' normal responses. This they do, though not always to the degree nor in the manner intended. Whether price controls are in principle (if entirely effective), or in practice (given all the repercussions), desirable depends on their aims, achievements and costs.

Price controls change the time sequence of cost and price increases. If firms normally pass cost increases on as soon as they are incurred, as though more expensive materials and components went immediately into production instead of stock being rotated in order, price controls could change the routine. Where they wait either for some indication of competitors' policy, or have a haphazard or leisurely routine for pricing, the passing on might be speeded up. On balance, however, there is some deceleration. This reduces cash flow and profitability somewhat, at the same time perhaps as it makes pricing decisions more systematic. This in turn, together with the reporting procedures required by the controllers, makes many firms (some of them very large) much more aware of changes in their own production costs. This at least must provide better opportunity for controlling costs, and at best encourages it.

At times of high activity and expanding markets, many suppliers push up prices faster than unit costs, even with some vigorous competition. In much manufacturing and distribution, unit costs are moderated anyway as demand and sales increase, so wider profit margins can be taken merely by increasing prices at the same rate as previously. Firms whose unit costs include too much managerial inefficiency or mistaken policies on pricing or use of resources might be forced or encouraged to drop unprofitable lines or methods more quickly where a prices policy cuts short the free upward drift of their prices. A fierce price control, like the allowable cost regime with productivity, can actually deprive *source* firms of funds or return for cost-saving investment, thus suppressing the efficiency it is supposed to encourage. But at the same time, the same rules can have the opposite effect in other firms. Instances of the one or the other do not establish the net effect. Whatever the particular Price Code rules did, it is difficult to believe that price control generally does not induce greater efficiency. This is after all what market-determined prices are supposed to do in competitive industries, and one advantage of competition over monopoly. The Monopolies Commission has documented cases where monopolies incur the wrong costs rather than exploit their customers by charging high profits. Case by case examinations, of the NBPI kind, show some of the scope for this, and can even assist with remedies on occasion.

On the other hand, price control can contribute to inadequate investment. Again the comprehensive codified policy is more likely to have this effect, even with exceptional price increases to provide investment funds or return. The special investment relief was more use to the largest firms with on-going investment programmes than to smaller ones with distinct projects occurring intermittently. But this may work in different ways. Lower revenue provides less for reserves. Worthwhile investment could be inhibited, if interest rates are high, or the firm too highly geared, or investors generally cautious. There are, however, enough financial intermediaries other than banks or equity subscribers to provide a fairly wide choice of terms. Lower prospective revenue reduces the potential return to investment. But the general level or rate of interest of demand also influences, more strongly probably, prospective yields. The state of confidence also influences investment decisions; price control may be bad for confidence. But in general the prospect of less inflation should be good for confidence.

'Distortion' of trade is something else associated with price control. Strictly speaking, unevenness of control distorts trade rather than control in principle. The distortion consists of changing the pattern of output, and possibly therefore altering competition. If some products or firms are subject to control and others not, or not so effectively, the uncontrolled lines or firms become more profitable than controlled ones. Output of uncontrolled goods rises relatively to controlled goods or firms. As the controlled items are presumably more important to the customers than the uncontrolled, damaging distortion follows. Thus runs the argument. The major 'distortion' embodied in the Price Code was intended to have this effect: exports were excluded to allow prices, profits and output to rise as much as world markets would allow. The other major distortion followed from concentrating control through notification and delay on larger firms. Wherever the border line is set, there are some firms in some trades just below it. 'Large' has to be defined relatively to all enterprises; large relative to competitors in one industry may be only medium-sized or small nationally speaking. Initiative in competition or price leadership may come from the large, relative to immediate competitors, or from the thrusting interloper rather smaller than the sleepier established giants. If it does, there is no reason for concluding that competition which is more damaging to the large or selectively controlled as a result of the control, gives a better use of resources or choice of products than competition with no control, or even-handed control. Moreover, the main thrust may come from the large controlled firm, and this may be hampered by selective control. If the competition has a net benefit, its inhibition is a loss. However, the fact that a surprisingly large proportion of the firms reviewed did not change their sales and marketing policy, in respect of product or price differentiation particularly, at least suggests more caution in deploying the argument than unqualified logic would suggest.

Price controls which bite effectively may result in less consumer choice or convenience. This partly follows from distortion of trade, assuming that consumers' choice and convenience were or would be maximised in the absence of control. Partly it follows from pressure on costs. Reducing the profitability of whole product ranges leads to intensified search for cost reductions. Average costs can be reduced by removing the most costly lines or outlets from the range altogether (provided enough overheads can also be lopped). Of the lines that continue, some costs are easier to control or reduce than others, notably standardised lines rather than non-standard. Another general way to reduce costs is to reduce working capital, especially in distribution. If this is done by better stock control, this is an unequivocal benefit. If it means reduction of the lines carried, or shelves filled less continuously, service to consumers suffers.

Finally, there are the political or social arguments for and against control. These are outside the confines of this book, though not outside the purview of those who have to decide on or design the controls. With or without the politics, price controls have or can have effects both beneficial and damaging to the interests of enterprises or consumers. The net result must be a balance of unlike advantages and disadvantages—if only we knew more about ranking or measuring them.

Note on Further Reading

Prices and Incomes. Cmnd 2639 (1965).
Prices and Incomes Policy, an Early Warning System. Cmnd 2808 (1965).
Prices and Incomes Standstill. Cmnd 3073 (1966).
Prices and Incomes Standstill—the Period of Severe Restraint.
    Cmnd 3150.
Prices and Incomes Policy after 30 June 1967. Cmnd 3235 (1967).
Productivity, Prices and Incomes Policy in 1968 and 1969. Cmnd 3590
    (1968).
Productivity, Prices and Incomes Policy after 1969. Cmnd 4237 (1969).
The New Inflation, Jones (1973).
Price Theory and Price Policy, van Meerhaeghe, (1969).
Price Commission quarterly reports.

NBPI Annual reports.
The National Board for Prices and Incomes, Mitchell (1972).
The Operation of Stage Two of the Counter-Inflation Programme.
   Cmnd 5267 (1973).
The Counter-Inflation (Price and Pay Code) Order 1973 (no. 658).
Review of the Price Code. Cmnd 5779 (1974).
Modifications to the Price Code. Cmnd 6540 (1976).

Chapter 10

Prices and Consumer Protection

Governments have been drawn into general concern about price formation and pricing practices, wider than RPM or prices and incomes policies. As consumers have been recognised as a politically notable group, a public interest in prices and quality has been acknowledged. 'Quality' itself takes on wider meaning the more seriously consumers' interests are taken. Consumer protection is understood to cover fair dealing, redress for complaints, and national minimum standards of design or performance for almost any goods or services. At the same time consumers have become more widely represented, to exert a distinct 'consumer interest' into many aspects of policy.

Whether 'consumers' should be taken to include commercial and industrial buyers as well as household customers is a question not easily decided. All buyers feel themselves frustrated at times, when faced with monopoly sellers. The largest industrial customer may have some common interests with domestic consumers. On the other hand, large firms buying from large enterprises have remedies or command the attention that small consumers cannot do themselves. Consumer protection usually means *domestic* consumer protection, following the Moloney Committee (1959-62) on consumer protection, which decided to exclude even small businesses, caterers or hotels and boarding houses from its purview. However, it is as well to bear in mind that consumers do have some common interests, depending on the context of the problems.

CONSUMER AFFAIRS

Advice
In a market economy, the customer is supposed to dominate competitive markets by discriminating choice, so that he selects the best value for money given his needs and preferences. With clearly distinguished standard goods, this is reasonably close to a function

we can recognise as shopping. If there are few dimensions of quality, and little technical content to assessing them, consumers can, and mostly do, discriminate among supplies accessible to them. (Fresh food is an example: freshness, size, appearance and lack of damage are enough to make reasonable choices.) But the more the dimensions of quality and the greater the technical content, the less can domestic consumers assess their choice and hence value for money. Moreover, learning by trial and error is no longer appropriate when large, infrequent purchases of durables take up a considerable part of household expenditure. Consumers need advice about value, whether fitness of purpose or durability. Industrial or commercial consumers also need advice; but they have access to research and testing facilities of their own or through trade associations. Domestic consumers have a particular need.

The market system produces advice but it is mostly biased, or downright misleading, since producers and distributors have an interest in selling (rather than considering a no-sale option), and in selling their choice (rather than the well-informed consumer's choice). Unbiassed advice, distinguishing better from worse sources of supply, necessarily involves discrimination among firms. Government departments (in the UK) fight shy of discriminating— and probably for good reason. Official selection or rejection for quality or cheapness would be worth a great deal commercially, and such power would be deeply resented. Moreover, departments need the tolerance or co-operation of firms in other policies, and goodwill (or lack of badwill) would not be likely to be forthcoming while such a function existed, a function, be it said, not obviously appropriate to officials.

Consequently, consumer advice was first developed by independent organisations, notably the Consumers' Association producing *Which?* each month since 1957. Their main activity is testing groups of products and recommending 'best buys', including keen prices (and where to look for them), but also analysing quality differences so that consumers can choose more reasonably to meet their individual needs. It soon appeared that there were many more aspects of quality besides performance that merited advice. The law about marking and labelling, and safety from various hazards and additives also affected consumers' welfare. Even fresh fruit and vegetables may have colouring, pesticides or other odd chemicals on them, unseen to the purchaser but perhaps not to be preferred.

The Moloney Committee on Consumer Protection was appointed in 1959, with terms of reference 'to review . . . the legislation relating to merchandise marks and certification trade marks, and to consider and report what changes if any in the law and what other measures, if any, are desirable for the further protection of the consuming public'. The Committee proceeded to report at length, covering many things from labelling and compulsory minimum standards for many particular goods, to rights of redress of complaints, advertising standards and conditions for hire-purchase agreements. Consumers' interests should be permanently represented by a statutory Consumers' Council. A decade later many of the recommendations were still to be implemented, in spite of the existence of the Consumer Council.

The Consumer Council, appointed by government but largely independent of it, proceeded to give advice as much to the government as to consumers. Consumer advice was more concerned with design and performance than with best buys. To government departments the Council was a pressure group, trying against a degree of indifference to get the Moloney report more fully considered, and gradually being consulted on consumers' views on many kinds of legislation.

How permanently the consumer had 'arrived' politically was demonstrated by a mistake. In its initial enthusiasm for tidy administration and saving the taxpayers' money, the incoming Conservative government abolished the Council. This prompted surprisingly widespread criticism. Moreover, it deprived the government itself of consumers' representatives to consult over the mass of legislation still working its way through. Consumer advice was left to the Consumers' Association, although local authorities in some areas were beginning to provide some consumer services.

The government made amends for its apparent slight to consumers with the Fair Trading Act (1972), and the establishment of the first Minister of Consumer Affairs. The many functions of the Office of Fair Trading (OFT) fall to be discussed below, in consumer protection rather than advice. The government which followed (the Labour government of 1974) turned the consumer affairs division into a separate Department of Prices and Consumer Protection (DPCP), with a Secretary of State in the Cabinet. Advice to consumers was again supported, this time through CACs run by the larger local authorities, financed partly by DPCP. The CACs carry information of a general kind about a wide range of consumer goods (including copies of *Which?*), and monitor prices locally. A selection of shops are visited by Consumer Protection officers, and current prices recorded for standard consumer goods. The CACs aim to be a focus for any kind of consumer problems.

Consumer protection

Consumer protection refers to complaints procedures and general standards of safety or fair trading. Complaints about nationalised industries are dealt with by the consultative consumer councils (see p. 199 below), where they exist. Complaints about transport fares have to go to the industries, complaints about services to the consultative councils. Complaints about goods or services from the private sector usually have to go to the retailer or supplier of the goods, in the first instance. Advice on getting faulty or unwanted goods replaced is given mostly by the CACs.

Complaints or suggestions of a more general kind, concerning the policies followed by suppliers or producers, are less easy to make. Concerning nationalised industries, the consultative councils may take up general issues. Concerning private sector products, the OFT should take up any that prejudice consumers' interests; but this would not include pricing, unless some particular practice were either monopolistic exploitation or doubtfully honest. DPCP is the only body which can protect consumers from prices being generally too high, or rising undesirably or unnecessarily fast. The DPCP is responsible for the prices policy, and the Price Code, or whatever else governs general pricing behaviour. The NBPI and the Price Commission have both regarded themselves as protectors of consumers' interests. The powers the Price Commission has, more particularly to recommend remedies for harmful practices, depends on the design of DPCP; DPCP also has the role of implementing recommendations made by the Price Commission or the Monopolies Commission (provided the government as a whole will agree to DPCP plans).

Protection from harm has increased steadily since the start of *Which?* and the report of the Moloney Committee. Fireworks, drugs and flammable clothing are obvious hazards, which have been subjected to considerable control, either of design or sale, to protect consumers, especially children. In the case of actions detrimental to consumers' interests 'in respect of health, safety or other matters' (as well as economic interests, or unfair practices), the Director General of the OFT may seek assurances from the offending trade that the danger will be removed (or refer the matter further if the assurance is not given).

Advice and protection both have costs. Some of the costs are borne by the community, in the form of the expenditure of public authorities on, for instance, the CACs and the OFT. But some are borne by producers, where new standards require different materials (with less fire risk, or less risk of chemical harm), or better packing (for drugs, for example); and where higher standards of protection for the customers means more returned and replaced goods. The direct effects must be to increase prices somewhat above what they would otherwise have been. Few would presumably deny that the benefit was worth the cost (certainly not judging by the extraordinary unanimity of political approval for consumer protection). However, there is the further question of what the indirect effects may be. Greater awareness on the part of producers or traders of the qualities that consumers or the community on their behalf expect, and a greater probability that negligent or indifferent attitudes to their products will give rise to complaints and compensation, may well encourage the generally alert managements, if not competitive ones. Alertness to quality may not always bring lower prices: it can hardly make them higher (apart from the legitimate cost of the better quality).

Better information and less misleading information has been required of traders since the Trade Descriptions Act (1968). False marking, misleading descriptions, misleading indications of price are all subject to penalty, and this applies to services as well as to goods. Information marks, such as marks of origin, must be displayed if this is required. This Act has been one of the more important in making consumers better informed about day-to-day purchases, as well as the more complex durables reported on at length. It has probably also been a great deal more valuable than anything else to the majority of shoppers, who do not read articles or go out of their way to special offices before they buy.

Unit pricing and standard packaging
A particular kind of consumer information long advocated by all consumer representatives is *unit pricing*, namely, the display of prices in terms of a simple unit of quantity (per pound, kilo, metre, and so on). Pricing in eccentric quantities or packs effectively reduces most consumers' discrimination to the level of comparing prices for precisely the same quantities, a very narrow range of choice.

One of the measures prepared by the then new Consumer Affairs division in 1974 was a Unit Pricing Bill, giving the minister powers to implement schemes for specific trades by Order, after due consultation. This was on its way through Parliament at the dissolution—with support from all sides of the House.

The incoming government of 1974 put through the Prices Act (1974), a clause of which at last provided these powers. In view of all the support, one must question why it took so long in coming— and why its implementation was exceedingly slow. The reason is the difficulty of describing exactly what goods are affected, consulting with perhaps dozens of trade associations, and providing for every little quirk of business that might make some innocent practice actionable, or allow a culpable one to escape. (A favourite example is the butcher who charges different prices for a whole joint, or parts of it.) There are also costs of adaptation to be considered in respect of firms selling non-standard sizes or weights.

Display of prices can also be required under the Prices Act, a necessary corollary of unit pricing as well as an elementary piece of consumer information in its own right.

Standard packaging is an alternative to unit pricing, and sometimes a preferable alternative. Under the Weights and Measures Acts, Orders may be made prescribing the standard quantities in which certain goods may be sold. Butter, tea and sugar (sold retail) have long been sold in standard packs. Standard packaging of many foods (breakfast cereals, jam, biscuits are obvious candidates) may be more informative to consumers than a unit price on an odd pack, price-marked with a different price. In this respect the Prices Act supplemented the Weights and Measures Acts. Consultations over standard packs are no easier or quicker than unit pricing. Long arguments can be conducted about the appropriate standard, weight or liquid volume, for instance, punctuated by fears that the consumer may not appreciate that differences in quality may affect weight/volume ratios. However, a certain amount of progress is discernible, if only because some of the more enlightened retailers have decided as a matter of social policy to anticipate the trend of legal requirements. Increasing EEC activity in consumer affairs, especially over standard quantities and price marking, may serve to maintain the momentum in member countries.

Representation

Since the establishment of the Consumer Council (1963) consumers have had growing representation at political levels, the 'consumer' being almost always understood to be the domestic consumer, with the brief interval of 1970-2.

The OFT is a much more powerful consumer-oriented agency than any other, as it has considerable initiative without having to wait for ministers' direction. The Director General has a duty to review practices in consumer goods trades to discover possible harm to consumers. A Consumer Protection Advisory Committee was also appointed to support him. If they do indeed agree with his view, the Director General may recommend that the minister implement his proposals by Order. A consumer interest can now be represented to government in a specific legal form, difficult to resist.

The OFT was left in being by the next government, but

consumers were additionally represented by the National Consumers' Council (NCC) set up in 1975. This is also independent of government and has a small staff of its own, including some research capacity. The NCC has about twenty members, appointed by the Secretary of State after consultation with various consumer organisations. Its function is to report on a very wide range of consumer matters, including prices and pricing practices. Care was taken to see that the weakest of consumers, the poor and old, are explicitly represented, even over-represented, a redress for previous neglect of their special interests.

Consumer interest in a wider sphere of policy was added by making the chairman of the NCC, in a personal capacity, one of the independent members of the National Economic Development Council, on which ministers, unions and employers discuss major economic policies. Such representation has helped to bring the idea of consumer-members on the boards of large companies a little nearer reality, along with 'industrial democracy' in the form of worker-directors.

Industrial consumers are represented more by the OFT than by any other organisation. The Director General also has the duty to review commercial practices in order to discover monopoly or restrictive practices. As Registrar of Restrictive Practices he may issue an Order stopping a practice made illegal by the Restrictive Practices laws, and he may refer monopolies to the Monopolies Commission, subject to a veto by the Secretary of State. His powers to investigate harm to consumers are not restricted specifically to domestic consumers, though they mainly concern 'consumer trades'.

Nationalised industries' consumer councils
Consumers' interests are most likely to be treated too lightly where the market presses least, in monopolies. The danger was thought to be particularly great in the statutory monopolies. As public services, most of them are in any case of particular importance to consumers, industrial or domestic. The nationalised industries were therefore obliged, by their statutes, to set up consumer consultative councils.

All the members of the consumer councils are unpaid representatives, except the chairman who is paid for part-time work. All have a staff of their own. They reported originally either to the controlling board of their industry or to the minister to whom the board reports. They started off with varying powers and functions, and these have been amended at various times in the course of reorganisation of the industries. One of the biggest changes affecting them all was the transfer of administrative responsibility for them from the departments with industrial responsibility to the DPCP (1975). At the time of the transfer their constitution was as follows. The electricity industry had area consultative councils, whose chairmen were members of the Area Electricity Boards. There was no national council. The gas industry had a National Gas Consumers' Council, and area consumer councils, whose chairmen lost their seats on the Area Gas Boards in the reorganisation of 1972. There was a Domestic Coal Consumers' Council, including merchants as well as consumers. All of these could and did discuss prices on the occasion of changes proposed by the industries but without having great impact on the decisions.

The transport industries were much less well covered. Overtly there was plenty of representation. A Central Transport Consultative Committee was supplemented by eleven Transport Users Consultative Committees. However, the latter discussed proposed rail closures almost exclusively. Neither type of committee could discuss fares. There was no systematic representation for bus users, except that the TUCCs could discuss bus services replacing rail services for two years after the change. Air passengers on domestic lines had a council; the Civil Aviation Authority and the British Airports Authority had both set up users' councils; but again there was no co-ordinated machinery for air transport users.

The Consumers' Council reported on the councils in 1968, recommending many changes, especially in the obligations of boards or ministers towards them. Shortly afterwards the Post Office Corporation (1969) was given the Post Office Users' National Council (POUNC) which remedied some of the weaknesses. The POUNC was given an unusually generous staff, of career civil servants, and the PO was *obliged* to consult it about any major change, including price changes. In addition POUNC could review any matter it thought worthwhile. With a dynamic chairman, and the use of consultants, it soon developed functions beyond the rest. A Select Committee on Nationalised Industries reported on *Relations with the Public* (in 1971), and was very critical of the work of the councils as being too much concerned with complaints and too little known to consumers (in spite of their long existence). The POUNC it found much more purposeful in concentrating on important aspects of consumer affairs. At least their view had some effect, in that the Gas Act of 1972 also obliged the BGC to consult the NGCC on important matters including prices.

The transfer of the councils to the DPCP allowed some uniformity of policy to be developed, as well as making them more independent of the industries. The NCC was given as its first major task a review of all the consultative councils. The NCC's criticisms were on much the same lines as those of the Consumers' Council and the SCNI: too much attention to complaints (for which the CACs might be more suited anyway); too little attention to or powers to consider important general issues. The NCC's solution was to centralise the councils, and supplement them with proper arrangements for bus and air passengers. The national councils should have access to joint research facilities; the boards of the industries should be obliged to inform them of all major developments in price or service, with time to consider them before they were put into operation; and the councils should have powers to require the minister to put their recommendations before Parliament in the event of the minister not agreeing with them.

The nationalised industries' consumer councils are not suited to give consumers advice; that has to come from the industries, or other consumer advisory bodies. They do provide protection for individuals in dispute with the industries. On general matters, they have so far acted as sounding boards for the industries to get a sense of how some consumers react to their arguments and activities. But it remains to be seen whether they can represent a consumer interest more independently, with access to a Consumer Protection minister rather than the industries' minister, and with clearer rights and powers.

It is very doubtful whether the increasing representation of consumers has yet affected pricing practices, or even particular prices. Like advice, the more important effects are probably indirect, and perhaps slow in coming. A specific consumer voice in policy at any level makes it more difficult for producer interests to be served entirely or all the time. Producers are often interested most in high prices, or frequent price increases. Consumers' interests are in low prices and increases infrequently. Pricing in the less competitive sectors may eventually be modified.

CONSUMERS AND PRICE CONTROL

Price control is anathema to firms and very appealing to consumers. Doom is forecast by the former, something near a panacea for households' financial stresses by the latter. Neither is anywhere near the realities. Like any other intervention in markets, price control is a policy to which enterprises and consumers will respond according to the various pressures of demand and supply; the economy will not, so to speak, stand still while so fundamental an intrusion as an *effective* price control is thrust upon it.

On the supply side, a price control will tend to discourage supply. The control squeezes the gap between unit costs and average revenue. Either profit margins must be lower, or some costs must be squeezed. If neither of these can easily be done, or cannot be sustained for long, resources will go out of production. Capital will move elsewhere; labour may be unemployed. So much for the bare bones of the conclusions to be drawn from the workings of the market system. But the system is not so simple. Where there is monopoly, or where prices are administered (set by a policy decision, not closely related to current unit costs), a price control may not result in resources leaving production. It must result in incomes of the producers being reduced (assuming they know their own business best, and that their income does not rise with lower prices); but they may just endure it, if they were previously enjoying monopoly surpluses. The control then redistributes welfare between consumers and producers, and between the non-producers (such as the old and young) and the gainfully occupied. The control may also lead firms to seek factor substitution more urgently, to preserve their income with lower average revenue.

We must remember also the distortion possibility, noted as an objection to prices policy (p. 190 above). Price controls cannot cover every product; multi-product firms will find it relatively more profitable to produce non-controlled rather than controlled goods.

On the demand side, consumers will be led to consume more than they otherwise would, which may be the object of the policy. However, if the unwanted price rise occurs because of a real increase in the cost of the inputs, the substitution of alternative consumption or reduction of waste of the goods in question is sooner or later desirable. The price control would inhibit such long-term adjustments. The other side of the distortion argument is that consumption of non-controlled goods may actually be discouraged, unless the price-controlled goods are also in short supply. Again this is too stark a picture of what may happen. Consumers take time to adjust their expenditure. Some is a habitual or necessary commitment, not easily changed for reasonably small price differences. Loud complaints about shortages lead retailers to try to redress the balance, in order to preserve their customers' goodwill.

Whether the responses to price controls are worth enduring depends partly on the circumstances. The more price competitive markets are (including factor markets), the less worthwhile the possible distortions (and the more likely they are to occur). The less competitively prices are determined, and the less actively discriminating the customers, the more likely it is that price controls are endurable or worthwhile.

If price controls are the *only* policy being considered, the disadvantages will be considerable; but this is rarely the case. Price controls are a supplement to rationing, in conditions of acute shortage. They may be a quick way of supporting the weaker consumers through painful adjustments that cannot be accomplished through income changes. They may above all be a supplement to other policies designed to reduce the degree of effective, working monopoly among producers.

The range of prices for identical goods is one reason for consumers' interest in price control, especially when steep or rapid price increases make them more noticeable. The Labour government of 1974 came to office committed to establishing and requiring the display of 'fair' (retail) prices. Price display was not difficult; fair prices proved a disappointing impossibility. A fair price has to cover the costs of some given or presumed 'reasonable' range of shops. The range of costs between shops, even in one area, is formidably large. The range of prices is not usually so large, and part of the difference is accounted for by differences in the service rendered in the selling.

There is a conflict of interest between shops, as well as between consumers. A fair price for small shops can be far above a tolerable price for the multiples or no-service cash-and-carry stores. A fair price for supermarkets would bankrupt neighbourhood and rural shops. Non-mobile consumers or those outside the crowded city areas have a primary interest in the survival of the neighbourhood shops, and the smaller units of the multiples. Mobile or city dwellers have more interest in concentration of trade in large-scale operations. There cannot be a fair price for them all. Fair prices, approved prices and recommended prices all hark back to RPM; they do give security to shops and consumers, but at the expense of higher prices than the more efficient can afford, behind which less efficient operators may shelter. It does not follow that administered or recommended or supervised prices are wrong *per se*; there are other objectives of economic or social policy than enterprise efficiency, and more particularly, than approaching greater enterprise efficiency without regard to the speed of the approach. It does mean there are costs to weigh in the balance.

SUBSIDIES

The Prices Act 1974 also gave the Secretary of State powers to subsidise the prices of certain foods. The food subsidies were part of an agreement with the trade unions to seek a voluntary incomes policy. At that time (early 1974) import prices were rising fast due to the 1973 boom. Farm product prices were rising at home also, as prices were adjusted to EEC levels. Food prices were expected to flatten out in a matter of months. It was intended then to modify and smooth the increase by subsidising prices during the remaining boom, and gradually withdraw them later when the increase subsided.

Subsidies may be used to promote the welfare of either producers or consumers. If the price elasticity of supply is low, and lower than demand elasticities, a subsidy will probably increase producers' incomes; in face of virtually fixed supply (short term), any extra revenue is likely to increase the prices of the supply. If supply elasticity is high (where competition among suppliers, surplus capacity or weak bargaining position makes it so), a subsidy benefits distributors or consumers. If there is competition among distributors, prices are kept down, and consumers benefit from the subsidy. But if price elasticity is low and competition not keen, distributors may get some of the benefit.

A subsidy intended to benefit consumers cannot subsequently be used to support producers, unless margins are also controlled. This lesson was learned in 1975 when subsidies on bread (paid to producers, but having the effect of reducing prices to consumers) were increased to cancel a rise in price due to increasing costs. Most of it was promptly passed on to retailers in the form of bigger discounts, part of it going on to consumers, still happily discriminating among cut-price bread, while the producers took lower profits. An Order (under the Prices Act) freezing margins had to be imposed *for the benefit of producers*, quite the opposite of the intention of the power. But this inhibited competition among retailers. So in 1976 an Order fixing uniform maximum retail prices was amended, making them dependent on the discounts the retailers could bargain from the bakers, leaving the producers to cover their costs as best they could. The workers in distribution then took a hand, refusing to deliver to shops cutting prices below the retail price based on the old fixed margin, on the grounds that smaller shops unable to get the larger discounts would stop stocking plant bread, putting the van salesmen out of a job. Price control or fiercer price competition means less resources employed; and the human 'resources' do not always like it much.

Suitable items for subsidy have to meet three conditions. They must be necessities, widely used, to get the right welfare effect. They must be in adequate and fairly elastic supply, so that a nominally consumer subsidy does not go to producers or importers. They must have a fairly low demand elasticity, so that increasing consumption does not cost too much in subsidy, or ruin the producers of near substitutes. So the list of those eligible is quite short. Milk, butter, cheese (cheddar-type only), tea, bread and flour qualified (butter at the expense of the better margarines nevertheless); but not meat. The extreme scarcity of war conditions makes 'meat' desirable, almost regardless of the kind or cut; with reasonable plenty this is not so, and demand elasticities for any one kind are high.

The great weakness of subsidies is that they are either indefinite, open-ended and increasingly expensive to maintain, or temporary and limited but causing higher price increases when they are taken off than would have occurred. Only if subsidies coincide with a short-lived burst of inflation can they be removed painlessly.

Taking off the subsidies involved in supporting increasing deficits in the nationalised industries created serious social problems. The energy industries' costs were still rising steeply (1974-6) at the time, and employment falling. The government felt compelled to respond by urging cross-subsidisation between small and large consumers to modify the regressiveness of the withdrawal of the subsidies (overriding the objections of the marginal cost purists). The extra revenue required by the gas and electricity industries was sought by increasing the commodity rates more than the standing charges, thus reducing the average price for small consumers a little below the level the industries would otherwise have set. This 'tariff-tilting', towards something nearer average cost pricing, mild though it was, caused heated controversy between producer and consumer interests. The NCC favoured not only tariff-tilting but flat-rate tariffs. The SCNI would clearly have liked to be convinced of the practicality of such a policy, had it not been persuaded by the resource-allocation arguments against it. The NEDO Study managed to remain on the fence, though reporting the industries' 'resentment' of government interference with pricing generally. The full regressive effect of the electricity price increases was somewhat mitigated by government payment of a quarter of the electricity bills of social security beneficiaries for the winter of 1976-7 (the industry then having considerable excess capacity, partly as a result of the steep price increases of 1974-6).

PRICES AND WELFARE

Distributional effects

Welfare, or real income, depends as much on prices as on money income. The distributional effects of money transfers receives much attention, and money transfers have been used as the main means of altering distribution. However, as the problems of larger and larger transfers of money have become more pressing, the distributional effects of price changes have begun to be noticed. Both the food subsidies and the tolerance of large deficits in the energy industries were policies intended to have welfare effects as well as contributing to counter-inflationary programmes.

The RPI, the numerator of welfare measurement, measures weighted average price changes. However, the poor and the rich have different expenditure patterns. It is possible that the price indices of poor households' expenditure move in a different way from those of richer households. It is indeed argued sometimes that the poor or large families have been made worse off by differential price increases. Two separate price indices for pensioner households have been compiled since 1968. These show little difference from the average index; though differences in price increases for short periods can be significant. There is, however, no separate index for poor households as such (though pensioners are largely in the below-average income groups), nor for large families, though the FES does distinguish expenditure for income groups, size of family and region.

In spite of persistent low growth and a precarious balance of payments, the 1960s were years of generally rising consumption, especially in the form of the consumer durables. Both cars and electrical goods grew relatively cheaper, under the joint influence of technical advances in production and growing international competition. Running costs were also falling quite markedly in real terms, largely due to cheap oil. Petrol and electricity were both cheap enough for consumption to increase several times faster than average incomes. Had this been all, the above-average income households would have done much better relatively than they did. The below-average, and especially the really poor, were to some extent protected by food and clothing prices rising only sluggishly (food prices being kept down to world levels, and clothing subject to increasing competition); but they were burdened by housing and coal prices rising relatively fast.

However, the 1970s have seen different trends. Food prices started to accelerate relatively fast as producer subsidies were reduced and the EEC system of market support introduced. At first fuel prices rose only slowly during price initiative, at the expense of ever-increasing deficits. Then from 1974, as the deficits were eliminated and costs escalated, the trend turned sharply upwards. Housing costs still went up relatively fast. Of the items more than proportionately important to poorer families, only clothing prices still increased at notably below-average rate. The food subsidies helped to bring the price experience of poorer households near to the average of the richer ones. Over a short period (five years or less) the differences in trend are quite marked. But over a longer period few if any differences seem to persist.

Imperfect but necessary policies

Prices policy is primarily a counter-inflation technique. It can be argued, therefore, that it is necessary for national purposes, even though its effect on individual enterprises is undesirable. However, there is more to it than that. The basis of prices policies or controls has to be costs. If prices were fully determined by costs, prices policies could not be effective, other than as efficiency studies.

Price policies are based on the assumption that a good many prices or price increases are so loosely determined that controls can push them lower than they would otherwise be. This assumption is clearly justified, not only by the calculations of how much the price level was lowered, or how much potential revenue was taken out of intended price increases, but by the various ways in which price increases come about. The same assumption was made by the CBI; it was they who proposed and operated the price initiative limiting price increases voluntarily, and persisted with it in spite of the absence of the hoped-for reciprocal 'pay initiative' from the TUC.

So prices policies can relate prices more closely to costs, or to costs differently defined. But this leaves costs too little 'accountable'. Wherever price, product and service are closely interlinked, as they almost always are, costs are not independent of price. Moreover, where product and service are fixed, it does not follow that costs are beyond comment, or irrelevant to the public interest. Monopolies, the classic exploiters, are at least as likely to incur the wrong *costs* as to charge excessive prices. Similarly the indifferent performers exploit their customers by being ignorant or careless about their operations, that is, their costs, as often as about their prices.

Nationalised industries and public services, as well as the large assemblers in manufacturing, face a similar problem over their purchases—of knowing whether even the lowest, or slowest inflating price is justified. Their usual remedy is to centralise buying to give themselves maximum bargaining advantage, and then deal with a short list of rival suppliers. At any one time, one supplier will have the best product, most reliable service or lowest price. But standards change very quickly, for internal or external reasons. Being relegated to third supplier instead of first on major contracts for a national organisation is as powerful a sanction against a lethargic management as any. Also, it may be the smallest (feasible) supplier that comes up with the innovation or cost-saving or new idea about more efficient use. It is often not price as such that causes question or change, but the quality of the product or the regularity of supply. Where alternative suppliers are not available, even a public authority may be left like the DHSS buying tranquilising drugs from Roche, with no remedy but a long unsuccessful negotiation over prices, eventually culminating in a Monopolies Commission investigation (it took ten years to get some restitution politically negotiated).

So long as consumers at any stage want assurance about the reasonableness of prices they cannot get for themselves by bargaining, it seems highly likely that governments must continue to give it. In the public interest, that of suppliers as well as consumers, appropriate pricing principles should be encouraged. Those right principles relate to costs, plus adequate profits. The relevant costs are those of the most efficient or least-cost producer. Prices should encourage the right responses from consumers in the light of continuity of supply. Prices below marginal cost should be looked at askance; those above justified for a good specific reason. If only the world would stay stable, the right pricing principles would give the right results. As it is, the right pricing principles have their place in public policy only as one in a collection of conflicting principles. The consumers' interest is in low and stable prices.

The government's peculiar role is to ease the economy out of aggregate problems, a task which enterprises cannot do. In this role governments intervene in the market sectors, influencing prices by rules and regulations in general prices policies, and particular price controls. To all these interventions individual enterprises or households react, directly as the law requires, indirectly as their own interests and problems dictate. The reactions take time; both producers and consumers have commitments and routines not quickly changed. Nevertheless the market system is as notable for its adaptability, for good or ill, as for its great variety. Neither pricing principles nor prices policies are easily applied; but imperative need keeps them at the centre of political as well as commercial or academic discussion.

Note on Further Reading

Final report of the Committee on Consumer Protection (Moloney). Cmnd 1781 (1962).
Relations with the Public, SCNI (1971).
Consumers and the Nationalised Industries, NCC (1976).
Theory of Price Control, Galbraith (1952).
Report of the Cost of Living Advisory Committee (1968).
HC Debates on the Prices Bill, Committee Minutes on Clause 1 and 2 (subsidies and control of margins) (1975).

Index

36-45
183
189
193

39
41
42

203